# The Case for Mark
# Composed in Performance

# The Case for Mark
# Composed in Performance

ANTOINETTE CLARK WIRE

CASCADE *Books* · Eugene, Oregon

THE CASE FOR MARK COMPOSED IN PERFORMANCE

Biblical Performance Criticism Series 3

Cascade Books
An Imprint of Wipf and Stock Publishers
199 W. 8th Ave., Suite 3
Eugene, OR 97401

www.wipfandstock.com

ISBN 13: 978-1-60899-858-6

*Cataloging-in-Publication data:*

Wire, Antoinette Clark.
    The case for Mark composed in performance / Antoinette Clark Wire.

    Biblical Performance Criticism Series 3

    ISBN 13: 978-1-60899-858-6

    xii + 226 p.;  23 cm. Includes bibliographical references and indexes

    1. Bible. N.T. Mark—Criticism, interpretation, etc. 2. Bible. N.T.—Performance criticism. 3. Storytelling. 4. Oral tradition. I. Rhoads, David M. II. Title. III. Series.

BS2585.2 W58 2011

Manufactured in the U.S.A.

# Contents

# Contents

# Series Foreword

The ancient societies of the Bible were overwhelmingly oral. People originally experienced the traditions now in the Bible as oral performances. Focusing on the ancient performance of biblical traditions enables us to shift academic work on the Bible from the mentality of a modern print culture to that of an oral/scribal culture. Conceived broadly, biblical performance criticism embraces many methods as means to reframe the biblical materials in the context of traditional oral cultures, construct scenarios of ancient performances, learn from contemporary performances of these materials, and reinterpret biblical writings accordingly. The result is a foundational paradigm shift that reconfigures traditional disciplines and employs fresh biblical methodologies such as theater studies, speech-act theory, and performance studies. The emerging research of many scholars in this field of study, the development of working groups in scholarly societies, and the appearance of conferences on orality and literacy make it timely to inaugurate this series. For further information on biblical performance criticism, go to www.biblicalperformancecriticism.org.

The current volume by Anne Wire makes a compelling case for understanding Mark as a composition arising over time through repeated performances by many favored storytellers in early Christian communities, lifting up especially the role of women in the origin and development of Mark's gospel. In challenging the common view of the Gospel of Mark as the literary creation of a single author, Wire makes a major contribution to gospel studies by creatively constructed an alternative paradigm for the emergence of Mark.

# Preface

I found myself intrigued by the Corinthian women prophets when I worked to reconstruct their stance from Paul's argument with them in 1 Corinthians. And I relished the stories of the disabled who claimed healings from Jesus. But the gospels as whole narratives I found alien. I think now this was because scholars have used each of the gospel themes and traditions to characterize one of the four men who wrote these books toward the end of the first century. I was supposed to be interested in the spirituality of John or the Christology of Luke or the genre of Mark. But when I asked where their material came from, I was told this was beyond the reach of scientific investigation, off the map, in the area marked on the margins of old maps, "Here be Dragons."

Now the study of oral traditional literature has opened up this area to exploration. We realize that ancient authors did not get their stories from flights of imagination but from traditions they had heard, and that under special circumstances these traditions had been cultivated into narratives that characterized and sustained particular movements. The question is how we can recognize such living traditions and what we can find out about the processes in which they were shaped. This study makes the case that the gospel called Mark is such an oral tradition by finding evidence of the process of its composition in its external form as a variety of Greek manuscripts and in its internal form as specific language, episodes, and story patterns. Now I read Mark as the communication of a movement of people through the voices of its gifted composers. We can hear their voices not only in its most formative decades but also in its continued telling, its limber manuscript tradition, and its interpretation since that time. I could not be more attentive to how these voices speak or what they are saying.

I want particularly to thank all the people, many cited in the notes, whose writings have opened up for me the possibility of hearing this tradition. Special thanks are due to Annette Weissenrieder, Robert Coote, and all the scholars whom they gathered in April 2009 for the conference at San Francisco Theological Seminary on The Interface of Orality and Writing in the Shaping of New Genres. Also I benefited from Werner Kelber's invitation to attend the conference at Rice University in April 2008 on Orality and Literacy in Judaism, Christianity and Islam.

I want to thank David Rhoads and Mary P. Coote for their reading of the manuscript, David Rhoads and K. C. Hanson for their careful editing, and Heather Carraher for her typesetting. It is published thanks to Cascade Books and their series on Biblical Performance Criticism.

# Abbreviations

| | |
|---|---|
| *b.* | Bablyonian Talmud (*Babli*) |
| BETL | Bibliotheca ephemeridum theologicarum lovaniensium |
| *BTB* | *Biblical Theology Bulletin* |
| *CBQ* | *Catholic Biblical Quarterly* |
| *EvT* | *Evangelische Theologie* |
| *ExpTim* | *Expository Times* |
| *HTR* | *Harvard Theological Review* |
| *Int* | *Interpretation* |
| *JAF* | *Journal of American Folklore* |
| *JBL* | *Journal of Biblical Literature* |
| JSNTSup | Journal for the Study of the New Testament Supplement Series |
| *m.* | Mishnah |
| *Neot* | *Neotestamentica* |
| NovTSup | Novum Testamentum Supplements |
| *NTS* | *New Testament Studies* |
| P. Oxy. | Oxyrhynchus Papyrus |
| *t.* | Toseftah |
| WUNT | Wissenschaftliche Untersuchungen zum Neuen Testament |
| *y.* | Jerusalem Talmud (*Yerushalmi*) |

# Introduction

## The Case for Oral Composition and Its Significance

Unless we are completely naïve, we listen to a story with a mind to whose story it is and why he or she tells it in a certain way. We may know the speaker, or someone has told us about the author, so that hearing their story broadens our understanding of them and we see the story they are telling from their perspective. Even when we read something with no name attached, we construct a general idea of who wrote it from where we find it and what it says, and in this light we take it as reliable or not.

### Gospel Composition

The New Testament gospels were not signed by their composers. Titles were added when the gospels were copied together in the early second century: "According to Matthew," "According to Mark," "According to Luke, "According to John." Stories were developed about the writers from a few references to these names in early Christian writings. Irenaeus identified the gospel authors with the four living creatures of the Apocalypse: lion, ox, man, and eagle.[1] Early Church mosaics show medallions of four men. Medieval illuminations show each author at a desk with quill pen in hand. Recent literary studies of the gospels have further characterized the four authors: Matthew a scribe intent on righteous conduct, Mark a radical with an ironic bent, Luke the storytelling historian, and John the revealer of symbolic meanings. These pictures help us, as the animals, mosaics, and illuminations helped people of earlier times, to distinguish and personalize the gospels. And just as those depictions showed the evangelists as apocalyptic, Roman, and Byzantine figures respectively, we in the recent West discover four

1. Irenaeus *Against Heresies* 3.11.8; Rev 4:6–11; Ezek 1:5–14.

1

authors with a variety of perspectives on the story of Jesus—reflecting our world of diversity where "it takes all kinds." Are there ways to understand how the gospels were composed that are less projections of ourselves and more open to the voices speaking to us?

It is now recognized that most ancient texts that have survived were not written by an individual but took shape in other ways—through song or recitation, in collections of stories by clan, court, or temple recorders, or in inscribed praises and curses. In each case the story was composed more for communal honor than for individual expression. The final stages of a text were of minor interest because the reciting, compiling, or inscribing took their value from the tradition that was being transmitted. This was true of Israel's Torah and Prophets, where authorship was not ascribed except to the story's hero. These anonymous traditions are the authorities to which the gospels appeal, and the gospels in turn are written without signature.

But how were the gospels composed? I will argue that they were composed, not by individual authors with pens in hand, but orally in performance; that is, they were shaped in the telling. We are shaping stories all the time as we tell them, and we can accept this origin for many stories about Jesus. But in our culture we do not tell extended narratives and cannot conceive of an entire gospel being shaped in recitation. Accepting such a scenario requires an understanding of oral tradition—the practice of shaping and transmitting in performances the tradition by which a people interprets its life. An introduction to recent study of oral tradition follows.

## Two Forms of Composition

First, however, the question arises as to whether it makes any difference in our understanding of a surviving text if it is composed in the act of writing by an individual author or is composed over time in an oral performance tradition. Since the content of the text we are reading does not change with our theory of authorship, is it merely a technical and superficial matter how that text is composed? To show that it is not, I ask what is distinctive about a story shaped in its telling.

For one thing, an oral tradition is made of sounds, whereas a writer's text is made of shapes. The shapes last longer and can be moved around, but the sound has its own advantages. As a physiological reality produced by a human voice and received by a human ear, the sound has a force among humans beyond whatever it is signifying. Before the electronic age, the voice was never anonymous. Rather, the spoken words were made by a certain speaker who stood behind what was said or who represented the person who did. In this sense a spoken statement is always social, always in context, whereas writing can be composed elsewhere and be read alone. While writing allows the reader time to reflect without pressure to respond, speaking represents someone's commitment and it challenges listeners to take an immediate stand.

More important, the sound is understandable to everyone raised in that culture, whereas the shape of written letters requires a text to be read and someone who is able to decode it. In the Roman East the only texts for the majority of people were coins and occasional words on graves or buildings, or trades people might keep a list of items on wood or clay. But land deeds and books came only with wealth. The current estimate of literacy for Jews in Roman Palestine is three percent.[2] This three percent would read aloud to make out the meaning of each row of letters through hearing themselves make the sound, and some people could overhear them. By contrast, the spoken word reached everyone.

The most basic difference between an author's text and an oral-traditional story is in the relation of the composition to the tradition in which a people's culture is passed on. Authors may draw on given traditions in the process of a story or an argument, but they do so in order to make their own particular statement. Performers of tradition are understood to be transmitting a given tradition of the community. Yet we have no external standard of what is traditional, so the difference between authorial and traditional composition cannot be calculated from how much each one is indebted to that tradition. Only the people in a specific culture and location where a story is at home can gauge its adequacy to their tradition.[3] These listeners have heard the story

2. Harris concludes from his study of literary and material remains and educational options that ancient Mediterranean literacy does not exceed 10 percent except in principate Italy (*Ancient Literacy*, 22). Hezser concedes to Bar-Ilan that Jewish literacy in Roman Palestine cannot be much more than 3 percent because the majority of Jews lived in rural areas (*Jewish Literacy*, 35–36, 496; Meir Bar-Ilan, "Illiteracy in the Land of Israel," 55–56).

3. So Nagy: "What the poet tells is true or false, depending on when he tells it: the local traditions on which the poet's immediate audience has been reared constitute the

regularly, whether in a family or work setting, a seasonal celebration, or a religious ritual. They will object if the tradition is violated by the performer and they will look to another teller.

And how do they know the tradition is violated? In transmitting a tradition, it is not exact wording that is required—except perhaps for a punch line or a refrain—so much as an accurate and effective evocation of the familiar story. This means that the performer must use traditional language and traditional ways of speaking and must "get the story right" in its opening, its progression and its climax. The leeway granted to the teller comes in how much the scenes are drawn out or condensed, sharpened or softened to suit the particular time and place they are being told. Listeners are not checking words but expecting to hear the familiar tradition and to realign their lives by it.

## Mark as Performance Tradition

If tradition is characterized by its capacity to retell the story by which people recognize themselves, what would it mean to say that the gospel of Mark was composed in performance? It suggests that to demonstrate such composition we need not turn back to some original moment when the tradition was first spoken, a moment that in any case is out of our hearing. Instead, we can listen for evidence of the process of composition that takes place whenever it is performed among traditional hearers. This may be seen in the way tellers preserve the tradition with incremental changes only, changes that keep it recognizable to its traditional audience. If the shape of the tradition is generated over time in oral performance, interpreters can focus on repeated performance events in which this composition occurs.

Lest this give a false impression that the teller is the originator or innovator of the tradition, it must be said that the teller's point is to reassert the tradition. Any adjustments of words are made to tune the tradition more sharply to the hearer's ears. No traditional teller, no matter how mature and constructive in performance, presents himself or herself as its creator. The story asserts its authority, not as the speaker's authority, but as the tradition's authority of which the speaker is the

---

ultimate criterion of 'truth.'" *Best of the Achaeans*, 3.

4

instrument.[4] Although the teller embodies the tradition and keeps it alive, being in fact the presence of the tradition in the flesh, the tradition is understood to precede him or her and is expected to sustain itself through other tellers who come after this one.

It is this respect, which the tradition demands and receives, that requires of us a different way of understanding than we bring to authored texts. Such respect reflects some kind of identification with that tradition, whether it be a cultural classic, religious canon, or crucial local report. And this respect generates the tellers' re-composition that preserve the tradition over time. Even where writing has intervened, it takes speakers to bring the tradition back into effective human communication.

When we hear Mark as the story of a community told by several favored oral performers rather than as the product of a single writer, we understand it differently in several ways:

1. The single author thesis assumes that Mark was written by a literate person in the second half of the first century, which meant at that time by an urban male shaped in the Greek language and Hellenistic culture. By contrast, the thesis of composition in performance allows for composition over decades by a number of favored tellers. Special attention may have been given to a man or woman who had known Jesus, to an older person respected for traditional knowledge, to someone in whose home the group gathered, to a good storyteller, to an aggressive propagator of the movement, or to a person with physical qualifications for public speaking in height, strong voice, or clear speech.

2. The single author thesis presses us to seek one consistent vision in the entire text, often found in contrast to source material. Composition in performance suggests that more than one favored teller has put his or her imprint on the conception as a whole, leaving a rich and complex web of tradition. It follows that the text cannot be read as a response to a single historical and social setting; rather, the text reflects multiple contexts of composition. Yet because respect for a tradition increases with time, its early shaping provides the basic form and content that also points in new directions.

4. Ibid., 6.

3. The single author thesis implies something near the freedom of a modern novelist to "tell it as he sees it." Composition in performance, however, presumes the heavy weight of tradition. In this scenario, not only is the story of Mark told in structures and language that have long been traditional in Israel and the Near East, but what is being told is absorbed by the telling into the rhythm and the authority of the tradition, which in turn supports the memory of the teller. The story that spawns a community also motivates the group to monitor further telling and to reject renditions that it does not recognize as constituting itself.

4. Whoever writes down a performance tradition is subject to the same monitoring. Research on media transitions notes how the suspicion of a new medium causes innovators to be especially conservative. As the first printed Bibles meticulously imitated the script and the illuminations of hand-written manuscripts,[5] and Kindle takes the shape of a book, so we can expect that the early handwriting of Mark did not veer far from its performance tradition. As such, the written Mark will reflect the oral traditions and embody the oral performances that lie behind it.

## Twentieth-Century Rediscovery of Oral Tradition

### *Oral Traditional Epic*

A major turning point in the study of Homer occurred in the mid twentieth century when Milman Parry and Albert Lord recorded Serbo-Croatian singers reciting epics for hours based only on life-long hearing.[6] These expert singers in the oral tradition said they were telling what they had always heard, but the tapes showed that each rendition had characteristics unique to that performer and even to that particular performance. From observing these firm and yet flexible traditions, Parry and Lord developed a theory of composition in performance according to which these people over generations had shaped their stories into works of art. Singers learned the narratives through years of hearing and practicing the art until they cultivated their own repertoire of

5. Clanchy, "Looking Back from the Invention of Printing," 12–13.
6. Parry, *The Making of Homeric Verse*; Lord, *Singer of Tales*.

the old stories. Lord analyzed the recurring formulas, themes, and story patterns that characterized these oral compositions—"formulas" being his term for repeated phrases with rhythmic effect, "themes" being what he called the recurring episodes or scenes, and "story patterns" signifying for him the sequence of events that make up whole oral narratives.[7] He found analogous ligaments in Homer's epics where phrases were reused, episodes stereotyped, and tales framed by story patterns such as that of the warrior who returns home unrecognized. He concluded that the Iliad and the Odyssey were not composed in writing but orally in this kind of traditional process.

The proposal that the renowned Homeric epics were composed in performance provoked fresh research in the study of Homer and of epics world wide. International conferences were held with scholars in Europe, Asia, and the Americas; oral traditional journals were established; and many traditional texts were published.[8] Particular attention was given to the interface of orality and writing in the study of past oral traditions, because it is through literature that some early oral traditions have survived.[9] When classicists took the oral thesis as a denigration of Homeric art, John Miles Foley responded that the oral teller's metonymy—in which one formula, scene, or story pattern comes to stand for a complex network of tradition—is a form of art as significant as metaphor.[10] He argued that such "immanent art" is obscure only to outsiders who do not share the tradition that is evoked by its special phrases and ways of speaking. Gregory Nagy cautioned critics against thinking of tradition as a performance followed by its proliferation. For him "the evolution of the fixed texts we know as the Iliad and the Odyssey may be envisaged as a cumulative process, entailing countless instances of composition/performance in a tradition that is becoming streamlined into an increasingly rigid form as a result of ever-increasing proliferation."[11] Here proliferation tends not toward dissolution but

7. Lord, *Singer of Tales*, 30–123.

8. Foley, ed., *Oral Tradition in Literature*; Honko, Handoo, and Foley, eds., *The Epic*; Honko, ed., *Textualization of Oral Epics*; and the journal *Oral Tradition* (edited by John Miles Foley; 1986–); see especially vol. 14 (1999) on Jewish traditions.

9. Foley, ed., *Oral Tradition in Literature*.

10. Foley, *Immanent Art*. For an introduction to his concept of immanent art, see his *How to Read an Oral Poem*, 109–24.

11. Nagy, *Best of the Achaeans*, 10.

toward stability as different versions meet each other, a process that he thought occurred in recitations of Homer at the Pan-Athenian festival.[12]

## Folklore and Ethnopoetics

This ferment of research on epic traditions has been matched in folklore studies by a sharpening focus on performance.[13] Whereas at one time catalogues of folk stories were taken as sufficient evidence of a people's oral culture, now it is recognized that a performance is far more than words. When, where, and how the teller speaks are just as crucial. Such factors include dress, stance, rhythm, speed, volume, and tone, as well as the auditors' role in the performance as seen in how they receive it. Various efforts have been made to fashion written signs for these performance factors,[14] and recent technological advances allow more of a performance to be recorded. Yet the better our recording becomes, the more we realize how much of a performance is not accounted for.

The oral register of speech can also be signaled within a written text, for example, by figurative language, parallelism, special formulas, archaic speech, appeals to tradition, and other evocations of the past.[15] But the focus of folklore studies has shifted away from ancient traditions no longer being performed toward traditions where performance can be seen and heard today. It is ironic, if understandable, that extensive oral traditions in millennia only marginally literate get less attention in performance studies than do small pre-literate oral traditions today.

Here a further step is taken by ethnopoetics, a practice among scholars of Native American traditions to take old recorded stories and rituals and reprint them in stanzas that better reflect their internal forms and meanings. Dell Hymes has identified in early records of Chinook coyote tales certain particles that signal the beginning of a new section, and certain repetitions of words and phrases that segment material into units.[16] By such observations of "measured verse" he has been able to

12. Nagy, *Poetry as Performance*, 107–12.

13. Dorson, *Folklore*; Ben-Amos and Goldstein, eds., *Folklore*; Baumann, *Verbal Art as Performance*.

14. Fine, *Folklore Text*, 166–203.

15. Bauman, *Verbal Art as Performance*, 3–58.

16. Dell Hymes, *"In Vain I Tried to Tell You."*

---

reprint stories in lines and stanzas that show both rhythms of sound and patterns of meaning.[17] Similarly Dennis Tedlock has used his own recordings of Mayan rituals and old records of their wisdom to produce texts that can be taken to Mayan ritual specialists today for consultation and correction, calling his work ethnopaleography.[18] Hymes and Tedlock are also particularly sensitive to the way their own presence and perspectives can skew the traditions they transmit, making their research doubly important for students of other inscribed traditions.

The question remains whether the difficulties outweigh the promise of recovering any gospel texts as oral tradition. Should we assume we are dealing with an author's product whenever a tradition has been recorded, even where no author appears or where authorship is mentioned in opening or closing of what otherwise seems to be a traditional composition? Or have scholars of oral-traditional literatures, European folklore, and Native American stories made a sufficient path across rough terrain that it is now appropriate at certain points in New Testament studies to test the thesis of composition in performance?

## New Findings in Early Jewish and Islamic Oral Tradition

Scholars in the history of Israel's traditions recognize the role of oral tradition in the generation of their materials, but few propose oral composition of extended texts.[19] Post-biblical Jewish legends are collected but only occasionally analyzed as a genre of oral tradition.[20] More has been done with motifs that surface now and then in writing and that suggest tenacious oral traditions continuing over centuries. Here Odil Hannes Steck's study of the killing of the prophets is a classic, as is now also Jon Levenson's work on the binding of Isaac and on resurrection.[21] Hindy Najman has analyzed "Moses discourses" from Deuteronomy to Jubilees and the Qumran Temple Scroll to uncover rhetorical uses of

17. Hymes, "Tonkawa Poetics."

18. Tedlock, *Popol Vuh*; Tedlock, "From Voice and Ear to Hand and Eye."

19. Niditch, *Folklore and the Hebrew Bible*; Niditch, *Oral World and Written Word*; Yassif, *Hebrew Folktale*.

20. Ben-Amos, "Narrative Forms in the Haggadah"; Ben-Amos, *Folklore in Context*, 38–85; Wire, *Holy Lives*.

21. Steck, *Israel und das gewaltsame Geschick der Propheten*; Levenson, *Death and Resurrection of the Beloved Son*; Levenson, *Resurrection and the Restoration of Israel*.

old traditions for new purposes, implying that there were oral practices that made such persuasion possible.[22] Yet seldom can submerged traditions be reconstructed from those that have surfaced in writing sufficiently to let us hear what was spoken and how and why.

However, hopeful signs for reorienting the study of gospel composition are coming from recent breakthroughs in certain streams of rabbinic and Qur'an research. Longstanding theses about the generation of the Mishnah and the Qur'an have been challenged, and new, more complex proposals are taking their place.[23]

## Recent Study of Oral Torah in Judaism

Scholars of early Judaism are rethinking the rabbinical tradition that God gave Moses two Torahs, the written one in Scripture, and the oral one in the rabbinic learning whereby each generation of disciples memorized its teachers' rulings. Jacob Neusner displayed the great variety of rabbinic pronouncements concerning the Oral Torah, suggesting many different practices.[24] Martin Jaffee then demonstrated that the thesis of an Oral Torah from Moses parallel to the written Torah became widespread only in the third or early fourth century as a legitimation of the rabbis' living tradition, possibly against Christian interpretations of Hebrew Scripture.[25] This left open the question of how the rabbis' teachings were generated before that time. Addressing this question, Jaffee compared the parallel rabbinic debates in the Mishnah and Tosefta and proposed that the common traditions behind both were cultivated by different rabbinic groups as they deliberated orally and wrote anthologies, resulting in these two distinct though still related documents. The Mishnah was then further explained and rationalized over centuries in the shape of the Jerusalem and the Babylonian Talmuds. Yet it is not clear to me how Jaffee features this incremental oral composition of

22. Najman, *Seconding Sinai.*

23. I give below only a cursory review from outside these disciplines and recognize that more traditional positions are still held by many respected scholars. Other innovative work such as that by Bruce Chilton on the Aramaic Targums will be considered where it impacts the interpretation of Mark.

24. Neusner, *What Exactly Did the Sages Mean by "The Oral Torah?"*

25. Jaffee, *Torah in the Mouth.*

tradition taking place simultaneously with what he calls the memorizing of written debates.

Elizabeth Shanks Alexander takes this analysis further by showing that the early rabbinic legal traditions in the Mishnah and Tosefta reflect a continuity that is not literal or linear.[26] In the two collections she sees common overarching structures and fixed phrases used to struggle with similar concerns, despite the fact that the arguments are configured quite differently. The two collections do not share a specific course of argument, but they do share certain principles of law and a way of deliberating about them, including some memorable phrases. The variations are of the kind seen in different oral performances of a tradition and they indicate that the Mishnah does not take itself as a fixed authority. Its fixed authority is the achievement of later sages whom we read in the Talmuds. They learned from the Mishnah its practices of deliberation but used them to apply the Mishnah as a fixed authority—intentional in every detail—to the different questions of their times. Of particular interest to Alexander is the way these later Amoraim or "explainers" ignore many key principles of the Tannaim or "repeaters" whose traditions shaped the Mishnah. Flexible oral practice had established the authority of the Mishnah. However, once this text was no longer taken as a script for practice but as an authority in its own right, each of its phrases became necessary and each repetition a potential new principle. Here Alexander sees the influence of Greco-Roman rhetorical schooling on rabbinic practice, in that Greco-Roman teachers required students to rework traditions to resolve all possible legal ambiguities.

The work of Jaffee and Alexander among others has shown that even the highly structured legal debates of the rabbis reflect oral practices that continued to shape the material during times of writing, as writing in turn influenced the debates. This mutual influence between writing and orality shows why the ultimate dogma of literal oral transmission from Moses cannot be projected back as the principle behind these tenacious and yet long limber traditions. Nevertheless, oral Torah is not a bad name for the rabbis' practice of speaking to people's ongo-

---

26. Alexander, *Transmitting Mishnah*.

ing need for rulings, which seems to be what kept the traditions fluid both before writing and after.

## Recent Study of the Qur'an as Speech

In Qur'an studies it is the definitive authority of the Qur'an as writing that has made study of its oral dynamics difficult. Yet early controversies over how Muhammad's revealed recitations were collected show that the Qur'an was not written during his lifetime. This leaves a certain space for diachronic study of its forms of speech. Angelika Neuwirth has proposed possible liturgical roots of the many psalm-like passages that could reflect the Prophet's style, as well as liturgical practices behind the more developed late-Meccan recitations of biblical stories that are framed in paraenesis and praise.[27] And she finds linguistic markers of orality in "quantitative regularities between verse groups" that assist in the recitation of early short suras, reminiscent of the "measured verse" Dell Hymes found in the Chinook coyote tales.[28] She also sees an oral process in the rhymed "clausulas" that developed at the end of more simple units, giving a moral comment and an appropriate blessing of God.[29]

The priority of the Qur'an as oral recitation (*qr'n*) over its written form is being argued not only on linguistic but also on theological grounds. In a study of *al kitab*, the book, which has the authority of God's voice, Daniel Madigan shows that the Qur'an does not simply identify itself as the *kitab*. Only when it is recited is it called the *kitab* that represents God's authority and knowledge.[30] In this connection Nicolas Sinai claims that certain early Qur'anic suras "posit a transcendent source document, participation in which is supposed to invest Muhammad's recitations with a mediated kind of scripturality."[31] Proposing that this "scripturality" was a cultural bar set by the Jewish and Christian canons presented as divine revelation, Neuwirth sees the transcendent *kitab*

27. Neuwirth, "Psalmen"; Neuwirth, *Studien zur Komposition*; Neuwirth, "Von Rezitationstext."

28. Dell Hymes, *"In Vain I Tried to Tell You."*

29. Neuwirth, *Studien zur Komposition*; Neuwirth, "Zur Struktur der Yūsuf-Sure."

30. Madigan, *Qur'ān's Self-Image*, 13–52.

31. Sinai, "Quranic Self-Referentiality," 114–15, quoted in Neuwirth, "Two Faces of the Qur'an," 4–6.

concept itself reflecting the priority of orality as a communication process in specific exigencies. As an example she translates the Qur'anic creed spoken: "He is God, one, God the Absolute. He did not beget, nor is He begotten, and there is none like him."[32] She argues that this line reworks phrases from both the Shema and the Nicene Creed in a polemic for the universal, unbegotten, and unmatched God. In this way, the Qur'an's divine address is revealed to be in dynamic relation to human situations, as the Prophet interacts with listeners. It is oral in both its flexible vocal characteristics and in its tensions with other differently situated revelation claims in and outside the Qur'an.

## Implications

In these ways, critical scholars in Jewish and Islamic texts are shifting fixed assumptions about speech and writing as they recognize how essential was oral address to changing settings in the production of their foundational texts. The relevance of this work to research on Christian texts is too multifaceted to lay out here. At the least, it is likely that the gospels are also witness to oral dynamics that have been dismissed as inaccessible or irrelevant. Like the Mishnah and Tosefta, the gospel texts show certain deviations in parallel passages that are characteristic of oral tradition but have been interpreted largely in terms of literary dependence and authors' intentions. Yet we will be hardpressed to match Alexander's claim of an essential continuity between the performance tradition and its written record and interpretation. She argues that the Mishnah's deliberative ethos, if not its principles, triumphs in the Talmuds. Can we say that the gospels' native ethos (is it story? prophecy? proclamation?) is sustained for other times by its conversion into religious and, more recently, literary canon? The discussion of Qur'anic orality also raises the question of the extent to which the acts and sayings of Jesus in Mark evidence an address to different people that is sustained in new situations by its tellers, writers, and interpreters.

## Recent Research in Gospel Oral Tradition

Waves of awareness of oral tradition have from time to time lapped lightly across the modern study of gospel traditions, but there has been

32. Qur'an Sura 112; Neuwirth, "Two Faces of the Qur'an," 8–9.

no sea change in the way that the gospels are interpreted as interdependent texts of literary authors.

## Form Criticism

The first wave came with the form-critical work of Martin Dibelius and Rudolf Bultmann in the early twentieth century.[33] They brought into gospel studies what Europeans had learned from their national folk traditions and what Gunkel had discovered in Genesis and the Psalms, namely, the way traditional speech reflects its social functions. While Dibelius focused on preaching and teaching as the crucibles that shaped the gospel materials, Bultmann moved in the other direction, dissecting each kind of gospel saying or story to project possible situations that shaped its telling. Yet many aspects of oral tradition were not pursued, due perhaps to the trauma of the 1930s and 40s that left Dibelius dead and Bultmann reoriented on the theology of New Testament writers.

Other aspects of oral tradition were not fully pursued. First, the situations that gave rise to gospel speech forms were too narrowly conceived in terms apparently drawn from the preaching, catechesis, and mission of German state churches. A broader view based on the way parable teaching and prophecies of salvation and judgment functioned in Israel's crises could have led Bultmann and Dibelius to reconstruct communal situations more appropriate to mid-first-century political and religious settings.

Second, on the assumption that four individual evangelists composed the canonical gospels, they focused on tracing the smaller units of tradition used by these writers back to "original" oral forms and settings. This distracted them from attending to the more accessible process whereby stories and sayings are transmitted differently in different settings, making each telling one actual if provisional instance of a performance tradition.

Third, both Bultmann and Dibelius conceded that the individual units of tradition may well have been combined as they were transmitted. Dibelius spoke of the evangelists' freedom being greatly exaggerated, and Bultmann said that "the composition of the Gospel only

33. Dibelius, *Formation of the Gospel Tradition*; Bultmann, *History of the Synoptic Tradition*.

completes what was begun in the oral tradition."[34] Yet they did not press this insight toward inquiring how the whole story of Jesus may have been orally configured or to what extent the surviving gospels may represent instances in the journey of whole accounts being composed by favored tellers. It seems that their interest in recovering single sayings and actions of Jesus was greater than their readiness to hear the complex stories that were being told.

## Recent Study of Gospel Orality

The most recent wave of research on the gospels as oral tradition began with Werner Kelber's 1983 study, *The Oral and Written Gospel*, which proposed that the writing of the gospels put an end to a lively oral tradition.[35] Soon after, in an Edinburgh dissertation Thomas Haverly argued on the contrary that Mark preserves an orally composed tradition.[36] This unpublished work provides the first detailed analysis of Markan formulaic phrases and traditional scenes in the mode of Albert Lord's work on Slavic and Homeric epics. Joanna Dewey soon began studying many aspects of Mark as oral tradition.[37] She sees Mark's narrative structures to be characteristic of performance. Its addition and aggregation, repetition and enfolding, its agonistic tone and sound echoes, its measured variations from other gospels all point toward an early connected oral narrative.[38] She has recently proposed that the gospel of Mark may owe its survival after Matthew's and Luke's rewritings to its continued circulation as a popular oral tradition.[39] Dewey's broader research in ancient storytelling, alongside that of Holly Hearon, also provides a sharper view of possible settings where the gospel was told, with special focus on women's telling.[40] Meanwhile, Pieter Botha of South Africa has

---

34. Dibelius, *Formation of the Gospel Tradition*, 3-4; Bultmann, *History of the Synoptic Tradition*, 32.

35. Kelber, *The Oral and the Written Gospel*.

36. Haverly, "Oral Traditional Literature and the Composition of Mark's Gospel."

37. Dewey, "Oral Methods of Structuring Narrative in Mark."

38. Dewey, "Gospel of Mark as an Oral-Aural Event."

39. Dewey, " Survival of Mark's Gospel."

40. Hearon, *Mary Magdalene Tradition*, 19–42; Dewey, "From Storytelling to Written Text," 76; Hearon and Maloney, "Listen to the Voices of the Women"; Hearon, "Storytelling in Oral and Written Media Contexts."

produced a series of articles over two decades that shows how problematic it is to understand the gospels as Roman-period literary texts, as well as the promising way an oral tradition thesis suits Mark's style and themes.[41] Also the work of Richard Horsley and Jonathan Draper on Q as oral tradition pointed in a parallel way to Mark as a performance tradition. This work was developed further in Horsley's monograph on Mark, and with Draper and John Miles Foley in a recent collection of articles on orality in Mark.[42] And now Tom Thatcher has edited a volume that looks back on the twenty five years since Kelber provoked this research and ahead to new issues rising.[43]

The wider question of what an oral tradition approach might mean for gospel interdependence has been framed by James D. G. Dunn.[44] He observes from comparing the gospels that most material survives in multiple forms that reflect the flexible firmness of oral tradition—identity at key points, especially in direct discourse, and difference in the various ways things are told or elaborated. This confirms Bailey's research on storytelling in modern traditional communities that shows how themes that are crucial for a community's identity persist while expression varies with the performance situation.[45] Dunn has therefore called for altering the default setting of gospel study. It should now be assumed that gospel traditions have been transmitted orally except where extended identical wording requires an explanation in terms of literary interdependence. For him this means giving up the idea of a single original form for each saying or story, since Jesus' impact on people was "diverse in character from the first."[46] Other scholars are carrying this work further by means of statistical studies and by comparing the gospels with analogous parallel traditions.[47]

41. Botha, "Mark's Story as Oral Traditional Literature; Botha, "Greco-Roman Literacy"; Botha, "Social Dynamics"; Botha, "Mark's Story of Jesus"; Botha, "New Testament Texts."

42. Horsley with Draper, *Whoever Hears You Hears Me*, 123–94; Horsley, *Hearing the Whole Story*; Horsley, Draper, and Foley, eds., *Performing the Gospel*.

43. Thatcher, ed., *Jesus, the Voice, and the Text*.

44. Dunn, "Altering the Default Setting."

45. Bailey, "Informal Controlled Oral Tradition"; Bailey, "Middle Eastern Oral Tradition."

46. Dunn, "Altering the Default Setting," 172–73.

47. Mournet, *Oral Tradition and Literary Dependency*; Baum, *Der mündliche Faktor*.

## The Present Situation

Yet in most research the default setting has not changed, and the literary paradigm in gospel study holds fast. Some scholars may be drawing back from specific theories of synoptic interdependence, but they do so by focusing on a single gospel as an author's literary statement, as if research can ignore whatever preceded. The few of us who do see in the gospels an extended process of passing on tradition by incremental recomposition in performance tend to couch our proposals in modals with qualifying adverbs, and our suggestions weigh lightly against a century of literary analysis and files of lecture notes.

Enough research has been done that it is time to make the case for Mark as an orally composed tradition. This does not mean that we revert to a naïve picture of pure orality untouched by writing practices. Mark refers explicitly to written texts and to reading. Rather, it is a concerted effort to show that composition in performance can best explain how the text was generated—including the scribe's transcription as another instance in the expression of a still active tradition. Only such an argument can shift the default setting in the direction of Mark as a performance tradition and at the same time challenge those who read the gospel as one writer's achievement to defend their thesis.

In making the case for gospel oral composition, there would be advantages to beginning with a comparison of all the gospels in their sameness and difference.[48] Albert Lord has argued that the kind of flexible wording and ordering of stories in the gospels is witness to oral rather than manuscript traditions.[49] As expected, oral tradition is most stable where there is frequent use of traditional phrases, stylistic parallels, and direct discourse of key characters. But the complexity of the tradition made Lord doubt that any of the gospels could have been formed by a single author working from discrete sources in a manuscript tradition.[50] And he concludes, "The question of primacy is not a sensible one."[51] Yet the very complexity of the tradition makes it too great a task to work on four gospels at once. This leads me to set aside

---

48. For such an attempt concerning the Synoptics see Baum, *Der mündliche Faktor*.

49. Lord, "Gospels as Oral Traditional Literature."

50. Ibid., 80.

51. Ibid., 84.

for now the argument from gospel multiforms and work to make the case for Mark as a performance tradition.

## Major Objections to the Oral Composition of Mark

I will organize my arguments as a response to objections that face any proposal of Mark as a tradition composed in performance. This will allow readers to focus where their questions lie. The first set of objections rise from the external form of Mark. These will be addressed in Part 1.

1. As a book in print in the Christian canon, Mark is interpreted to claim authority for contemporary movements, in this case movements representing marginal groups whose social power is based on the spoken word and community life.

2. As a translation of a Greek edition, Mark is based on two finely-copied fourth-century parchment codices of the whole Bible, far removed from any performance tradition.

3. As a written document of whatever origin, Mark is demonstrably not a performance to be heard, but a book to be read.

4. As a Greek document, Mark can hardly be transmitting an oral tradition begun in Aramaic-speaking villages.

A second set of objections rise from the internal content of Mark and will be addressed in Part 2.

1. As a prose narrative, Mark was not recited in poetic meter nor sung so as to be readily memorable by oral performers.

2. As an account of recent events, Mark was not an ancient legend that would inspire repeated telling.

3. As a narrative of one man's life with certain consistent motifs, Mark was not the loose chain of episodes that might be expected from traditional tellers.

In Part 3 I will test my arguments against the above objections by taking soundings in Mark at three points where previous study has struggled to answer pressing questions of interpretation: Who is this Jesus? Is God's kingdom arriving? Is the good news left untold? I will be asking what the thesis of Mark composed in the telling can contribute to unraveling these knots.

In the Conclusion I will project two possible historical scenarios for the generation of the Markan story in order to stretch our imaginations. Finally I will summarize the case by beginning with the internal form of Mark and its apparent early telling to trace its development toward the book we read today.

# PART 1

# The Written Text of Mark: External Evidence of Composition in Performance

Initial objections to the thesis that Mark was composed over time in the oral tradition of a community come from the fact that we receive it as a written text translated from the Greek language as part of the Christian New Testament. None of this seems to require or even suggest composition in performance. I have broken down the problem into four parts and will work my way backward, beginning from the book that we hold.

First, Mark is part of the Christian canon. As such, it has a history of nearly two thousand years of veneration and, more lately, of detraction. Every interpretation of it takes place in this context and cannot escape being a claim on whatever reputation it has in the Christian churches and in the wider culture impacted by Christianity. This makes each reinterpretation of Mark suspect as a power play by some group claiming its authority, in the present case perhaps a contemporary group identifying itself with oral tellers of the gospel against established literary methods. In the United States I think particularly of feminist, womanist, and mujerista interpreters; black, Latino, and Asian-American theologians; Christian activists and practicing oral preachers and performers. All of these privilege oral and communal knowledge over literary and theory-oriented research. Meeting this objection is the task of chapter 1.

Second, the Mark we read is the translation of a modern Greek edition of this gospel, which itself stands on a narrow base. Early manuscripts of Mark are particularly few and fragmentary, and full manuscripts survive only from the fourth century when Mark is part of an elegant volume apparently prepared for the Roman emperor. Chapter

2 will ask if we have access to what a first scribe wrote, let alone to a speaking voice that he had heard.

Third, the Mark we know is not a flexible performance tradition but a written document received by readers—even when they read the book aloud to us. How can we understand what we do not have? Should we set aside the question of oral origins as something beyond our reach and accept the simpler thesis of a single author of this written text?

The chance for a simpler approach to an historical problem is significant, but in this case it needs to be resisted because it is based on modern assumptions about written texts. Before printing, each text was a precious and unique manuscript accessible to the few who were trained in reading and writing. Composing was done aloud, either while communicating or shortly before, and the occasional writing was done by dictation. Communication was always by speaking, even when a message had been written and was being read aloud for hearers. In his study of Homer Albert Lord said: "People did not wait until there was writing before they told stories and sang songs. Moreover, when these genres first appeared in writing, their metric base, their poetic and compositional devices, were already fully developed and none of them could have been invented by any one person at any one time. They are too complicated for that."[1] It may be that the simple theories that suit our experience are not adequate and we must settle for more complex proposals. This effort requires attention to historical context, to who composed documents in the Roman East of the first century, how and for whom they did so, as well as who wrote them down, how and for whom they did so. Only then can certain probable hypotheses be proposed about the origins of Mark. A review of this context for the writing and receiving of Mark and the consequent probabilities concerning this document is the task of chapters 3 and 4.

Fourth, Mark is written in Greek, yet the narratives are set in a time and place where the spoken language was Aramaic. So the major characters in Mark are quoted in a language they were not speaking. How then could the Greek Mark be the tradition that was composed orally as it was generated and transmitted in Aramaic-speaking communities? Chapter 5 will take up this problem.

1. Lord, *The Singer Resumes the Tale*, 1.

In all, the written text of Mark that we hold in our hands would seem to be many times removed from its pre-canonical functioning, its initial transcription, its probable Aramaic roots, and the performances in which it was composed. Yet we can only begin where we are, with our English Bibles that translate surviving Greek manuscripts. From here we trace our way back through the manuscripts to their writing, to the tradition's transition into Greek, and toward the gospel's composing. We find, in fact, that some kind of composing was going on all the way through this process.

# 1

# Mark Found in the Christian Canon

## Canon as Cultural Treasure

In considering Mark as part of an authoritative canon, a first response to the charge of a power play must be a concession that, yes, the thesis of Mark's oral composition reflects particular contemporary interests. If Mark were read today as a long-term product of several tellers and many listeners in communities gathered to risk the commitment it demands, it might challenge people now to an active communal response rather than to individual meditation on the meanings of an author. Because the listeners who favored such tellers would have represented a wider range of the society than the very few who learned to write, the tellers might be young or old, female or male, slave or free, Jew or Gentile, literate or not, and what they said and how they said it could appeal more broadly in that day and perhaps also in this. In addition, the open-ended quality of a traditioning process in which all performers tell the given story to convict their hearers would press contemporary interpreters of the written text to tell it more effectively in today's new, and yet also analogous, contexts. The single author thesis is of course also a reading strategy that reflects particular contemporary interests, and whether the scholar is sensitive or oblivious to this dynamic is not the determining factor.

Though no reading of the past is innocent, some approaches are more adequate to the ancient evidence and our contemporary needs than are others. This means that it is crucial that the field be kept open for different proposals to be considered on their merits. As new perspectives are brought to bear, research is stimulated and what has been assumed in a generation or a culture may appear as the emperor without clothes. For this to happen, there must be not only broad review of previous research and close reading of primary sources but also attempts to state the case for new frameworks of understanding. The case for Mark composed in performance has been gaining ground through the recent work of many, including Haverly, Botha and Dewey, Draper, Horsley and Dunn, and represents a disruptive and positive contribution to understanding Mark today.[1]

I am pointing here toward an understanding of canon as a cultural treasure chest in which old gems are preserved by being recut to shine with new facets. This is bound to meet objections on all sides. First I address objections from the religious side, then objections from critical theory.

## Objections from Religion

Those who see the canon as the rule of faith will object to the flexibility of oral tradition. What is to prevent Mark from changing into something not at all itself? And how do cultures like ours with multiple canons—Protestant, Catholic, Jewish, Islamic, and the Great Books of Western Civilization among them—manage to maintain their distinctive character? Do they not move toward a melding of traditions that violates the very function of a canon to let people know who they are and how they act?

The concern that a flexible tradition will lose its character comes from the assumption that truth is unchanging. If this is the case, any flexibility threatens truth, which must maintain its original form at all costs. In a print-based culture, we imagine that exact verbal transmission will supply this permanence, especially when a tradition is walled in as a canon. Yet it is common knowledge that Jesus was not an author and the tradition about him was carried orally, at least for some years. Therefore much attention is given to eye-witnesses who are reliable, confirm each other, and produce written records at an early stage.[2] Though we do not have these original documents, we have so many

1. See Introduction, section: Recent Research in Gospel Oral Tradition.

2. Byrskog, *Story as History*; Bauckham, *Jesus and the Eyewitnesses*; Bauckham, "The Eyewitnesses in the Gospel of Mark."

later copies that we think we can figure out where errors arose and reconstruct the original sayings and actions of Jesus.

None of this historical work is insignificant, yet it cannot be said to have secured the tradition in its original and inviolate truth. The danger is not that the oral story of Jesus was lost in the way a message whispered around a circle of people is garbled beyond recognition. These tellers were not repeating sounds hardly heard but were retelling a story that the listeners could affirm or correct. The danger in telling a story with one original truth is that it could take the hearers so little into account that they do not hear it addressing them and do not take it seriously—and soon it is lost. An effective oral tradition is retold to engage the hearers. Or, once written, it is interpreted to engage its readers. This engagement cannot dispense with the continuity of the tradition, but it allows sufficient flexibility for it to be heard in a new setting or a new generation. Historical analysis of the tradition is itself an important effort to engage the modern era with the biblical texts. But it does not need to project an inviolable origin that cannot be historical and that threatens to calcify the tradition.

Jan Assmann distinguishes two kinds of tradition: the stream of tradition that sustains the known world through repeated but flexible story and ritual, and the tradition once written and dammed up canonically that represents the permanence of transcendent authority and requires interpretation in order to impact daily life in new times.[3] New interpretation of a canon is no threat to its people. Rather, interpretation is the way the dammed up stream of tradition aerates itself to keep the lake fresh and life-giving within its canonical bounds. These interpretations earn long-term impact when they do justice both to the text they interpret and to the age in which they speak, to the tradition at stake and to the people seeking to live by it. We do see interpreters who bend the text to their power, as well as texts that serve death and not life, witness American slaveholders preaching the New Testament epistles. But there were and are counter-witnesses as heard in the African-American slave songs and narratives[4] and as heard in the early baptismal confession: "Neither slave nor free . . . for all are one in Christ Jesus" (Gal 3:28). The challenge to the historian is to hear the full con-

3. Assmann, *Religion and Cultural Memory*, 1–30, 122–38.

4. Hopkins and Cummings, *Cut Loose Your Stammering Tongue*; Courlander, *A Treasury of Afro-American Folklore*, 301–412.

flict in the text and among the interpreters and to expose the interests being expressed.

Because it is not finally the text or the present context but the living tradition where these two meet that has what Assmann calls the formative and normative effect, it comes down to active participation in the tradition. This means respecting both how it is immanent in daily life through special ways of speaking and how it transcends any single person's choices and orders a whole that one can only struggle to understand and embody.

And what of the dangers that other traditions in today's collided cultures pose to this symmetry? Does "true religion" or consistent living require us to withdraw into enclaves where purity can be achieved, if at the cost of influence? No tradition speaks on this question with one voice. However, most traditions make claims wider than an enclave can encompass: "In you all the families of the earth shall be blessed" (Gen 12:3); "The good news must be announced to all nations" (Mark 13:10); "Our God and your God is one" (*Qur'an* Sura 29). If these are heard not as pretexts to dominate but as responsibilities to bless, announce good news, and praise God, then an interface with others is essential to all these traditions, difficult though it is for each tradition not to universalize its own lens for what this means. It seems that the one God whom these traditions confess juxtaposes the traditions in a way they cannot easily escape.

## Objections from Postmodern Theory

The most vocal opposition to a tradition-challenged life in our time comes not from those on the religious front who petrify their canon to preserve it but from those on the postmodern front who reject every authority. Wesley Kort has argued that Western culture has often shifted its functional canon, first having oriented itself to the Bible, then shifting onto nature, then focusing on history and most recently lifting up literature as its scripture or lodestar.[5] Now the postmodern move deconstructs every gauge of value, "not reading anything at all as though it were scripture," as Kort puts it.[6] This free fall may be exciting, but it

5. Kort, *"Take, Read,"* 19–67.
6. Ibid., 69.

has its down side. Images ignore what they image, random persuasion rules, and even the constructing self is subject to political and economic manipulation.

Kort challenges his readers to seek a reappearance of the Bible as Scripture in the work of Maurice Blanchot and Julia Kristeva.[7] In no sense do they downplay the bankruptcy of modern culture. In fact, they accentuate it and take it in different ways as the context of their interpretation. Blanchot attends to Western culture's craving for answers, for unanimity, and for functional results to the point of genocidal violence. Kristeva experiences her world as internal alienation from all others and the self. The two call for exit, divestment, abjection, and waiting in the desert. But they practice these actions in part by flash frames from their biblical traditions. Blanchot sees Abraham leaving his known world, Jacob wrestling all night with the angel, Israel in exile. Kristeva sees Jesus' abandonment, suffering, and death. Kort stresses that tradition here is not being used to provide answers, which in today's situation would only exacerbate the cultural and personal plight. Rather, traditional resources help to illuminate "the whole catastrophe," expose the deceit, and allow space for a sign yet to come of mutual recognition and new life. Here one might say the Jewish and Christian canons become living traditions through the lens of these writers, who do not flee their postmodern worlds but find themselves driven to reading their biblical traditions in and through these worlds.

Kort calls this centripetal and centrifugal reading, centripetal reading being the deep penetration into the tradition for any hint of salvation for soul and body, and centrifugal reading being the movement out from this center to the farthest reaches of the shifting human dilemma.[8] The two ways of reading are not seen at odds but as necessary to each other, practices prone to a kind of oscillation.

From here, one can reflect back on the canonically-oriented interpreters and consider if they may not be reading in responsible relation to their very different worlds. Is there, then, no standard of right reading other than meeting the needs of an interpretive community, as Stanley Fish's view threatens to leave us thinking?[9] Even Fish recognizes

---

7. Ibid., 97–117.

8. Ibid., 29–30, 128–33.

9. Fish, *Is There a Text in This Class?*; Kort, "Take, Read," 80–85.

the possibility of mutual persuasion, which I think concedes a certain power that shared traditions have to serve as the fulcrum of this debate. What is necessary for effective interpretation is not only engagement with the full reaches of the specific world in which one interprets, but also readiness to hear and speak with interpreters from other places and times who dig deeply into common traditions. It is not that unanimity will quickly come or should come, but rather that the breadth of a living tradition may be revealed as it is exposed in different interpretive worlds.

The readiness to dialogue with other interpreters provides a challenge both to closed doors and trackless space. Interchange requires interpreters to demonstrate the appropriateness of their readings, not only to the people they speak for but also to others interested in the tradition they represent. Such dialogue encourages interpreters to recognize each other as people who have something to teach and to learn. New interpretations need not be dismissed as arbitrary power plays, but can be received as stimuli to fuller explorations of a living tradition. Positions being debated need not exclude each other. Mark can be interpreted as a tradition composed in the telling in a way that does not exclude a writer with a vision, and literary theories can recognize that the vision does not begin with a writer, nor end there. Composed in the telling, Mark belongs to all its composers.

# 2

## Mark Found in Manuscript

When reading ancient books in translation we assume that the editors have determined the original text from the surviving manuscripts and that the translators have done their best to put the text into our language. At most we compare several translations—or if we know the ancient language, several different manuscript readings—to consider the possibilities at crucial points. Largely, however, we take the printed text as the object of our interpretation. This is encouraged by those who refer to the Nestle-Aland Greek edition of the New Testament as the "standard text" and its widespread translation in the United States as the "New Revised Standard Version." At the same time many different translations are in public use, and text critics are now questioning if it is possible or even advisable to reduce thousands of Greek manuscripts, not to speak of ancient translations and quotations, to one virtual original. In addition, Mark presents its own acute textual problems. I am asking in this chapter how recent efforts to find and translate the Greek text of Mark contribute to our understanding of Mark composed in performance.

I take up three special problems of the Greek text of this gospel. First, Mark is the New Testament writing with the most variations among its ancient manuscripts. At the same time, these manuscripts differ at several points that are especially sensitive for its literary and theological interpretation. Second, in spite of the discovery within the last century of more than a hundred early papyrus manuscripts of the New Testament, Mark appears in only one of these before the fourth century, a fragmentary manuscript ($P^{45}$) not characterized by adherence to any sustained type of text. And third, the early Greek manuscripts of Mark that we do have are characterized by what is sometimes called a "free text." It seems to have been acceptable for the early scribes to rephrase statements or clarify awkward places so that almost all the variants that characterize later manuscripts have already appeared in Mark in the early centuries.

## Variation among Manuscripts of Mark

The unusual variation among manuscripts of Mark is demonstrated by Kurt and Barbara Aland when they compare the Nestle-Aland 25th Greek New Testament edition with six other modern editions. They stress how similar the different New Testament editions are, averaging only 4.4 variants per page. But the gospels average 8.1, and Mark itself averages 10.3.[1] This greater variation in Mark has been explained in different ways. Kurt and Barbara Aland suggest that the gospels have been more difficult to reconstruct because they were copied more often than the letters, thereby introducing more variants.[2] Yet there is no evidence that Mark was copied more than the other gospels. The prominence of Matthew in the early church could account for greater variation among Markan manuscripts, since some of them were harmonized with Matthew. Even so, this explains only one kind of variant. Joanna Dewey has proposed a different explanation, namely, that Mark was particularly effective as a performance piece in early churches and continued to be told after other gospels were being written.[3] These performances clarified and adapted Mark's story in ways that were incorporated by copyists into written texts. The harmonizing of Mark with Matthew could then be seen as part of this broader pattern of performing Mark in new circumstances, including circumstances in which other gospels were being performed and heard.

Lest this issue of more variation in Mark be dismissed as of little literary or theological significance—as though it were only a matter of a word changed here or there in an unchanged story—consider the opening and closing of Mark. In these two places the number of vari-

---

1. Aland and Aland, *Text of the New Testament*, 27–30.
2. Ibid., 30; cf. Parker, *Introduction*, 149–51, 157.
3. Dewey, "Survival of Mark's Gospel," 505–7.

ants is staggering. Is the first line simply "The beginning of the gospel" (Irenaeus), or "The beginning of the gospel of Jesus Christ" (Sinaiticus [א] and Origen), or "The beginning of the gospel of Jesus Christ the Son of God" (Vaticanus [B] and Bezae [D])? Or, according to J.K Elliott's conjecture, is the whole phrase and the following quotation a later addition to Mark at the time it is given the long ending?[4] In some manuscripts Mark ends with the women in the tomb stunned to silence (Sinaiticus [א], Vaticanus [B]). In an Old Latin manuscript the women tell the disciples, who then spread the word of eternal salvation (Bobbiensis [k]). Still other manuscripts describe how the disciples refuse to believe the women, Jesus berates them, and yet he empowers them to tell the gospel to the whole creation (Ephremi [C], Bezae [D], Freer [W]), in one case after warning them about the Devil (Freer [W]). No papyrus fragment of Mark has been found that contains the beginning or the end, leaving the above manuscripts as our early witnesses. I will return to Mark's beginning and end in later chapters, but it is clear here that the variations are not trivial. There seems to be more than one Mark.

## Meager Early Evidence of Mark

This brings us to the second problem that characterizes the manuscripts of Mark: few manuscripts have been found. The discovery of over a hundred early papyri of the Greek New Testament since the twentieth century has yielded to date many second and third century fragments, eleven of Matthew, five of Luke, and sixteen of John—some of significant length in the latter two gospels—but only one fragment of Mark.[5] This papyrus (P[45]) gives us less than half of Mark 6—9 and shreds of four other chapters, and no line is complete.[6] Even the fourth and fifth centuries leave us only a single further papyrus manuscript of Mark's second chapter, but there are seven more pieces of Matthew, two of Luke, and four of John. Although dating is occasionally debated, no

---

4. Elliot, "Mark 1.1–3."

5. See the chart inside the back cover of Aland and Aland, *The Text*; Nestle-Aland, *Novum Testamentum Graece*, 684–89; and P. Oxy. 4401–4406, 4445–4448; 4494–4495; 4803–4806.

6. Kenyon, ed., *Gospels and Acts*, part 1, text: 3–12, 51–52; part 2, plates.

one doubts that early evidence for Mark is thin. At least in Egypt where the arid climate has preserved all the papyri, Mark must have been copied less often, perhaps because it was considered a less comprehensive account of Jesus' life, less elegant, less apostolic, less focused on Jesus' speeches, or possibly too familiar as an oral account. Furthermore, a relative neglect of Mark is found in the New Testament quotations of early church writers who cite Matthew eight times more often than Mark, Luke three times more often, and John four times more often.[7]

Yet none of the gospel papyri are complete enough to provide full texts for interpretation. They have served primarily to confirm the ancient roots of certain types of text more fully preserved in parchment copies from the fourth to ninth centuries. For example, the text of Luke and John in a mid-third century papyrus ($P^{75}$) is so close to the fourth century Vaticanus (B), and yet not identical, that their common source is projected to have come from the end of the second century.[8] Kurt and Barbara Aland take this type of text as the earliest accessible New Testament and categorize all other types as later and inferior.[9]

Others counter that, although most papyri are of this kind, there is equally early papyrus evidence of several kinds of text. Eldon Epp designates text types with letters of the alphabet drawn from names of key manuscripts, speaking of a spectrum of types in the first five centuries with some conflation between them.[10] In addition to the $P^{75}$/Vaticanus (B) text mentioned above, the quite different text of Codex Bezae (D) appears already in some third century Acts and Luke fragments ($P^{29}$, $P^{38}$, $P^{48}$). By the sixth and seventh century there are papyri with the more elaborate Byzantine type of gospel text found in Alexandrinus (A), which by medieval times becomes the dominant text. As for Mark, its third century $P^{45}$ fragments show the roots of most of the fifth century Mark of the Freer parchment (W). However, in demonstrating this last point, Larry Hurtado found that these two ($P^{45}$ and W) are not precursors of the C text type of the later Caesarean parchments ($\Theta$, 565, 700 f13).[11] In fact, $P^{45}$ and W join Codex Bezae (D) in placing Mark at

---

7. Llewelyn and Kearsley, *New Documents*, 260–62.

8. Martini, *Il problema*, 149, as reviewed in Parker, *Introduction*, 320–23.

9. Aland and Aland, *The Text*, 105–6.

10 Epp, "Significance of the Papyri."

11. Hurtado, *Text-Critical Methodology*, 63–66, 88–89.

the end of the gospels: Matthew John, Luke and then Mark.[12] Also destabilizing the theory of a few defined and sustained text types are some papyri different from any of these, for example, the recently published P. Oxy 4968 with a text of Acts that summarizes and conflates.[13]

In any case, since papyri survived only by chance, we cannot conclude that the one early Mark papyrus ($P^{45}$) and its associate W reflect the original Mark. In a fourth century papyrus ($P^{88}$), Mark's second chapter is close to a B type text. And by the end of that century (about 400 CE) Mark appears in Codex Bezae (D) in a text nearly as distinctive as Bezae's Acts.[14] And not long after that Mark appears in the more Byzantine Alexandrinus (A) gospels. So early Mark seems to have been as varied as the other gospels. The question is whether this variety developed over time from the author's original manuscript as it was differently copied, with the B kind of text being more carefully copied than others, or whether the earliest tradition was itself fluid. If the latter, more uniformity will have come only gradually as each church center validated its familiar text and, finally, as church consolidation in Constantinople established the Byzantine (A) text. This is not to say that one region could not copy its text more precisely, but in this case other regions would preserve a wider range of early tradition.

## The "Free text" of Early Mark

The third problem with the early Mark is its loose copying or "free text." Here the Mark of $P^{45}$ represents an extreme form of what is a general characteristic of early gospel manuscripts. Scribes of all the papyri and many early parchments ($\aleph^*$, W, D) introduce small changes which are not traceable from one manuscript to another but seem to be the copyist's contribution. Words are added or omitted, synonyms are substituted, grammar is shifted, or details are adjusted. Ernest Colwell studied the distinctive patterns of the scribes of the early New Testament papyri and proposed that the $P^{45}$ Mark was not copied letter by letter or even syllable by syllable, but phrase by phrase, seldom producing something senseless, but often dropping short words or reordering to simplify

---

12. Skeat, "Codicological Analysis."

13. Parker and Pickering, "New Testament 4968"; Parker, *Introduction*, 171–74.

14. Parker, *Codex Bezae*, 24–30, 247–48, 257.

and clarify.[15] This scribal practice seems to have been less a matter of self-conscious correction than a matter of shifting or replacing words that had come to sound awkward or improper. Barbara Aland calls it a "smoothing out in the widest sense," a kind of "oxidation" or "rust" found in all the copying of the early centuries, and she compares it to the way that manuscripts after the tenth century all have a Byzantine patina.[16] Nevertheless, she argues that the best papyri resist this "oxidation," and she thus characterizes the more flexible texts as corrupt texts.

Others, however, see the flexibility quite differently. The copyist may be shaping the message to be heard in a specific setting where language or thinking varies, as cannot be avoided in translation. Colwell sees missionary aims driving the flexibility of the early versions and bilingual manuscripts.[17] Parker speaks of a copyist choosing a more vernacular, "homespun" Greek.[18] Dewey observes that since the gospel story at that time was carried as much by voiced tradition as by text it is not surprising that the scribes are informed by more than the document they are copying.[19] When the flexibility that Colwell finds in the scribe copying $P^{45}$ phrase by phrase appears also in the Freer Manuscript (W)'s singular variants, Hurtado suggests that these are "texts made for popular consumption" with easier readings and more frequent harmonization.[20]

All of the above factors—the greater number of variants in manuscripts of Mark, the lack of a single sustained text type for Mark, and the freer copying of the early Mark papyrus ($P^{45}$)—suggest that Mark might be better understood not as a single document composed by one person on one occasion but as a specific tradition taking shape in an extended performance of voice and of hand. In other words, the marginal freedom to adapt the text in the interest of communication that characterizes Mark as performance is not halted by hand copying. In contrast to the much later transition from copying to printing, which

---

15. Colwell, *Studies in Methodology*, 108–24, esp. 117; see also Royse, *Scribal Habits*, 103–97.

16. "Glättung im weitesten Sinne," "Oxydation," and "Rostfrass." B. Aland, "Münsteraner Arbeit."

17. Colwell, *Studies in Methodology*, 166–67.

18. Parker, *Codex Bezae*, 255–56.

19. Dewey, "What Did the Audiences of Mark Hear?"

20. Hurtado, *Text-Critical Methodology*, 65–81.

shifts interpretation to the sermon or the commentary outside the text, the transition to hand copying sustains for some time the process of each hand's interpretive performance.[21] This fluidity continues at least until copyists shift their attention from preservation by effective communication to preservation in the archives, from the copying of stories carried by familiar phrases to the copying of syllables or even letters, as Colwell finds beginning in $P^{66}$ and $P^{75}$ respectively.[22]

These observations mean that what most text critics take to be the preservation of the text through "strict text" copying—as found in the third century Luke and John of $P^{75}$ and in the fourth century Vaticanus (B)—may be the beginning of something new. In cities such as Caesarea and Alexandria, people had begun to preserve the text by archiving, editing, and literal reproduction, and it was to these circles that the newly converted Emperor Constantine sent the following letter addressed to Eusebius:

> Victor Constantinus Maximus Augustus to Eusebius.
>
> In the City which bears our name by the sustaining providence of the Saviour God a great mass of people has attached itself to the most holy Church, so that with everything there enjoying great growth it is particularly fitting that more churches should be established. Be therefore ready to act urgently on the decision which we have reached. It appeared proper to indicate to your Intelligence that you should order fifty volumes with ornamental leather bindings, easily legible and convenient for portable use, to be copied by skilled calligraphists well trained in the art, copies that is of the Divine Scriptures, the provision and use of which you well know to be necessary for reading in church . . .[23]

Eusebius concludes, "Immediate action followed upon his word, as we sent threes and fours in richly wrought bindings."[24] Whether this means the number of copies sent at one time or the number of columns per page, many text critics suggest that our earliest close-to-complete Bibles, Vaticanus and Sinaiticus, were produced through this patron-

---

21. Kirk, "Manuscript Tradition"; Assmann, *Religion and Cultural Memory*, 101–21.

22. Colwell, *Studies in Methodology*, 115–18.

23. Eusebius *Life of Constantine* 4.36, in *Eusebius, Life of Constantine*, 166–67.

24. Ibid.

age[25] And, as Epp has recently conceded,[26] our present Greek text and modern translations are based largely on these two documents, and on P[75] because it resembles them. Yet if uncontrolled texts came before this controlled text, to use Colwell's terminology,[27] then the controlled text can only tell us about the one tradition that it controls and not about the uncontrolled traditions that preceded it.

## One Mark or Many

Stepping back for a broader view, we find in medieval times that only the Latin Bible was known, and that only to monks and learned clergy. When the first Greek editions were made from recent Byzantine type texts, they had tremendous impact through their printed translations, the Luther Bible, and the King James Bible. But the Byzantine Greek text on which these were based had been developed and codified in Constantinople. It then became the great feat of the modern textual critics over several centuries to wean the church from this medieval *textus receptus* and to substitute critical editions based on parchments from the fourth to tenth centuries. Now papyri can take us farther back to the second and third century and show earlier roots of several kinds of texts that keep no uniform shape. Here the one text type represented by P[75] and Vaticanus has shown itself most internally consistent and in Egypt most widespread, causing our present Greek editions and translations to be built on that base, and leaving others on the cutting room floor.

Three major text critics object. J. K. Elliott insists that, where manuscripts differ, the critic must not favor any theory about type of text and age of manuscripts but ask only what variant best explains the origin of all others within the context of that document.[28] C.-B. Amphoux considers the Greek gospels of Codex Bezae (D) to have been edited by Polycarp in Smyrna about 120 CE and preserved through Justin and Irenaeus, only to fade in influence as the church shifted focus from

---

25. Skeat, "Codex Sinaiticus"; and Elliott, "T. C. Skeat on the Dating"; cf. Epp, "Significance of the Papyri," 76–77.

26. Epp, "Ancient Texts and Versions," 10.

27. Colwell, *Studies in Methodology*, 164–69.

28. Elliott, "Can We Recover," 17–44; Parker, *Introduction*, 343–45.

teaching to liturgy.[29] This argument suggests that modern critical editions based on the Vaticanus have resurrected the wrong corpse.

The third objector, David C. Parker, has done the most detailed study of Codex Bezae, is an editor of the International Greek New Testament Project, and writes comprehensively about directions in textual criticism.[30] His position is more nuanced. He recognizes the strict copying and early roots of the $P^{75}$/Vaticanus tradition, while at the same time questioning whether it can be considered the original text. If what characterizes the earliest manuscripts is the multiplicity of variants, then this flexibility is foundational. For example, he calls the tradition that produces the Codex Bezae a "confederacy" with "similarity not in detail but in character. We have not a text but a genre [of manuscripts] distinct from all other types, but puzzlingly unlike each other."[31] He continues, "The character of text we have in Codex Bezae is very old, older than the writing of Gospels . . . The possibility that Mark at least was never officially published raises some interesting questions as to our precise task in reconstituting the text."[32] And in concluding *The Living Text,* he says that the manuscript, like the telling of the story, does not carry a tradition that must be reconstructed behind it, but it *is* the tradition at one point, a tradition that continues to have effect in both written and spoken forms.[33]

If this points in the right direction, then it is appropriate to provide for people interested in Mark, not a virtual original, nor even an effort to reconstruct "the best accessible text" as our texts and translations are, but rather several actual manuscripts representing performances of Mark. One could begin with the Mark quotations of either Irenaeus or Origen in their canonical order (artificial, and yet instructive), then follow that with the fragments of Mark in Papyrus 45, the Mark manuscript of Sinaiticus*, Codex Bezae's Mark, and finally the Mark of Old Latin Bobbiensis' and/or the Freer Manuscript (W). A configuration of this sequence could be done with translations on facing pages, and with manuscripts and translations pulled up simultaneously on line. A

29. Amphoux, "Schéma d'histoire"; Parker, "Professor Amphoux's History."

30. Parker, *Codex Bezae;* Parker, *The Living Text of the Gospels;* and Parker, *Introduction.*

31. Parker, *Codex Bezae,* 284.

32. Ibid., 285; Clark, "Theological Relevance of Textual Variation," 15.

33. Parker, *Living Text,* 203–13.

yet more comprehensive project of this kind called *Marc Multilingue* is underway in Europe, providing in its first volume seven early Greek manuscripts of each paragraph of Mark with seven facing French translations.[34] Succeeding volumes will repeat this procedure for the key Mark manuscripts of Latin, Syriac, Coptic, and other ancient versions. If this can be done without taking an alternate manuscript as the gold standard, Mark becomes accessible as our earliest scribes performed it by hand. Granted that voice and hand will not have performed identically, here in manuscript the performance can be made visible and can prepare us to feature the gospel's oral performance and early composition more adequately.

34. Elliott, Amphoux, and Haelewyck, "Marc Multilingual Project"; Amphoux, "Une edition 'plurielle' de Marc"; Haelewyck and Arbache, "Presentation"; and Amphoux, "Evangile de Marc"; www.safran.be/marcmultilingue; Parker, *Introduction*, 201–2.

# 3

## Mark Found in Writing: The Setting

The most basic challenge we face from the external form in which we receive Mark is simply that it is a written document in our hands, not sounds in our ear. How then can we say that this document was composed in the process of performance? For this we have to see the way writing functioned in the ancient world, then the way people communicated with each other, and finally the way stories were shaped and why some of them were written.

### Writing and Reading in the Greco-Roman World

How we write and read today warps our understanding of ancient practices. So I begin with a quick scan of Greco-Roman reading and writing—who wrote and read, how they did this, and why, granted that generalizations can only be general. Who wrote is the question of literacy and social power. How they wrote has to do with materials and methods. And why they wrote concerns their purposes, insofar as these can be reconstructed.

Recent studies of ancient literacy have sobered scholars who had assumed that the classical period offered broad education. Writing was used in contracts, military organization, and governing, but the large majority of people functioned without reading or writing. Formal education occurred when parents hired teachers, largely restricting literacy to elite males and to slaves or other scribes trained to handle records. William Harris has estimated that literacy crested, not in classical Greece where it reached only slightly over 5%, nor with some extension of education by the second century BCE in the Mediterranean East at about 10%, but rather strictly in Italy of the first centuries CE at 10% to 15%.[1] At no time did small town or rural people, whose field labor produced the wealth of the ancient world, read and write.

Catherine Hezser's study of Jewish literacy in Roman Palestine concludes similarly, following Bar-Ilan, that because Palestine was largely rural, Jewish literacy cannot have been much more than 3%.[2] Small groups of temple and sectarian scholars studied Scripture and interpreted for ritual and daily life, and the few urban families with wealth and Roman connections educated their sons, but people of means like Babatha and Salome Komaise's brother in second century Palestine did not even sign their names, and Bar Kochba dictated to scribes, signing only one surviving letter.[3] In general, reading and writing were not a part of life except in small scribal and ruling circles.

One reason for this becomes clear when we consider the materials and techniques of ancient writing. Scrolls were the primary form for written materials of any length, made from papyrus often exported from Egypt, with Torah scrolls and other major documents made from the yet more expensive parchment. The scroll format did not allow easy reference to an earlier statement or quick comparisons within a text, let alone convenient copying from an old scroll that tends to roll up. Small notes have been found on clay and wooden tablets, which in this time are beginning to be tied together into notebooks. From this notebook shape the parchment codex develops, which becomes the form used for Christian gospels. This book form was more convenient for writing, and it was cheaper because written on both sides, yet it was still unwieldy and heavy in the case of long texts. Inks were difficult to use, both for handling and for writing clearly on irregular surfaces. Derrenbacher says that desks did not come into use until the fourth century, which leaves all this happening with scribes sitting cross-legged on the floor.[4]

Most difficult from our perspective is the way letters appear on the page. There is no spacing between words in Greek at this time, no regular punctuation, no paragraphs or chapters, and no titles until the

---

1. Harris, *Ancient Literacy*.

2. Bar-Ilan, "Illiteracy," 35, 38; Hezser, *Jewish Literacy*, 34–36.

3. Hezser, *Jewish Literacy*, 184, 253–90.

4. Derrenbacker, *Ancient Compositional Practices*, 34–37; Botha, "New Testament Texts."

end of a document. This steady stream of letters would be hard to copy without losing ones place, and harder yet to read. In fact, reciting would require previous practicing of the text in order to distinguish words and sentences, virtually to learn it, so as to make it audible to others.[5] A literate letter carrier would want to practice reciting the letter on the road in order to be able to read it with affect. If we add the difficulties in reading that would come for us without eyeglasses and electric lights, the complications of the written medium become almost insurmountable.

In fact, we cannot grasp how these people read and wrote without recognizing that writing was strictly a surrogate for speaking or, better, an accessory to speaking. The composer spoke to a scribe who wrote the letter and the reader spoke again to bring it back to life for the addressees. Writing and, to a lesser extent, reading were skills of specialists in a world where people communicated by speaking. Quoting Ken Morrison, Botha puts it that texts "were never more than a 'variant of oral utterance due to the lack of procedures for transforming writing into text.'" Only with writing conventions of medieval and modern times like separate words, sentences, paragraphs and section headings was "speaking in text" changed into a visual "writing in text."[6]

Why then do people of the early Roman Empire write at all? What is the specific function of this practice for the people who use it? If we set aside the many reasons for speaking which will be considered below, it seems that the specific reason for writing something is to extend one's power, whether militarily, financially, commercially, or socially. By writing and reading, soldiers are enlisted and campaigns planned, people are registered for taxation and taxes collected, supplies are ordered and delivered on time, graves and buildings are inscribed and fame won. In short, the few who are literate are able to use their literacy, inefficient though it may be, to maintain their command of the resources that the society produces. Literacy and record-keeping not only confer a mystique that can be used to impress others but also allow a level of organization necessary to achieve and maintain dominance. So it may not be poverty or inefficiency in organizing schools that prevents wider literacy in Greece or Rome but rather the confidence that

---

5. Saenger, "Separation of Words"; Botha, "New Testament Texts."
6. Botha, "New Testament Texts," 627; Morrison, "Stabilizing the Text."

these skills belong in the hands of those that rule, while others do the labor that is their lot.

The question remains whether those who cultivate religious texts are an integral part of this process. Clearly they are expected to be so by those who profit from social control, witness the status of priests and scribes in each empire. Some religious leaders and other literates may see themselves operating against the grain in their interpretations and social practices, but they find themselves at least on an ambiguous periphery of power.

This analysis of the function of literacy to maintain power is supported by the widespread popular distrust of the written medium in the ancient world. Rosalind Thomas says of classical Athens that writing was accepted as trustworthy only in late stages of the city's development.[7] Jensen adds that since literacy did not come to Greece with a conquering foreign culture, its status even among the powerful was not high compared to that of Homer, whose tradition was sung and whose authority came from the Muses.[8] Nor was writing seen by the Greeks as an effort to establish fixed texts, Jensen claims, since they seemed unaware that oral texts were flexible. When they wrote on vases, coins, and gravestones, they made objects speak in order to secure ownership or incur fame, not primarily to make a message more permanent.

Among descendants of Israel, the written Torah was far more venerated than studied, but its traditions, like those of ancient Greece, were well-known orally. This happened through songs and stories of Abraham and David and Moses, shaped, as one can see in the Pseudepigrapha and Targums, to speak to the present time, and beginning from some stage in this period, read and heard as Torah in the synagogue. Writing other than the copying of Torah was disparaged and seems to have been associated with securing property in commerce, tax registering, debt records, and land deeds.[9] Hezser adds that the eventual writing of the Jerusalem Talmud, like the scribal codifying of law in the Roman context, was not a concession of access to the many but an effort by the few to secure their religious and political influence.[10] If we seek a reason

7. Thomas, *Oral Tradition and Written Record*, 27–32.

8. Jensen cites Plato in *Phadrus* 49–55 in "Albert B. Lord's Concept of Transitional Texts," 94–114.

9. Hezser, *Jewish Literacy*, 500–503.

10. Ibid., 435.

why a narrative like Mark becomes transcribed in writing, we must ask whose power such writing would serve at the time. But first, if writing was seen as a tool of a small literate group in ancient societies and hence not expected to be trustworthy, how did people communicate with each other?

## Communication as Speaking

Though we must make exceptions for other kinds of human physical contact such as fighting and feeding and lovemaking, communication in the ancient Western world is speaking. Or we can say, verbal communication is by the mouth. This takes three general forms: speaking in action, speaking in confirmation, and speaking assisted by writing. In the first category fall all the kinds of expressive, informative, and instructional speech of everyday life which I will not further delineate. This is by far the commonest form of speaking, also in our time. In the third category we will come to the least common form of speech in the ancient world, speaking that uses a transitional step of writing. Meanwhile, there is a second category of speaking crucial in traditional societies, the speaking that confirms what is already recognized. It appears in daily speech when we speak to reassure ourselves or others, but its classic role is in the areas of social, political, and religious life where cultural memory is fostered. Here people speak to remind themselves who they are and what they characteristically do. Though some changes occur when the tradition is brought into each new context, the primary purpose of this speech is not to innovate but to confirm.

Who speaks this way? This speaking belongs to communities, because it takes time for a tradition to develop, and an individual life is short. It is the people of a community who know their tradition that are the ones to speak it, and in any given community some people are taken to be more competent in the tradition than others. These people have learned to speak by hearing the tradition over time and by being encouraged to participate in the speaking of it. When a tradition is young, many participate, so that people have heard each other and come to favor a skillful speaker. In more established groups the older, more trained or more powerful may have the speaking roles. The speaking skill is many-faceted, involving not simply memory and voice but a grasp of the whole tradition, a grasp of the listeners' situation, and the ability to put the two together, to tell the tradition so that people claim it as their own.

How the tradition is told depends on the kind of tradition. Here the form critics had it right, that the situation determines the appropriate saying, whether a lament or curse or victory song or prayer of repentance. In these settings, the words spoken are often an integral part of a ritual action. The speaking may be done by the body as well as the mouth, but the purpose is to express loss or gain, grief or joy, within an overarching confirmation of life as the community understands it.

Narrative speaking of tradition tells the story of the group or of key events or figures that have shaped it or are anticipated to do so. Here the occasion also shapes the speaking in different ways. For example, the *4 Maccabees* memorial day speech in honor of the martyrs is nothing like the praise of Wisdom's deeds in Wisdom of Solomon 10 or the escapades of Aesop in the *Life of Aesop.* Yet each presents an oral event in which the values of a group are exemplified and confirmed. The focus may be on a wondrous beginning, a model character, a community-shaping event, or the defense of a course of action, and the story in each case draws people in to confirm what keeps them going.

Such speaking may be ephemeral, good for one occasion and gone again after it has had its effect. Or it is retained in the cultural memory and revived at appropriate times by those who tell it best. But in a few cases, speakers will use the assistance of writers, usually in order to speak to another time or place. When this happens, writing does not replace speaking. Rather, writing can make it possible for the speaking here and now to happen again there or then. A speaker may dictate a letter addressed to another place, which will then be carried and read to the people there. Or he dictates a speech to his descendants that will be spoken at a later time. In this way, sounds can speak through an object. The drumbeat or Morse code sends a distant message. A curse tablet can (it is believed) mediate invective. An inscription can cause someone to speak its words to others—so that the gravestone asks passersby a question from the dead or the temple dedication causes speakers to speak the donor's name to her honor. A speaker may practice a speech, so to speak writing it in his mind, and deliver it tomorrow. Or a speaker can dictate an agreement, a deed, or the royal annals that may be read later to a court or council when an issue is contested. In each case, speaking is assisted by some mediating tool. Nevertheless, the effecting start and the affected end of the communication is spoken. If at some time this pattern is broken so that the start or end is silent, such that someone composes a letter silently as he himself writes it or reads a gravestone silently and alone, this is an exception, not a normal communication.

In an environment where people communicate by speaking, composition is not identified with writing, not even in the literate and affluent classes of society. Pliny, for example, describes himself composing before daylight in his bed, then calling in someone to take dictation as he speaks. Later, he composes outdoors or even when riding around his estate, and then he dictates afterward to a scribe (*Letters* 9.34). Also for his friends he holds private readings of what he has composed to get their critique or praise (2.10; 3.18; 7.17). Or he gives the address in public, what Botha calls oral publication.[11] His communication is assisted by writing, but speaking remains his aim.

## The Writing of Traditional Narratives

In a cultural context where people communicate by speaking in order to carry out and confirm their lives, and where writing largely serves the rulers and fosters their power, it seems unlikely that traditional narratives would be written at all. And most of them probably were not. But once a culture is writing, some of its traditions do get written and the question is: why does this happen? and how does this happen? An adequate historical answer to these broad cultural questions is not possible here. But some sketch of the possible reasons for writing traditional stories and of the possible ways they get written is needed as a template for weighing how the specific performance tradition of Mark could have become the book of Mark that we receive.

It is not a sufficient answer to the question of why traditional stories get written to say that they can be used to serve the power of those who are literate. That seems to be true, but it is too general. Of what particular use is such writing, and for whom exactly? I propose three reasons why traditions that have long been told might be set to writing. First, the community faces a conflict and it serves one side of this conflict to put the tradition in writing. Second, those who know the

---

11. Botha, "New Testament Texts," 629–33.

story experience a crisis of such proportions—persecution, war, exile, death—that someone seeks to sustain the tradition through writing. Third, the tradition enters another social world where writing is used for such accounts.

The conflict theory has the advantage of assuming a power struggle, which could explain why literate people assert their control over the storytellers by presenting the tradition in writing. It assumes that the tradition is so embedded in the community that it cannot be set aside or much changed. But it could be retold in a certain way that curbs tendencies within it or that secures it against changes that could arise. But why is writing used to shape the tradition, since the oral story is already flexible and open to new performances? It may be sufficient from the perspective of literate people that readers will gain a certain priority in interpretation from having direct access to the story that others will lack.

The second alternative is that writing is a response to a great crisis. This reason for writing a familiar story seems likely for the first century when we read the account of Palestine's traumatic history in the second book of Josephus' *Jewish War*. At least it makes sense to those of us living in a print culture. When everything is in turmoil, we think a book could offset the loss of the storyteller, the meeting place, or even the community. But we forget the investment necessary to find a scribe and writing materials and time and space for writing in persecution, war, or slavery. And the product will not be a pamphlet that everyone can carry with them but a single heavy scroll, a large papyrus codex, or dozens of wooden tablets in no way handy for times of hiding or evacuation. In contrast, a story in the memory and in the mouth is highly portable and far more persuasive. In fact, a community's scattering in crisis could provoke the wider telling of their story. On the other hand, the impending or recent death of a much-loved performer might precipitate the writing of his or her story, whether as a writer's tribute to that evangelist (as suggested in the epilogue to the Fourth Gospel), or out of concern that the complex tapestry woven in a community not begin to ravel.

A third alternative is that the tradition enters another social world where writing is more widely used. Here the change from composition in performance to text-assisted performance would not be made to defend one view of its meaning or to tide the tradition over a crisis. Rather it happens because the story comes to people who expect a text. When disseminated forms of a tradition meet each other and their differences begin to rankle and get rounded off, this can raise the question of the "right story." In this vein, Nagy proposes that the Homeric epics became more uniform due to comparisons that arose when many people were performing them at the Athenian Pan-Hellenic Festival, leading eventually to transcripts being written that later came to be used by performers.[12] On the other hand, it may simply be that, where other authoritative traditions are available in writing, an influential group in a community may consider that writing would add stature to their performed tradition. Or a text could be useful to someone who is literate, such as a young performer impatient with learning by ear or a man of means wanting to ponder the story at home. The new text would not take the place of the performer in the community, but in time it could have an impact on the tradition being performed and limit the flexibility of its performance. Once the written form becomes the text's measure, interpretation will occur outside the story rather than in the way it is told.

Before taking up the question of why Mark itself was written, I need a further template of options for how oral traditions appear in writing, turning from motivations to methods. Here Foley has taken up from A. N. Doane four possible patterns: 1) a scribe transcribes a performed event; 2) a performer transcribes his or her own performance; 3) a literary author imitates a performance tradition; and 4) a scribe recomposes the story for his audience in a parallel way to what oral performers have been doing.[13]

On the first two options, Albert Lord observed that texts of oral songs cannot be transcribed well by hand without slowing down the performer, breaking the rhythm, and interrupting focus on the audience—barring, he adds, great infusions of wine, I gather for the singer, not the scribe. He concludes, "There is very little chance . . . that our written texts [in the Slavic tradition] were taken down during performance."[14] Concerning the second option, he observed that oral performers are seldom writers, and those who are literate do not reproduce their own songs well. Lord did defend his scheduled tape

12. Nagy, *Poetry as Performance*, 108–10; Foley, *Singer of Tales in Performance*, 76–78.

13. Foley, *Singer of Tales in Performance*, 74–75; Doane, "Oral Texts," 80–82.

14. Lord, *Singer of Tales*, 126.

recordings of prime Slavic singers, noting that gifted performers were glad to take all the time they wanted to sing. Yet at the same time, Lord claimed that changes he found in these songs were not due to a conscious aim at a new audience. He did concede, nonetheless, that such induced recordings were oral-traditional in a bit different way.[15] All of this points to the shifting sands under our feet when we think we have in writing—or can even now get—the song that is being sung or the story that is being told.

The safest way out in reading old texts would seem to be the third option of settling for an author who is making literary use of an oral register of speech. It is certainly common, especially in narrative genres, for writers to adopt a storytelling style. But it is also presumptuous to say that all surviving stories come from writers borrowing or imitating traditional patterns. Alain Renoir suggests that one can project a spectrum that ranges from a traditional poet writing for oral address to an audience steeped in the tradition to a poet with some traditional background writing for readers strange to an oral tradition.[16] To gauge where a text falls on this spectrum, he says, one must ask about the extent to which the composer is shaped cognitively and emotionally by the oral-formulaic tradition, the extent of familiarity with tradition assumed in the intended audience, and the extent to which listeners or readers are being addressed. Such care could allow some discrimination between more and less traditional writings. Yet, even so, it does not include the composition that takes shape outside the literary sphere in human speaking and that enters the literary sphere only late and perhaps awkwardly. Where we know traditions that are coming from sustained and close-knit communities with an active oral life, there must be a way to test the possibility that a tradition owes its shape to patterns developed in its performance.

Perhaps Doane's and Foley's fourth category of "scribal re-performance" can be interpreted to allow for this option. Doane writes: "I am proposing a fourth model: reperformance. Whenever scribes who are part of the oral traditional culture write or copy traditional oral works, they do not merely mechanically hand them down; they rehear them,

---

15. Ibid., 126–29. Compare also the induced transcription by one talented singer of the Tulu oral epic in South India as described by Lauri Honko and Anneli Honko in "Multiforms in Epic Composition."

16. Renoir, "Oral Formulaic Rhetoric," 116–19.

'mouth' them, 'reperform' them in the act of writing in such a way that the text may change but remain authentic, just as a completely oral poet's text changes from performance to performance without losing authenticity."[17]

The scribe here is not the proverbial slave or monk who copies letters by rote in a sentence (or even in a language) he does not understand. Here the writer is part of the traditional culture. Whether himself a performer of tradition or simply a long-term listener, he knows how it goes, and why. So, in writing, he takes on the responsibility of each performer to make the story heard in the present place and time. This means that one cannot call his work a transcript of a speaker's performance, since the writer may be performing for a somewhat different audience, and some turn of the tradition as recorded could come from his particular re-performance. Even a second or third copying by this person or by someone else within the tradition could have this character, witness some interpretive changes in early manuscript traditions.

Yet this is very different from saying that the scribe becomes the author of the text. I would not even speak of a spectrum of re-performance here running from the most incremental change of the tradition to an author's radically new conceiving of oral traditional material. Rather, two different things could happen that only an outsider to the tradition would confuse. On the one hand, an author makes a point or an image using stories or songs that suit his aim, as in Doane's third option above. Or, on the other hand, in the fourth option, a scribal performer reasserts for his traditional audience what has been handed down, with adjustments made so that it will work in the present setting. In this case, the scribe is one of the several composers-in-performance of this tradition, no less creative than others, but also no less intent than others to pass on the tradition that has come down without loss.

And what can "without loss" mean in a context where tradition is not static? Traditional performers have told Foley that they speak the tradition each time word for word, even though he observes changes. He explains this phenomenon by saying that the performers' spoken words are not our letters with spaces between but meaningful lines or episodes, the "bigger words" that are integral to the story. No viable performer omits what makes the tradition what it is; and no viable per-

---

17. Doane, "Oral Texts," 80–81.

former adds what is not true to it, no matter how much it is condensed or elaborated.[18] The listeners of the tradition do their part by adjudicating truth and vocally critiquing a performance that is not faithful to the tradition. Doane says that truth in an oral song "seems to mean validity of the stance of the story by bringing it into line with the stance of its audience."[19] Albert Lord, as often, hits the nail on its head: "All sounds [that make a certain point] are comparatively variable; within a measurable range they are the same. From the position of the receiver, sounds within that range may be recognized as 'the same' even if they actually are not . . . This characteristic of sound, the fact that its variability is understandable within a range of limits, belongs to all types of discourse; it is basic to orality."[20] This characteristic would seem to apply also to a written text shaped in scribal re-performance. The sound of the tradition, the truth of its "bigger words," could still assert itself through a new, if awkward, written format as soon as it is vocalized again. Or does the fact that it is now being read from letters on a page hamper the reader's recomposing in performance and take from the story its living flexibility? Perhaps not initially so, since the reader can flex the tradition. And yet in time this seems to happen.

18. Foley, *How to Read*, 17–20, 125–41.
19. Doane, "Oral Texts," 81.
20. Lord, "The Merging of Two Worlds," 19–20.

# 4

## Mark Found in Writing: The Event

Because traditions composed orally—in our day family stories, jokes, accounts of disasters—do not normally get into writing, an argument that Mark was composed orally begs some explanation of why and how it was written. Those who study ancient literacy seem to agree that writing served the power of the literate minority, but such writing could take a myriad of forms, and this observation provides only the broadest guideline for understanding how a specific text like Mark was written. More concrete indications may come from a study of its contents which will follow in later chapters. Yet it is possible from the general options outlined above for why and how ancient traditions were written to consider which ones suggest themselves as more likely in the case of Mark. A few have been proposed for Mark and received some discussion. Others have not.

### Why Mark Was Written

Of the conflict, crisis, and cultural explanations for why Mark was written, the model of conflict in the community has often been favored. The Lutheran tradition's contrast between theology of glory and theology of the cross was for years seen as the clue to understanding the writer of Mark who corrected the tellers of glorious miracle stories with the Pauline proclamation of the cross. Redaction criticism has since provided a method whereby many have understood Mark the writer to be standing against his sources or against opponents associated with the disciples or miracle workers or esoteric teaching.[1] In a wide-ranging study of oral tradition in early Christianity, Werner Kelber contrasted the oral speaking of the disciples, the family of Jesus, and the prophets with the written medium by which the writer of Mark sought to limit the power of these figures.[2] And although Kelber no longer speaks of a mutual exclusion of orality and writing, he does not want to rule out the idea that "Mark's particular problem with oral speech" was crucial to the origin of the gospel genre.[3]

Considering the common function of literacy in maintaining social power, as well as the many serious conflicts attested in the New Testament, we certainly cannot rule out conflict at this point. At the same time, there is no reason to explain all the tensions in the text from a writer's wrestling with the tradition. Incremental changes occur in many performances and tellers retain much of what has been passed on, so that inconsistencies and conflicts can be knit into the tradition before anyone writes. One could say that if performing this tradition were not already a way to press a certain point or give a certain twist to the story, a writer would not have the forethought or even the option of doing so. Mark may therefore be the result of multiple layers of conflict, a conglomerate, making it unlikely that a single major conflict can explain the tensions in the text.

But what kinds of conflict might potentially have provoked someone to write Mark down? If there were tellers with different renditions of Mark, a writer could hope to legitimize one telling by producing it in a written form that could be seen and touched—and even occasionally read when a reader was available. Kelber's thesis that the writer opposes other leaders who claim spirit-given power exercised in oral proclamation suggests more than a fixing of outside limits. It also suggests an exposé of present leaders who are represented by the disciples, Jesus' family, and the prophets. Is Mark then best read in this transparent sense? Or does Mark support the commitments of the disciples even when they fail to live them out? Perhaps a double vision is necessary to

1. See, for example, Lohmeyer, *Das Evangelium*; Marxsen, *Mark the Evangelist*; Weeden, *Mark*.

2. Kelber, *The Oral and the Written Gospel*.

3. Kelber and Thatcher, "'It's Not Easy to Take a Fresh Approach,'" 41 and 30. See also Kelber's defense of the conflict theory in "The Oral-Scribal-Memorial Arts of Communication," 250–52.

see in Mark both the power of God's Spirit and the weakness of those who embody it.

Recent theories of Markan authorship have more often relied on a crisis model of explanation than a conflict model, either a crisis of persecution in Rome that called for faithful witness in the face of possible martyrdom or crises associated with the Roman-Jewish war and the destruction of the Temple in Palestine. In the latter case, some have proposed that the writing took place in the early years of the war at a time of apocalyptic anticipation, which the writer seeks to temper. Others propose a post-war time of hopelessness when Jesus' judgments against the Temple can be shown to be fulfilled, or a time of backlash against Jews with Gentile contacts met by Jesus' call to preach to all nations before the end. It is no surprise that the tradition was reheard at each crisis of its people since they lived in a changing present time. Nor is it a surprise that these crises are less than explicit—my student said of Mark, "I see no signs of war here"[4]—since tradents are not remaking the story but rehearing it in another setting. Yet it would be surprising if it were only at the single point of transcription that the tradition was being directed for hearing in some new way.

To focus the question we can ask what kind of crisis might have brought on a transcription rather than another oral re-performance of Mark. It is tempting to think of the preservation of the tradition in times of turmoil. In this period the Qumran manuscripts survived because they were hidden in caves, some of them carefully placed in jars for their preservation. Yet these scrolls speak of reading during meals and studying all night, which suggests they were written for use in such practices, not for preservation, but we have no signs in Mark that its communities studied scrolls or read their own traditions. Even the words of Scripture in Mark are apparently remembered rather than read (see errors in 1:2 and 2:26). And it is Jesus' opponents whom he taunts, "Have you not read . . . ?"—implying they do not understand and carry out what they claim to read (2:25; 12:10, 26).

If Mark was not written for preservation in a crisis or for daily study, nor, as we saw earlier, written for handy carrying into another land in flight, exile, or slavery, how else would writing serve in a crisis? I can imagine that the death of a long-standing and particularly gifted

---

4. Marilyn Chilcote, 1979.

teller of the story might mobilize a literate participant to make a script. This would be more likely if the scribe were identified with the rendition he could remember and feared that it might be lost or compromised. Or as a son or disciple of the deceased, he might anticipate being asked to perform the story after its echo was no longer clear in his own ears. The question might then be: How much would his writing mirror his mother's or his teachers' voice? Or how much does he adapt his telling to the presenting situation of loss?

On the other hand, the transcription of Mark into writing could happen, not due to a community conflict or a general crisis, but because the story enters a writing and reading culture. Village listeners may not hear a short telling of the story differently from a long one; and the artisans in city shops may recognize the same story whenever they hear it. However, a person who normally recites lines from a written Torah or Homer may wonder at variations in a parable's telling or discrepancies in the Markan quotations. When a group that tells Mark also acquires a Greek text of Genesis or Isaiah or the Psalms, it may want its own story in a form that can also be opened up to read and rolled up to put away. Interpretation of Mark would then follow its reading, as with Genesis, rather than be integrated within its retelling. Or a script may be needed to train new tellers of Mark in more literate settings where traditional oral practices are unfamiliar.

Concerning likely triggers for the writing of Mark, all the theories seem to exaggerate the significance of writing as the turning point in the Markan tradition. Whether a conflict, a crisis, or an increasingly literate culture provoked writing, none of these were singular events. All were endemic in first-century Israel and its diaspora. The tradition must have been weathering them all over decades through the skill of its tellers or there would have been no narrative to write. To put this in another way, the task is much larger than identifying what provoked some one person at one time to write. It becomes the task of tracing from what we find within the gospel that has come down to us clues about why it took the shape it did, probably first in many voices through traditional forms, then in a few tellers known for their skill, and finally in a number who tell it on parchment—though these stages will have overlapped and the oral account remain dominant for decades. In this process caution must be taken not to focus narrowly on what is new at each stage if we find that the flexibility of the tradition in its changing contexts serves the tenacity of the tradition rather than vice versa. Then the historical question of the stages of the tradition's development becomes less central than the hermeneutical question of how the tradition is shaped in new contexts.

## How Mark Was Written

If we shift the question from why an orally composed Mark came to be written to how it was written, we are faced with options similar to those noted in the previous chapter for how performance traditions appear in writing. These can provide a spectrum to keep in mind as we turn to the content of Mark. Does our Mark descend from a transcript of a performance in process, from a performer's later self-transcription, from a writer's imitation of the tradition, or from a scribe's re-performance of the tradition? Weighing the first two—dictation to a scribe or self-transcription—the low literacy level in Palestine and in cities of the Roman East of 3 to 10 percent at the highest tells against self-transcription. Accomplished performers would not likely be the ones skilled enough in the scribal arts to put their own speech into letters on a line. And why would they want to do so? The scribe would more likely be a different person with other motives. And what would make the performer tolerate constant breaks in momentum so that a scribe could get it down, as the first option proposes? Also, too little in Mark speaks for the third option of a literary writer who imitates the tradition. The sentences are not woven together into literary periods, nor do the episodes build into crescendos. The lack of any authorial presence in Mark is unlike even the literature that imitates a speaking voice.

There is more reason to consider the fourth option of scribal re-performance. Here the focus is not on determining if the scribe transcribes his own performance or another's but on understanding the scribe as himself performing the tradition in the act of writing. In re-performance the scribe takes on responsibility to engage his audience with the familiar tradition in the present exigency. Far from setting himself apart from previous performers as an author or redactor, the scribe continues the ongoing composing of the tradition, preserving what has been passed down by incremental shifts that keep it focused where people are. At the same time, the change to a new medium of writing would constrain the writer to keep as close as possible to the familiar account.

The question is whether at the time of writing the traditional audience might include a person who is not only able and equipped to write its story but sufficiently versed in its compositional practices so that he can re-perform it as he writes. He must neither bore people with a wooden copy of a previous performance nor offend people with omissions or additions that do not reflect the tradition they know. If we assume that Mark has been transmitted in Greek for years and probably decades in increasingly urban settings, the likelihood of such people within its hearing circle should no longer be small.

Is there a tentative hypothesis here of why and how Mark is written? We can work backward from this proposal of scribal re-performance. The scribe writes from inside the community tradition—what outsider would be motivated to write?—and continues the practice of composition in performance, but with a reed and ink as mouth. This person is constrained in the same way as previous performers to move the traditional audience to renewed commitment in their present context. Being literate, he is almost surely male. He leaves no signature, in contrast to the intimations in Luke's prologue or Matthew's hints of kingdom scribes and a literate tax collector among the twelve. Nor is there any tribute to a dead tradent, as in the final lines of the fourth gospel. The dominant message of Mark does not seem to be an exposé of the Jerusalem circle of Jesus' friends and family or a warning against miracle workers or false prophets. These may be crusades from the past that have left their mark on the story. At the time of its writing Mark takes on the specific format that can eventually carry it into a world that is more literate and probably less traditionally informed. But the written Mark would have been unwieldy and very difficult to read. It was likely reserved in a case for symbolic value or used for pedagogical purposes in its early decades while oral performers continued their composing task.

It remains an open question whether the writer is simply a scribal hand at the right place and time to put this remarkable question mark of a gospel into a format needed for an extended journey. Can we find in this work not only the conflict and crises of the past decades but also a step being taken to assure a particular right hearing of its story in its own time of transition? It will not be possible in the scope of this study to sort out the incremental changes of the tradition that have occurred over its decades of composition. Instead I will focus on understanding the one performance we are reading, which, as Doane says, is "the manifestation of the whole tradition at that point,"[5] incorporating as it does all surviving layers of a tradition that is being re-performed in writing. In doing this, I follow the scribe most faithfully by not highlighting contrasts between this version and those that have preceded it but by taking the whole including its tensions as it is presented—a story started but not ended.

5. Doane, "Oral Texts," 89.

# 5

## Mark Found in Greek

Before Mark was written, it was already told in Greek. But the question remains how this tradition became Greek if the events that it recounts occur in an Aramaic-speaking world. Can it then be a tradition that was composed in performance by people shaping their stories and expressing their identity? Have the Greek-speaking performers of this story and their hearers chosen to orient their lives on an exotic foreign world? Or have the traditions undergone a cultural shift so that they no longer speak the same language as the people of their heritage? A rough analogy could be the way that the Greek Bible or Septuagint functioned for Hellenistic Jews in cities of the Roman East. The Jews of the diaspora recognized familiar stories now told in their new cosmopolitan tongue, while proselytes were drawn to a tradition and a people not their own. But can Mark, in something like a half-century, have been composed in performance at the same time as people strange to its native tongue came to hear it and it shifted languages? Could the tradition cohere and its composition continue across the gap between the Semitic and Indo-European language families?

I am not proposing that an original text has survived unaltered across the language change or that a story was cast over a language barrier by one group and caught by another. But it is possible that the text we read could be one instance of a firm yet flexible performance tradition that spread and took form in more than one language. In this case the continuity would be, not a continuity of certain words, but of a continuity of bilingual people who adapted the shape and form of their tradition in a world where cultures overlapped. Not only could one favored teller in a place give way to another, but the auditors could shift in such a way that a bilingual context leads to a language shift. The question whether this is the case with Mark is best addressed in three parts, from generic to particular: how do traditions cross language gaps? how were languages distributed across the Roman East? and how could the Mark tradition have become Greek without ceasing to be traditional?

## Traditions Crossing Language Gaps

There is no question that traditions cross language gaps. Although ancient traditions often survive in later forms of their first language, they also appear in new language forms. One need only think of Buddhism in China, Confucianism in Japan and Korea, and Judaism in Europe and America. Texts will have been translated in such a process, and yet the transition is not initially textual but cultural. The complexity of these transitions cannot be adequately discussed here, but several factors may be involved. One factor is the disruption of traditional patterns caused by technological and cultural changes that allow one group to get access to land, to consolidate power, and to undercut other state or local subsistence economies. With this disruption come shifts of peoples, as military, governing and religious leaders expand their influence, and as others move to survive, to protect themselves, or to improve their situation.

In this process bilingualism occurs when different language groups overlap.[1] This is not a single phenomenon but one that varies greatly depending on such factors as the genetic relation of the languages involved, the different levels of competence in primary and secondary languages, the purposes for which each language is used, and the social dominance of one language over the other.[2] It is widely recognized that a subordinate group more often learns the dominant group's language than vice versa and that balanced bilinguality—equal competence in two languages—seldom occurs unless cultural identification has become double.[3] Nonetheless, recent experience with simultaneous trans-

---

1. Hamers and Blanc, *Bilinguality and Bilingualism*, 155–79; Fishman, ed., *The Sociology of Language*, 314.

2. Silva, "Bilingualism."

3. Hamers and Blanc, *Bilinguality*, 20–54; Hezser, *Jewish Literacy*, 237–43.

lation has shown the remarkable facility of certain bilingual people to hear something in one language and speak it in another, particularly when translating into the mother tongue. Such oral speaking outshines competence in translation of documents precisely because it is colloquial, aiming for equivalent significance without regard to wording and giving weight to paralinguistic features such as tone, association, and implication.

The question then becomes whether, in the place and time when Mark was being composed, there was sufficient language overlap that tellers of this story would be ready and able to make it heard in a different language without losing the traditional sound of its speech patterns. This would require not just personal bilingual competence of speakers but also bilinguality of the primary traditions that shaped people's language competence in the way that the Septuagint reflects for Israel's biblical lore. At the same time it would require listeners who were not bilingual enough to hear the story in its first form in order to cultivate the transition. It bears repeating that the point is not that a document could be translated and yet keep its original form, but that a bilingual cultural setting could allow a tradition to be begun in one language and continued in another—without, of course, excluding continuation in the first language.

## Languages in the Roman East

Making sense of a society such as first century Syro-Palestine where many different languages are active cannot ignore history, even though actual origins may be forgotten and current use may shape how languages are perceived.[4] Hebrew was the language of the ancient texts of Second Temple Judaism and was used when reading the Torah and Prophets in this region and when scribal communities interpreted these texts as they did in the Qumran Habakkuk scroll and the Mishnah. That Hebrew represented the people's identity is also clear by its revival in movements of political independence, as can be seen in the coins and letters of Bar Kochba during the second revolt against Rome. Also later

---

4. Fitzmyer, "Languages of Palestine"; Hezser, *Jewish Literacy*, 227–50.

rabbis cultivated children's study of Hebrew to raise up Torah readers for the synagogues and sustain the identity of the people.

But Aramaic, the official language of the Persian Empire that returned to Palestine with the exiles, became the standard spoken tongue. It is attested in parts of Ezra, Daniel, the Qumran texts, and the Palestinian and Babylonian Talmuds. As a Semitic language with many variations that is cognate with Hebrew, it could have been taken by the people of Israel in Hellenistic and Roman times as a modern or daily-spoken form of their own tongue.[5] The Targums preserving the Aramaic interpretations of Hebrew Scriptures that followed the synagogue readings show that an Aramaic translation became necessary in order to communicate to most people what the Hebrew text meant.

Greek was the language of the next empire in Palestine, establishing itself after the conquest of Alexander the Great in the three centuries before Christ. Many old and new cities were colonized with Greek patterns of government and culture. Israel's struggle against this tide of Hellenization reflected in 1 Maccabees finally gave way and collapsed under the Hellenizing of the ruling Jewish families. The language of occupiers can last longer than the occupiers do, and Greek became the international language in the Mediterranean cities.[6]

Latin arrived in Palestine with the Roman armies the century before Jesus and represented the ruling Roman Empire. Occasional gravestones of Roman soldiers and dedications on buildings made it visible in Palestine, but it was seldom heard, because the Romans used Greek to speak with provincial elites. Perhaps the fact that Latin represented the imperial occupation and Hebrew represented the ancestral tradition gave comparative neutrality to the Aramaic and Greek languages left behind by earlier empires. Hezser has observed that the large majority of Jews in Roman Palestine had no ideological reservations against Greek nor attachment to Aramaic.[7] Yet insofar as Greek and Aramaic functioned in first-century Galilee as markers of the urban and rural social classes respectively, they must have carried that valence.[8] And

5. Watt, "Current Landscape of Diglossia Studies"; and Paulston, "Language Repetoire and Diglossia."

6. Mussies, "Greek as the Vehicle of Early Christianity."

7. Hezser, *Jewish Literacy*, 240–41.

8. How multiple language situations spawn social conflict is analyzed by Schjerve and Vetter in "Historical Sociolinguistics and Multi-lingualism."

that valence could also have helped motivate the retelling of Mark in Greek when the story got to the cities.

This turns me to the crucial question in multilingual contexts of how different languages are used and by whom. Catherine Hezser begins and ends her review of language use in *Jewish Literacy in Roman Palestine* by quoting from the Jerusalem Talmud *Sotah* 7.2 (21c): "R. Yonathan of Bet Guvrin said: Four languages are appropriately used in the world. And these are: Greek for song, Latin for war, Aramaic for mourning and Hebrew for speaking."[9] In this neat scheme each language has its function. "Greek for song" may be a third century rabbi's relegation of Greek to the ancient poets (or to schoolchildren's chants?), and "Hebrew for speaking" may assert the time of study or the weekly Torah readings. The link of Latin with war fits its restricted use among Roman soldiers and administrators in first century Palestine, and the association of Aramaic with mourning could reflect women's cries in the daily language of the people.

That Aramaic is taken as the common spoken language of Jews in the first century is clear in the Aramaic exclamations of Jesus quoted in Mark: to Jairus' daughter, "Little girl, get up!" to the ears and tongue of the deaf mute "Be opened!" and on the cross, "My God, my God, why have you deserted me?" Josephus describes himself standing on the walls of Jerusalem under siege calling the Jews to surrender in their native tongue (*Jewish War* 5.361–419). When the New Testament says that people are speaking Hebrew, they probably mean Aramaic taken as the spoken form of their language (Acts 21:40; 22:2; John 5:2).

What scholars contest is not the place of Aramaic as the common spoken language of first century Palestinian Jews but the extent to which Greek functioned as a second language.[10] Greek was the language of the Jewish Diaspora and its returnees in Palestinian cities as well as the language used by the Romans and the Herodians to rule and collect taxes. In addition, the coastal cities such as Caesarea apparently functioned in Greek, as did commerce across Lower Galilee between these cities and the Greek-speaking Decapolis. What is less clear is how widely Greek was used in the largely Jewish city of Jerusalem and in

9. Hezser, *Jewish Literacy*, 227 and 250.

10. After almost forty years, Fitzmyer's essay remains a solid general assessment: "Languages of Palestine"; see also Hezser, *Jewish Literacy*, 230–35.

Herod's new Galilean cities, Sepphoris and Tiberius.[11] Porter notes that half the Jewish graves in Jerusalem are inscribed in Greek and argues that Tiberius was "probably even more bilingual than Jerusalem," although this seems to conflate evidence from several centuries.[12]

However, once a significant Hellenizing of Jewish life is recognized in these cities, as can be seen in the material remains,[13] and in the vignette of Herod Antipas' banquet (Mark 6:21–29), the question becomes: How were Herod's cities and the more Gentile cities to the east and west related to the small towns and villages of first century Palestine where the large majority of Jews lived. Oakman, Horsley and Sawicki see conflict.[14] The pressure of Roman taxes and Herodian urbanization fell most severely on peasants whose labor was the main generator of wealth. They were caught in debt, land confiscation, high land rents, and tenuous day laboring, which alienated them from Hellenistic culture in local cities and in Jerusalem and Rome. Freyne recognizes peasant hostility against Herod's cities in Galilee but claims that Galileans remained close to Jerusalem because of the historical kingship and the Temple.[15] Others contend that although rural poverty was endemic in ancient Palestine the presence of Herod's cities would have raised employment prospects of local potters, masons and farmers, drawing them toward a measure of Greek competence to increase their production and sales.[16]

The opposing views in this debate about peasant attitudes to Galilee's cities may not be mutually exclusive.[17] If some villagers lost land and hope while others sought small profits from trade, this would intensify conflicts between rural people. Those who announced a new

---

11. On Sepphoris and Tiberius as Jewish cities, see Reed, *Archeology and the Galilean Jesus*, 42–55, 100–138.

12. Porter, "Jesus and the Uses of Greek in Galilee," 136, 147.

13. Reed, *Archaeology*.

14. Oakman, *Jesus and the Economic Questions of His Day*; Horsley, *Galilee, History, Politics, People*, 202–21, 238–75; Sawicki, *Crossing Galilee*.

15. Freyne, *Galilee from Alexander the Great to Hadrian*; Freyne, *Galilee, Jesus and the Gospels*.

16. Zangenberg, ed., *Religion, Ethnicity and Identity in Ancient Galilee*; Claussen and Frey, eds., *Jesus und die Archäologie Galiläas*.

17. For a spectrum of scholarly views and an evaluation of this kind, see Reed, "Instability in Jesus' Galilee," 343–44.

kingdom might well become alienated from their families and be run out of hard-pressed towns near Herod's cities where other people hoped to make the best of new opportunities.

## Mark as a Greek Tradition

The Greek of Mark has generated a wide range of research, and at least two aspects of this research could have implications for how an Aramaic tradition became Greek.[18] Scholars have disputed whether Mark's Greek is a distinctive kind of "Jewish Greek." Deissmann proposed from study of the Egyptian papyri that the standard Greek in the Roman East was the Koiné or common Greek that we find in Mark, with a later correction by Deissmann himself that some Semitisms are of course present in the Koiné of Aramaic-speaking groups.[19] Recently Moisés Silva demonstrated from comparative work that the structure of widespread languages does not change when new groups learn them, explaining why the phonology and syntax of the Koiné remained firm while different Palestinian speakers used their own phrasing and preferred expressions.[20] In any case, the Greek of Mark is not distinctive enough to allow us to recover an earlier Aramaic narrative.[21]

Another approach has been to claim that Greek was more widely spoken in first century Galilee than previously thought, with the implication that the story could have been Greek from the start. This has been argued on the basis of widespread use of Greek in Lower Galilee,[22] and from Jesus' communications with Pilate in Mark 15:2–4 that would have required Greek, assuming the accuracy of that story.[23] One can

18. For an introduction, see Porter's collection of articles: *Language of the New Testament*.

19. Deissmann, *Bible Studies*; Deissmann, *Light from the Ancient East*; Deissmann, *Philology of the Greek Bible*, 51, 62–65.

20. Silva, "Bilingualism," 223–26.

21. Yet Matthew Black's Aramaic retroversions in *An Aramaic Approach to the Gospels and Acts* are still useful in deciphering certain difficult sayings of Jesus. And this method is further developed by Bruce Chilton et al. in *Comparative Handbook*, where the Aramaic retroversions of sayings in Mark are given a literal English translation.

22. Sevenster, *Do You Know Greek?* For bibliography see Porter, *Language of the New Testament*, 24–25.

23. Porter, "Jesus and the Uses of Greek," 149–53.

concede the possibility that Jesus could have learned to handle Greek by working in construction in Herod's first capital of Sepphoris four miles from Nazareth. Or fishers from Magdala and Capernaum could be using Greek to sell fish in Herod's second capital of Tiberius on the lake. But no one has successfully argued that most accounts in Mark reflect a Greek-speaking world or were likely to have been generated in Greek.

A remarkable aspect of the Markan narrative is that Jesus' ministry takes place strictly in small towns and the countryside. Although Galilee is surrounded by cities on the coast and to the east, and Herod Antipas in Jesus' lifetime builds the two major cities of Sepphoris and Tiberius in the heart of lower Galilee—the first close to Nazareth and the second to Magdala—Jesus and his followers are never said to enter a city until his last week. Herod's cities are ignored, and other cities outside Galilee are represented only in their tributary regions, as in "the region of Tyre," "the villages of Caesarea Philippi," or "the region of Judea beyond the Jordan" (7:24; 8:27; 10:1). The "cities" referred to in Markan summary statements along with "villages" and "farms" to show Jesus' wide range of activity are apparently not cities but Galilee's larger towns (1:33, 45; 6:56).

This avoidance of cities in Mark could be explained in two ways. Either the worlds of the country and the city were so alien in language and culture and population that they never met, or there is an ideological critique of the cities being reflected in this telling of the story. The alienation of countryside from the city in the Roman East is mirrored in reverse in ancient literature where history, philosophy, letters, and novels all are limited to an urban world and its outlying plantations. So is Mark simply "another world heard from"? Yet there also seems to be an intentional polarization in Mark between the banqueting Herod Antipas and the hairy John the Baptist (1:4–8; 6:14–29), between the disciples awed by the stones of the Temple and Jesus turning over its tables and predicting that one stone will not be left on top of another (11:15–17; 13:1–2). Granted that no attack on the cities is explicit until Jesus enters Jerusalem, nonetheless this gospel falls in closely with accounts of prophets attacking urban leaders who exploit the peasants, and with rabbis who consider Tiberius polluted because built on a graveyard (Isa 3:13–15; 10:1–4; Hos 5:1–4; Amos 2:6–9; Mic 3:1–12; *y. Shevi'it* 9.1 [38d]). It seems safe to say that the Markan story presents Jesus over against the ruling urban culture and those who adjust to it.

If so, this gospel's locating Jesus' work in the countryside reflects its cultural alienation from the values represented by the cities and also makes programmatic Jesus' contrary announcement of God's kingdom.

## From Aramaic into Greek

How then might this once rural and Aramaic tradition have become Greek? At least three factors may have played a role. First, the disruption of society and the shifts in populations in first century Palestine through exploitation and suppression, then war, slavery, and flight, apparently propelled this rural Jewish movement by dispersion into urban fragments across several Roman provinces. Paul's letters already show multiple conflicting groups in Greek-speaking cities making some claim to the Jesus tradition and testing different ways it could engage new settings. We can see how scattered Jesus' followers were by the distinctive development of several narrative traditions about Jesus that emerge by the century's end in the different gospels. Although Acts gives the impression of a planned expansion of the gospel by divine agency and human organization, Jewish and Roman historians show that the trauma of the times made any continuity difficult and thereby intensified the struggle for survival, roots and common purpose. And Jesus' followers were only one group among many in Israel reshaping their stories after the Temple's destruction in 70 CE.

In addition to disruption, a second crucial factor is the specific bilingual situation in the first century cities where the Markan tradition was being performed. Because the study of bilingualism in the Roman East is recently developed[24] and because the gospels are only recently being considered as possible traditions shaped in performance, what can be said at the juncture of bilingualism and gospel as performance remains untested. Perhaps sociolinguistic study of different multilingual situations today could provide models for exploring language use in a Hellenistic city. Is it more like Switzerland with several language territories in stable mutual relation? Or is it like Singapore with a once-colonial international language uniting people who also speak their na-

24. Taylor, "Bilingualism and Diglossia"; Watt, "Current Landscape"; and Paulston, "Language Repetoire."

tive languages and dialects? Or perhaps like Scotland with a dominant language and a residual minority who can speak Gaelic?[25]

The differences in Greek cities would be further variables—whether in Palestine or Asia Minor, large or small, old or new, as would be also the status of the Mark-telling groups—whether largely citizen or alien, slave or free, male or female, Jew or non-Jew. One could assume at points of transition that the group includes Aramaic-speakers who brought the story with them as well as some Greek-speakers who were raised in the city and speak little or no Aramaic. All would speak some Greek, and most people outside the group would speak only Greek, or Greek along with some other native language in the area. Any of these factors could encourage those who tell the story to follow each piece with a Greek telling, or get someone else to do so, until the whole story was known in Greek. A Greek telling would be motivated not only by interest in clarity for listeners and outreach to others, but also by any sense that Greek was the standard language or proper way to speak in the city. People who speak Greek from childhood, such as Paul, would have a certain advantage, and the new form would tend to spread in cities until it might also be expected where Aramaic was known.

A third necessary element for language transition beyond social disruption and bilingualism is cultural overlap. As we saw, linguists find balanced bilingualism, in which people speak both languages with native competence, only where they are at home in two cultures, that is, where they have managed some kind of cultural integration. In contrast to the alienation between villages and cities in Galilee, people with Hebrew/Aramaic roots in many cities had learned to live in both an Aramaic world and a Greek world. They could speak traditionally in Greek because their tradition was already known in Greek, the Septuagint having been translated from Hebrew two centuries earlier. Many writings in this tradition were composed in Greek or translated into Greek from the second century BCE to the first century CE: Sirach; Wisdom; First, Second, and Fourth Maccabees; Tobit; and Judith, to name a few that have survived. In the late first century Josephus wrote *The Jewish War* in Aramaic and then translated it into Greek with help from native speakers. Institutions such as the synagogue were developing in this period where Hebrew, Aramaic, and Greek were used. It is

25. MacKinnon, "Power at the Periphery."

not surprising that the groups who knew Mark and heard the law and the prophets read or at least interpreted in Greek, had no trouble expressing their stories in Greek. In fact, the story of Jesus could be said to become more traditional rather than less traditional as it was integrated into the Hellenistic Greek shaped in the synagogue.

We have traced Mark back from our English Bibles with their variety and their shifting cultural weight to the Greek manuscripts. There we found many Marks, as the tradition was being hand-written and adapted in late antique and Byzantine contexts. The scribes of these manuscripts were constrained by the oral and then the written tradition that was well known, but they were still expected, like those who told the tradition before them, to make it speak to their present settings. Before it was written, Mark was being performed in Greek for people in Hellenistic cities who knew no Aramaic, thanks to bilingual Jews who had been used to hearing their Scriptures read in Greek. And before—and after—it came to be performed in Greek, it was performed in Aramaic in the regions of Palestine, Syria, and places east where Aramaic was the spoken tongue. I refer to these Aramaic performances as compositions because the story first took shape and developed here. But I also call compositions what occurred in the Greek performances and in the Greek and then translated "free text" writings of this tradition, as well as in modern dramatic and sermonic renditions. This tradition has stayed strong by being limber as each generation has made the story its own.

# PART 2

# Language, Scenes, and Story Patterns: Internal Evidence of Composition in Performance

We face here a yet more intractable series of objections to the thesis of Mark as a performance composition. They arise, not from the external form of Mark as a canonical translation of Greek manuscripts, but from what we might call its internal form as an extended prose narrative of recent events. The objections are, first, that Mark is not epic poetry or song, second, that it is not ancient tradition but news, and third, that it is not a string of oral stories but an integrated composition.

The first question seems to be whether Mark could have been remembered in its full length since it was neither recited in poetic meter nor sung to music. Its patterned speech does not meet Albert Lord's definition of the formula that he found characteristic of traditional literature, namely "a group of words which is regularly employed under the same metrical conditions to express a given essential idea."[1] But the issue is broader than how much a person can remember without meter. Mark is short as traditional sagas go, and its narrative detail and plot development make it memorable. The broader question is whether Mark's language is formulaic in the sense of traditional, that is, whether the words that have been chosen evoke foundational cultural meanings and whether the syntactic and structural choices in the storytelling signal an oral register—a speaking voice. This is the issue of Mark's "texture," following Alan Dundes' categories.[2] Does the language of Mark undermine the thesis of its composition and transmission through performance?

1. Lord, *Singer of Tales*, 30–67, quotation on 30.
2. Dundes, "Text Texture and Context"; Wire, *Holy Lives*, 10–18.

71

Second, it is argued that the Christian story was too new at the time Mark was composed to have cured into a functioning oral tradition. This is the question of the content of the gospel, what Lord called its themes and Dundes calls its "text."[3] I will be referring to these units of the Markan narrative as scenes or episodes. When we read these scenes one after another, Mark seems to be a report of many recent events rather than an evocation of the identity-shaping legends of the past that we expect to find in an oral tradition. Does the content of Mark, the kinds of episodes it tells, play against its being a cultural performance tradition?

The third objection is that Mark is a whole story, not a bundle of pieces, and the unifying elements seem to require an author who has drawn these particular stories together to address some exigency. This is the question of the genre of the book, or the story pattern as Lord called it for oral literature, that which gives the text structure and coherence and focuses its meaning. In this connection Dundes speaks of the "context" of a narrative because its unity is shaped in and will be appropriate to the context that it addresses.[4] Does the consistency in the Markan story make unlikely its oral composition by multiple tellers?

This series of objections concerning Mark's composition in performance rising from its texture, text, and context—its language, its episodes, and its overall unity—will be addressed here in Part 2. The questions will be: Is the texture of its language sufficiently formulaic? Are the themes, episodes, or scenes that make up its text traditional? And can successive performance contexts have shaped the story into a whole? Here hangs the case, I would say, because only the story as told in Mark can demonstrate the way it came to be shaped and the meanings it took on as it was told and retold.

3. Lord, *Singer of Tales*, 68–98; Dundes, "Text, Texture and Context"; Wire, *Holy Lives*, 10–13.

4. Lord, *Singer of Tales*, 99–123; Dundes, "Text, Texture and Context"; Wire, *Holy Lives*, 10–11; 16–18.

# 6

# The Language of Mark as Performance Tradition

## Mark as Oral Composition

Earlier efforts to demonstrate that Mark is an oral composition[1] have given priority to identifying its formulas and themes. This followed Milton Parry and Albert Lord who took Homeric formulas and themes as the best evidence that these epics were orally composed. Thomas Haverly's dissertation is most comprehensive at this point and a mine of proposals.[2] Yet the fact that he omits from formulaic tradition Jesus' sayings and Scripture quotations suggests that he takes Mark as a narrative framework for the gospel being transmitted, whereas Jesus' speech is part and parcel of the narrative tradition, in fact, some of the more formulaic aspects of it. Pieter Botha's articles recognize that the sheer quantity of formulaic language cannot demonstrate oral communication.[3] He calls for taking formulas as textual symptoms of the compositional technique that is a process and not a product, a process found in many kinds of folklore. The challenge in the study of formulaic language, he says, is to get beyond labeling certain phrases as formulaic to finding language clues to the hearers' contextualized participation in the tale-telling process.[4] Dewey's work stresses the oral structuring of material in Mark, such as the echo patterns within the stories and

---

1. For a fuller introduction to recent research on Mark as oral tradition, see Introduction, section on Recent Research in Gospel Oral Tradition.

2. Haverly, "Oral Traditional Literature," 141–325.

3. Botha, "Mark's Story as Oral Traditional Literature," 311–17.

4. Here Botha (ibid., 326–31) refers to Foley, *Oral Tradition in Literature*, 1–18, 217.

between stories.[5] In her view it is patterns like these which show the written text to be a transcription of a performance or a further development of a story-telling tradition.

What seems clear is that, although Slavic and Homeric epics may be characterized by formulas such as the heroic epithets, and themes such as the banquet, these particular patterns do not provide a universal method for identifying orally composed literature. The same regularities are unlikely to appear elsewhere. And to understand the nature of the regularities that we do find, we must ask not only how they function to assist reproduction of the stories but where they come from, or at least how they are sustained. Are they taken simply as survivals from "old times"? Do they last because of their "catchy" sounds, whether by repetition, rhythm, or meter? Or do they reflect the way people talk?

## Mark as Speech, and Special Speech

Granted that the language of tradition generally sounds old and has a certain rhythm, yet the clue to what distinguishes it from literature may be that it is spoken language. Here I follow the work of Egbert Bakker, a classicist who does not rely on formulaic phrases in characterizing Homer but identifies the Homeric epics first of all as speech.[6] He understands speech through discourse analysis as developed by functional linguists such as Bernstein, Bateson, and Halliday.[7] Bakker's approach has been shaped particularly by Wallace Chafe's observation and description of the way people talk.[8] Writing usually proceeds in sentences and paragraphs, but Chafe's *Pear Stories* showed that when people of different cultures and languages were asked to tell a simple story that they had seen on a silent film, they did so in a running stream of short phrases following each other without much syntactical connection at all.[9]

---

5. Dewey, "Oral Methods," 32–44; Dewey, *Markan Public Debate*, 8.

6. Bakker, *Poetry in Speech*; Bakker, *Pointing at the Past*.

7. Bernstein, "Elaborated and Restricted Codes"; Bateson, *Steps to an Ecology of Mind*; Halliday, *Explorations in the Functions of Language*.

8. Chafe, *Discourse, Consciousness and Time*.

9. Chafe, "The Deployment of Consciousness."

> And then a boy comes by
> on a bicycle
> the man is in the tree
> and the boy gets off the bicycle
> and . . . looks at the man
> and then uh looks at the bushels
> and he . . . starts to just take a few
> and then he decides to take the whole bushel [10]

On the basis of Wallace Chafe's hypotheses concerning human speech Bakker makes proposals about Homer as oral performance that are suggestive for texts like Mark.[11] Bakker begins with Chafe's proposal that speech occurs, not in sentences, but in short "intonation units" of about three to seven words. This follows the pattern of human consciousness that, like human vision, focuses on only a small part of what is presented at any one moment. Consciousness moves quickly on, as does vision, to a new focus, and then to another, producing speech that is a flow of word-units only loosely linked to each other by "and", "but," or simple juxtaposition. Chafe also notes two other important features of speech. The "one new idea constraint," identifies that each "intonation unit" presents no more than one new idea. The "light subject restraint," observes that the subject or topic of the phrase is always "light", i.e., given or assumed in advance, allowing the new idea in the predicate or modifiers to have the weight of novelty. These characteristics of speech are not restricted to primitive or immature speech but are found to distinguish spoken from written language generally.

Bakker then identifies how Homeric parataxis follows a pattern such as this: short phrases or clauses loosely linked together, normally taking a half line that notes some aspect of an event or scene or confirms a person already mentioned. He translates into speech units an example from the *Iliad* of the first appearance of Andromakhe:

> so she spoke, woman housekeeper,
> and he rushed from the house, Hektor
> the same way again
> along the well-built streets.

10. Ibid., 28.

11. Chafe, *Discourse*; Bakker, *Poetry in Speech*.

When he reached the gates
going through the great city
the Skaian <gates>,
thereby he was to
go out into the plain,
there his richly dowered wife
she came running to meet him
Andromakhe
daughter of great-hearted Eëtion,
Eëtion who lived
under Plakos rich in woods,
in Thebe-under-Plakos,
ruling over Kilikian men. Of him then the daughter
she was held by bronze-helmeted Hektor.
<it was she> who came to meet him then,
and a maid came with her
holding a child at her bosom
tender-minded, just a baby,
cherished son of Hektor,
similar to a beautiful star,
him Hektor used to call Skamandrios,
the others Astuanax.
For on his own he defended Ilion, Hektor.
(*Illiad* VI 390–403)[12]

At the same time Bakker recognizes that Homer is not just ordi-nary speech, but is what he calls "special speech." Here Bakker speaks of a "gradual regularization of the intonational contour of the speech units into rhythm."[13] The expected rhythms of speech have been chan-neled more precisely toward recurring patterns or formulas in a pro-cess geared for traditional reception. He sees this happening in Homer when the mutual expectancy of the two parts of each split line becomes stylized into hexametric periods, also when the enjambment that only occasionally breaks this pattern is clustered in critical passages for a specific anti-metric effect. In addition, Bakker investigates other pat-

12. Bakker, "How Oral is Oral Composition?" 40.
13. Bakker, "Study of Homeric Discourse," 301.

terns in Homer to determine the role of each in this tradition-building "special speech," such as the role of particles, of framing followed by close-ups, and of deixis, verb tenses, and ring composition.[14]

This work of Chafe and Bakker suggests a different approach to investigating Mark as tradition. The first question would be, not whether Mark has the requisite formulas and themes of oral composition, but to what extent Mark has common characteristics of speech. If so, one can ask if this becomes "special speech" in any sense, speech stylized by a process of transmission in ways that have become traditional.

There is strong support for taking Mark's language as speech from linguists studying this gospel. James Kleist calls this "the spoken gospel," one characterized more by "sameness of expression than by constant variation," and he presents it in short, paratactic lines of speech.[15] Marius Reiser identifies many characteristics of Mark's style as common in spoken Koine Greek, such as repeated words, direct speech, diminutives, double negatives, and interjections.[16] After detailed study of Mark's verbs that occur prior to subjects, parataxis with *kai*, and asyndeton, he concludes that this is the Koine found in popular novels, diatribes, and pseudepigrapha that are the closest examples of literary languages to the spoken Greek, especially so in their dialogues.[17]

Though I cannot provide a comprehensive study of Markan language here, I will take up four features of Mark which indicate that Mark is characterized not just by human language in general but by the way people speak. These are parataxis, the continuing "and," simple word choice, and quoted speech. I will consider in each case whether this feature has been enhanced into any patterns that can be identified as special or traditional speech. This should allow a review of key aspects of Mark's language, not as orality that is deficient in literary style or that has no written record, as literates tend to think of orality, but as language best characterized as speech according to recent studies

14. Bakker, *Poetry in Speech*, 54–206; Bakker, "Study of Homeric Discourse," 300–303. "Hexametric periods" are the full lines in Homeric poetry having six metrical feet (long or stressed syllables), each line formed from two cola, the half-lines shown above. "Enjambment" occurs when a colon extends from one line to the next. "Deixis" refers to the use of deictic or demonstrative pronouns that point at something.

15. Kleist, *Gospel of Saint Mark*, 167–70.

16. Reiser, *Sprache und literarische Formen*, 58–64.

17. Reiser, *Syntax und Stil des Markusevangeliums*, 34, 163–68.

in discourse analysis, and speech that in some repeated way has taken special forms to become traditional. I translate the first twelve verses of Mark as a reference point for the following chapters, taking each phrase as the next speech unit and not trying to construct sentences.

> **1**$^{:1}$ The start of the good news of Jesus Christ[18]
> $^2$ as it is written in Isaiah the prophet
> look I am sending my messenger before your face
> who will construct your road
> $^3$ a voice crying in the wilderness
> prepare the Lord's way
> straighten his paths
> $^4$ John was there baptizing in the wilderness
> and announcing a baptism of repentance
> for a forgiving of sins
> $^5$ and they were going out to him
> all the region of Judea
> and all the Jerusalemites
> and they were being baptized by him in the Jordan river
> confessing their sins
> $^6$ and John, he was wearing camel hairs
> and a hide belt around his hips
> and he was eating locusts
> and wild honey
> and he was proclaiming saying
> $^7$ he is coming, the one stronger than me, after me
> his sandal strap I am not good enough
> to bend down and untie
> $^8$ I baptized you in water
> but he will baptize you in holy Spirit
> $^9$ and it happened in those days
> Jesus came from Nazareth of Galilee
> and he was baptized in the Jordan by John
> $^{10}$ and right when he went up from the water

18. The phrase "son of God" does not appear in the original Sinaiticus, Koridethianus, a Coptic manuscript, Irenaeus, or Origen. Several critics consider it more likely added than omitted by later scribes. See chapter 15, n.3.

he saw the heavens torn open

and the Spirit coming down on him like a dove

[11] and a voice came from the heavens

you are my son, the loved one

in you I delight

[12] and right then the Spirit threw him out into the wilderness

[13] and he was in the wilderness forty days

being tested by Satan

and he was with the wild beasts

and angels were looking after him

[14] but after John was handed over

Jesus came into the Galilee

proclaiming the good news of God

[15] and saying the time has come

and God's kingdom is arriving

repent and believe the good news. (Mark 1:1–15)

# 7

## Language as Parataxis and the Continuing *Kai*

In this chapter and the next I take up four features that characterize Mark, not simply as language, but as speech: parataxis, the continuing "and," simple word choice, and direct speech.

### Parataxis and Doubling

The setting of two phrases together without subordinating one to another—parataxis—has often been noted as a characteristic of Markan style. It appears not only in direct discourse where it often dominates, but also in narrative and teaching. Discourse analysis identifies these phrases as "intonation units" that characterize speech, thereby shifting our attention away from efforts to excuse or explain an unpolished literary style and toward hearing what this juxtaposition might signify. For example, the classical question of whether "The start of the gospel of Jesus Christ" is a title applying to the whole story that follows or a reference to John the Baptist as the beginning of the story cannot be closed in either direction. One need not permanently exclude the other, since the meaning depends on the speaker's voice and pausing as to how it will be heard. Yet parataxis should not be seen as obscuring the relationships within a text, since the text is speech and the speaker's meaning will be plain.

Yet if parataxis is so constant in Mark that we who read unvoiced speech settle for phrases strung in a loose chain, are there no patterns that repeat themselves and allow the ramble to become a path with signposts and direction? Rhythm does build up at key points, though nothing as tight as meter appears. Dell Hymes has challenged those working with transcriptions of Native American spoken accounts to look for co-variation of form and content, and to do this not only in single lines or verses, but in larger units.[1] Hymes has taken Chinook stories that were previously published in literary paragraph form and re-presented them in sense-units that reflect their own features and relations. Opening particles along with changes of people, place, and time set off the different units of a story, and repeated actions follow numerical patterns. He finds that patterns of threes and fives dominate the measured verse of Colombia River coyote tales, in contrast to balanced sets of twos and threes in the Finnish Nativity Song dictated by Arhippa.[2]

It takes only a quick look at the above piece of Mark to show that it falls in a tradition where the pair dominates, whether in synonymous or antithetical parallelism. Every comment seems to need another one mirroring itself in some way to be complete. There is an echo for John the Baptist's task in the conflation of Scriptures (to be a messenger, to prepare a way). The same is true for his message (to prepare, to make straight). All of this is presented before he comes baptizing and announcing. The origins of those who come to hear him are given twice and their response twice, as are what he wears and what he eats. Finally, the one he announces is compared to himself, and that one's task to his own. All the doubling comes to a head in this extended parallel of John and Jesus, both of them predicted, proclaiming and drawing great crowds in Mark's first chapter.

But the focus quickly shifts onto the second of these two figures with Jesus' double vision of the sky torn open and Spirit dropping down, the double audition, "You are my son, the one I love! I delight in you!" and the double accompaniment in the time of testing. Only then does Jesus come announcing God's good news, claiming the time fulfilled and the kingdom coming, and challenging people with the double task of repenting and trusting the good news. More follows with the calling of two fishers doubled to four, and the two acclamations of his teaching framing his first act of power (1:16–20, 21–28). By this time, what Hymes calls the "measured verse" of Mark is already set and it sustains

---

1. Hymes, "Sung Epics and Native American Ethnopoetics."
2. DuBois, *Finnish Folk Poetry and the* Kalevala, 41–53.

the continuing story in a "special speech" that is no surprise, considering the place of parallelism in Israel's tradition.

Frans Neirynck in his *Duality in Mark*[3] makes a comprehensive catalogue of each occurrence of thirty different kinds of duality in Mark. He shows that the second statement or question often adds further precision to the first, concluding that these "double step expressions" cannot be explained from different sources or redactions and are best taken as a Markan characteristic, adding that "this does not exclude indebtedness to tradition."[4] In his effort to determine an author's manner of writing, Nierynck could be describing ways in which the spoken story has become shaped in the dual rhythms of its cultural tradition. These parallel statements, inclusions, and echoes in Mark—whether they are identified by us as traditional rhythms of speech, as measured verse built on pairs, or as double-step expressions of the one delivering the gospel—show that additive parataxis is a key ligament of the "special speech" in the Markan tradition.

At the broader narrative level, this doubling does not exclude the common folklore pattern of tripling—seen, for example, in the three passion predictions—as well as multiple other rhythmic patterns.

## The Continuing *kai*

A second characteristic of Markan speech is the heavy use of the particle *kai* ("and"), often omitted in translations as being redundant in English.[5] It is such a staple of everyday speech that it could be dismissed as a simple boundary marker, a sound that keeps straight where one thing ends and the next starts but beyond this bears no more weight than the "he said" "she said" interspersed in a dialogue. Yet its constant appearance in Mark, diminishing only somewhat in later chapters, suggests that more is involved. It has been proposed that *kai* signifies not just a stall between units or their coordination but an assertion that what follows is added to and continues what preceded it.[6] If so, the

3. Neirynck, *Duality in Mark*, 75–136, 45–72.

4. Ibid., 72.

5. For particular attention to *kai*, see Kleist, *Saint Mark*, 152–53, 137–41; Reiser, *Syntax*, 100; Rüegger, *Verstehen, was Markus erzählt*, 58–71.

6. On an equivalent function of *de* in Homer, see Bakker, "Homeric Discourse," 293–301.

steady forward movement of this story is evident in more than the sheer quantity of this particle and the use of *kai* becomes a special quality of this telling of the gospel. As such, *kai* is "special speech" in Mark, expressed in at least three ways: in the particular prominence it receives, in the way it is intensified by other words and phrases, and in its role in the temporal and spacial map that the story presents.

The prominence of *kai* beyond sheer numerical count appears in the high percentage of narrative units that begin with *kai*. Here it would seem that a new place, time, or action would allow a more independent start. But according to Kleist's division of narrative units, four out of every five units of Mark begin with *kai*, six of seven in the first twelve chapters.[7] In Neirynck's Greek text with its larger units indicated by the capital letters he chooses to retain from the Nestle 26th edition, more than seven sections out of every eight begin with *kai*.[8] So this conjunction not only holds phrases and clauses together to make stories. It also binds the stories together into a continuing account from the gospel's pronounced start to its strange end. Once begun, no piece of this gospel is finished. There is no stepping back to see the view. Rather, the trek is relentless until the story stops in a dead end so sudden that it catapults the hearer beyond the story that has been told.

Second, *kai* is given special force by other particles, most conspicuously by *euthus*, which appears over forty times in Mark. The King James translation of *euthus* as "straightway" is supported by the word play with the cognate adjective in the opening quotation, "straighten his paths." This meaning in more contemporary diction appears in the words "direct" or "right", as in "directly" or "right then", that suggests cutting through the standard stalls and obstructions that mire down anything new. The strictly temporal translations, "suddenly" or "immediately," hardly do justice to the unstoppable progression of what is straight or right. Once narrative momentum is gained by repeated use of *kai euthus*, the latter word becomes less prominent. But it reappears significantly in the final burst of events at Judas' betrayal, the cock crow, and the plotting of the high priests, which now appear as inescapable in their progression (14:43, 45, 72; 15:1).

---

7. Kleist, *Mark*, 3–89.

8 Neirynck, *Duality*, 139–91.

Third, *kai* is the most constant indicator of the time and space map of this tradition. Though time references in Mark are seldom exact, the events told are all anchored in a single time sequence, for example, in the way John's arrest is given as the time after which Jesus appears in Galilee. The only flashback in Mark is the episode of John's death, set at the time when Jesus' identity sparks questions whether he is John raised from the dead (1:14; 6:14–29). The single time line is supported by a single place map: multiple journeys around, across, and away from the one Galilee town and lake, ending in the single journey to Jerusalem. The continuing initial *kai* locks each piece into the time and space of this world. This pattern presents the narrative as a report of events in real space and time, not as a story about something that happened once upon a time. Of course this does nothing to assure the accuracy of what is told, but it does sustain the stance of a blow by blow report. It is within this report framework that the wondrous events can be presented as experiences of real people, not as entertainment fiction. The repeated *kai* plays a key role in keeping Jesus' announcement of "God's good news" in real space and time.

It turns out that this particle as used in Mark is not just "pliable and good-natured *kai*" as Kleist names it.[9] It is a staple of common speech that has been set off here as special or traditionalizing speech by its prominent place at the beginning of most units, by its intensification with *euthus*, and by its pervasive claim to continue a report of a certain place and time.

9. Kleist, *Saint Mark*, 152.

# 8

## Language as Simple Diction and Spoken Discourse

In this chapter I will deal with two other features of Mark's special speech: simple word choice and the direct quotation of characters.

### Simple Diction

Mark is known for its simple diction and repeated use of the same words or phrases, a characteristic of common speech in any language. But how can simple vocabulary become special or traditional speech without losing its simplicity? This can happen by distinctive uses of the same word: "the mortal came not to be served but to serve," or by repeated use in a progression of meanings: "you can make me clean . . . be made clean . . . he was made clean" (10:45; 1:40–42). Recurrence of the same word in different contexts links the fate of different characters, as in the term "handed over" in the following lines: "After John was handed over, Jesus came into the Galilee"; "the mortal will be handed over to the high priests and the scribes . . . and they will hand him over to the Gentiles"; "And they will hand you over to the Sanhedrin" (1:14; 10:33; 13:9). It is also the case that common verbs can be built up upon each other to describe a scene more vividly than any bouquet of adjectives: "The woman, frightened and trembling, knowing what had happened to her, came and fell before him and told him the whole truth" (5:33).

In other contexts, spare and strong use of the one prominent Markan adjective builds up its power: "a great windstorm" becomes "a great calm" and a "great fear" falls on them; "a great herd of swine" suffocates in the sea; the unclean spirit "crying a great cry" is expelled from a man; Jesus "with a great cry" expires; "and they said to each other, 'who will roll away the stone from the door of the tomb for us?' and they looked up and saw the stone had been rolled away, for it was very great" (4:37–41; 5:11; 1:26; 15:37; 16:3–4). This sharp restriction in the variety of words channels them deeper through reverberation and the respect accorded direct speech. It is this kind of restriction, recurrence, and rhythm in the diction of Mark that make this speech not only plain but also special, able like salt to mold and preserve a tradition.

## Direct Discourse

A further signature of Markan language is the direct discourse in which the storyteller speaks with the characters' own voices. Hardly a scene lacks direct speech, and voice can even be given to people's thoughts (2:7; 5:28). Short phrases spoken by a character would seem to be the most colloquial part of a narrative, apparently immune to stylization in traditional patterns. Yet the parts of the Markan story that speak aloud for a character do take on special force in several ways, of which I will consider four. Direct discourse becomes special speech by repetition, by transcription, by putting questions, and by voicing authority.

The repetition of spoken words is most obvious in Jesus' not just double but triple passion predictions and subsequent passion teachings (8:31—9:1; 9:30, 41; 10:32–45). Though there is narrative gain from the triple telling in the disciples' increasing disorientation, the effect of the repetition is equally to establish the prediction in its repeated, if varied, cadence. This sets up the coming violence as foreseen and encompassed by the final words, "and after three days he must/will rise" (8:31; 9:31; 10:34). Parallels between these prophecies and later Christian confessions further suggest some early stabilizing of the traditions that summarize Jesus' final days. A very different kind of repetition appears where Jesus speaks the same word in many different stories: "your trust has healed you" (5:34); "don't fear, only trust" (5:26); "all things are possible for the one who trusts" (9:23); and, a second time, "your trust has healed you" (10:52). Here his voice reaches beyond single individuals to challenge those in need to trust and claim for themselves the good news.

Transcription of a native voice is a second way certain speaking is highlighted in Mark. The words Jesus shouts—"talitha cum" and "ephphatha" (5:41; 7:34)—are not likely to have been transmitted to display the storyteller's bilingual competence. Listeners will have wanted to hear the sound that healed and be able to pass it on, all the more if they didn't understand it. In Jesus' cry to God from the cross—"Elōi, Elōi" (15:34; Ps 22:2)—the sound will carry the emotion with a weight that the meaning alone and even the authority of this Psalm's tradition cannot match. It is not only the esoteric (or childhood familiarity?) of a foreign tongue that attracts but also the intimacy that comes from hearing the sound this man made *in extremis*. These words are surely marked as special, tradition-bound speech.

Jesus' questions seem unlikely candidates for tradition, being parts of longer interchanges and often leaving answers in the air. Yet this gospel presents Jesus first and foremost as questioner, and his proverbs and parables also function as questions to hearers. Over and over Jesus meets questions with questions: "How can Satan cast Satan out?" "Who are my mother and brothers?" (3:23, 33). Granted that these questions require the interchanges in order to make sense and each is quickly told, but the narrative as a whole becomes a rising crescendo or, better said, a gaping hole of questions. Soon there are responding questions: "Who then is this that the wind and the sea obey him?" "Where did this one get all these things?" and then Jesus' "Who do you say that I am?" (4:41; 6:2; 8:29). Whether or not the gospel ends as a challenge questioning hearers, it remains distinctive among the gospels for setting the question Jesus puts to his time and place in the center of its narrative structure. The rising tone of voice left in the air after a question is one marker of this story's special speech.

As one would expect, voices of authority are attributed the special weight of tradition in this gospel, the centurion who may speak in wonder and even Pilate and the high priest who ironically acclaim Jesus (15:2, 32, 39). But Jesus' own speech takes the central place of authority, particularly in those promises and warnings set off by the phrase, "Amen, I say to you . . . ," or better translated, "I tell you the truth . . ." This appears only seldom until it occurs four times on his last night (14:9, 18, 25, 30). And nothing can trump the voice from the heavens that draws on the long-standing tradition of the beloved son to express

God's delight and desire: "You are my beloved son. In you I delight!" and "This is my beloved son. Listen to him!" (1:11; 9:7).

The most complex invoking of an authoritative voice may come when Jesus cites Scripture. Other than the citation that opens the gospel before John or Jesus has appeared to speak (1:2–3), Scripture is cited when people speak to each other, particularly when Jesus speaks. He teaches with lines known from Scripture: "To those outside everything is in parables so that they might look and look and not see, and hear and hear and not comprehend" (4:12, quoting Isa 6:9–10; cf. Mark 13:24–25). Yet the most explicit reference to texts occurs when he argues with his opponents: "Isaiah prophesied beautifully about you hypocrites, as it is written, 'This people honors me with their tongues but their hearts are far from me . . .'" (7:6). Note that Jesus appeals here less to words on a page than to the story Scripture tells, "Haven't you read what David did when he was caught out hungry with his men, how he entered God's house . . ."; "Haven't you read in the book of Moses about the bush, how God said to him . . ." (2:25; 12:26). The repeated opening line that makes these quotes a question, "Haven't you read . . . ?" need not mean that Jesus learned Scripture from reading but that those who present themselves as its authoritative readers do not understand it and do not act on it, hence: "Haven't you read this Scripture, 'The rock that the builders culled has become the cornerstone?'" (12:10).When Jesus refers to Scripture in this way, the authority of Scripture, the authority of Jesus, and the question from the reality on the ground that subverts his opponents' authority all come into play at once. By speaking in the voice of Jesus quoting Scripture, the gospel teller makes new tradition from old.

In all these ways and many others, the spoken language that forms the texture of this gospel is intensified into something distinctive, into a special speech that signals tradition. These are not the formulas of Homer but the formulas of another tradition with its own rhythms and force, making its own claims to shape the identity of those who speak and hear it. Even before the storyteller in Mark begins to impersonate the characters by speaking for them, the introductory narrative manages to refer to the act of speaking by using six different Greek words. What brings this on? Is it the imperial context where no one dares to say what they think that makes speaking out so newsworthy? If we simplify the opening and use only one English word, "speak," we would have:

The start of the good speaking about Jesus Christ

as it is written in Isaiah the speaker,

look, I am sending my speaker before your face . . .

a speech speaking in the wilderness . . .

there was John baptizing and speaking of a baptism of repentance. . .

and all came out . . . and were baptized, speaking out their sins . . .

and John spoke, speaking, a stronger one is coming . . .

and Jesus came . . . and there was a speaking from heaven

"you are my son, my loved one . . ."

and he was spoken to by Satan forty days . . .

and Jesus came into Galilee speaking the good speaking of God and
   speaking . . .

repent and trust the good speaking.

Although this way of putting it obscures a real difference between speaking as prophecy and shouting and proclamation and confession and testing and telling news, nevertheless it does signal that the following narrative of Mark, not only in its form but also in its content, will be all about something being "spoken."

In answer to the presenting question whether Mark can be an oral tradition without meter or song, the response must be that it is not the metric formula *per se* that marks oral tradition. It is, first and foremost, the short and loosely-linked "intonation units" of speech rather than the sentences and paragraphs of literature that mark orality. And when these units have been practiced over time in a people's tradition, they establish measured rhythms or "special speech," in Mark's case a pattern of duality that joins the distinct units by means of *kai* into a continuing account of speaking and hearing a certain good news that can heal and effect God's kingdom.

# 9

## The Scenes of Mark as Performance Tradition

I move now from traditional language that Albert Lord called formulaic, which, following Bakker, I have characterized as special speech, toward considering the longer units that Lord called themes, here called episodes or scenes. There is no question that Mark is episodic, moving from one scene to another in a way that often reads like a road trip. Lord called these units "themes" because their repeated patterns show that a few kinds of scenes dominate and these scenes carry the meanings of the storytellers in traditional forms. Parry and Lord observed that those who recite epic poetry will tell you that they do so word for word, just as it was given them, even though recordings show variations from one performance to another. Foley has inferred from this that the "words" meant here are not our contiguous letters separated by spaces on a page. They are units of storytelling that cannot be omitted or distorted without substantive loss.[1] It is these "bigger words," whether phrases, motifs, or entire episodes, that Foley identifies as the nodes that can evoke a whole nexus of a tradition among those who live by it. By means of a metonymy that works *pars pro toto,* the part representing the whole, the listeners are quickly clued in to much wider implications and deeper layers of tradition.

In Homer's epics one familiar episode is the banquet. Foley has observed that banquet scenes do not mean simply that a host has invited guests to a meal with all the rituals that entails, but they signify that someone seeks to mediate a conflict so that the narrative can pro-

---

1. Foley, *How to Read,* 11–21.

ceed in a way that hitherto has been blocked.[2] In each case the scene is developed so that there is some novelty in the story, but there is much more that is reliable in the way a banquet scene will be told that secures what it traditionally signifies. Any scene told will have a familiar form and will bring up certain traditional associations for those who know it. My question is whether the traditions about Jesus have aged enough and the communities they address have enough in common for the repeated scenes to have familiar forms and to evoke a specific tradition.

The simple answer is that only our narrow vision makes us conceive of Jesus as the founder of a new tradition. Without question in the first century, and even in the fourth century when the Christian canon was confirmed and also today where Christianity is practiced, those who follow Jesus see themselves as part of a very ancient tradition. The story of God and Israel had many, even competing, renditions in the time Mark was shaped, and it was in terms of this story that Jesus mattered. This story in turn was an integral part of a much wider and more complex world of ancient stories that Israel did not always hear as foreign.

I will review five repeated scenes in Mark—exorcisms, controversies, healings, the vision of a voice from heaven, and the vision of one coming on the clouds—and ask how these scenes are formed in a way that shows their traditional significance. It is too bold for me to claim the competence of the Markan audience to grasp the full meaning of these scenes, but in the context of the whole story that is aimed at them, these scenes can be pathfinders toward some of what they would understand. I ask how the repeated scenes make immanent, *pars pro toto,* the transcendent art that grounds a people's life, as John Foley puts it when he speaks of the epic performer's "immanent art." Or, to use Dell Hymes analysis, how do the measured rhythms of a recurring episode evoke by their covariation of form and content the good sense that sustains the world? And in all of this I must ask how a certain tradition is drawn upon and then shaped in Mark, possibly evoking only certain aspects of its potential, or even in some way resisting expectations. The question remains whether these accounts of Jesus' recent actions and claims plow deeply enough into the ground of a people's mentality that news can in only months, years, and decades become tradition.

2. Foley, *Homer's Traditional Art*, 169–87.

# 10

## Scenes of Action:
## Exorcism, Healing, and Controversy

### Exorcism Scenes

Though exorcism stories do not appear in the Hebrew Bible, they are widespread among Jews in the Roman East by the first century (Tob 8:2–3; Genesis Apocryphon 20; Matt 12:27/Luke 11:19; Josephus *Jewish Antiquities* 8.45–48) and become associated in Greek texts with eastern Mediterranean wonder workers (Lucian *Lover of Lies* 16; Philostratus *Life of Apollonius* 3.38; 4.10, 20). The four exorcism stories in Mark have a common basic form involving a direct conflict between Jesus and an "unclean spirit" or "demon" that has occupied a person or place and threatens to kill (1:21–28; 4:35–41; 5:1–20; 9:14–29). Jesus is accosted on arrival by the spirit's defensive uproar and he can engage it first with almost clinical questions before rebuking and forcing it out. Those whose lives are at stake cannot take part in the struggle, being immobilized by the possession, but they can demonstrate their liberation afterwards by sitting, standing or speaking, or the unclean spirit may show its destructive power in the place where Jesus sends it.[1]

Exorcism stories have a more prominent place in Mark than in other gospels, not appearing at all in John or the Gnostic gospels, and told in Matthew and Luke only where following Mark and there abbreviated if not omitted. In the Markan tradition Jesus begins his ministry

---

1. For further analysis of the exorcism stories in Mark and Philostratus, see Wire, "Structure of the Gospel Miracle Stories," 89–92. On the gospel miracle stories more broadly, see Theissen, *Miracle Stories*.

by calling four disciples and exorcising an unclean spirit. This exorcism is remarkable for its location in the midst of Jesus' synagogue teaching, a location accentuated by the crowds marveling beforehand that "he was teaching them as one having authority, not as the scribes," and saying afterward, "A new teaching with authority! He commands even the unclean spirits and they obey him" (1:22, 27). An exorcism story can apparently be told in a competition over teaching authority.

The next exorcism story suggests a different use. The disciples, afraid for their lives, wake Jesus who is asleep in a storm at sea. "He rebuked the wind and told the sea, 'Silence! Shut your mouth!' and the wind fell and there was a great calm" (4:39). Berated by Jesus for their lack of trust, the disciples say to each other, "Who then is this that the wind and the sea obey him?" (4:41). When Jesus casts this life-threatening wind/spirit out of the sea, this story shows that his trust in God gives him power over whatever kills and this exposes the disciples' fear in contrast.

The third exorcism follows immediately and ends with another assertion of Jesus' access to God's power. Jesus instructs the man to go tell his own people "what the Lord has done for you and how much he has had mercy on you," and the man "sets out to proclaim in the Decapolis what Jesus did for him" (5:19-20)—without mentioning the man's misunderstanding of Jesus' instructions. Because exorcism stories are often told to praise the exorcist, the man's (and the teller's) praise of Jesus might be taken as traditional. But it is Jesus' attribution of the healing to God that grounds the story in Israel's tradition and identifies Jesus' foundation in that tradition throughout this gospel (cf. 6:41; 9:29; 10:18; 14:36). Meanwhile the story alludes in three ways to the Roman military occupation: in the unclean spirit's name, "Legion," in its begging not to be sent out of the country, and in the pigs that stampede and drown—arguably fuel for the Roman military. What God has done against imperial power is here attributed to Jesus.

The final exorcism story gathers up a number of the motifs already seen (9:14-27). The scribes dispute, the disciples are powerless without trust and prayer to God, and even the child's father has only conditional hope, saying, "If you can, help us." Jesus responds, "If you can! Everything is possible for one who trusts!" and with an elaborate command he orders the unclean spirit out. It shouts and convulses the boy so that many say he has died, but Jesus raises him and he stands up.

Coming close to Lazarus' resurrection in the Fourth Gospel, this story incorporates the power to give life to the dead within an exorcism story, without breaking the mold.

Even apart from the many other references within this gospel to unclean spirits, demons, and Satan, the exorcism story as traditionally told sharply dramatizes a direct and unmitigated opposition between life-giving and death-dealing power, and all the opposition that Jesus faces is drawn into one of these stories. But characterizations in each story are distinctive. The scribes simply lack the authority to get beyond words to action. The disciples follow Jesus but lack trust in God who gives life and are paralyzed. At the end of the gospel the disciples deny and betray Jesus, and the scribes take action to condemn him, making their integration into the exorcism stories a premonition of the gospel's final conflict between life and death. It is appropriate that the Romans who crucify Jesus are identified directly with unclean spirits that pollute the land they occupy and the exorcism of this "Legion" shows they are bound for destruction. Just as dramatically, the wind that threatens death any day at work and the illness that haunts one's vulnerable child are overcome (4:35–41; 7:24–30). The storytellers thus incorporate into the exorcism stories the full range of annihilating threats a person can meet, not softening but sharpening the dangers involved. In the face of these, Jesus acts as the one who knows the Lord that has mercy, is willing to pray as his disciples are not, and trusts that God can do everything (5:19; 9:29; 10:27). In this way Jesus' struggle and victory in the exorcism stories prefigure his death and resurrection and show what it means to follow him and to trust God.

## Controversy Scenes

The so-called controversy scenes in Mark represent another traditional and repeated pattern. Here Jesus meets legal and religious authorities and contests their interpretations of God's requirements. I will focus narrowly on what the tellers of Mark seem to be signifying to their traditional hearers in these accounts rather than investigating practices of oral controversy in Israel and the Roman East or fitting Mark into a history of literature about teachers who field questions. To limit the scope without making an arbitrary selection of scenes, I will focus on the two parts of Mark where many controversies are told, early in the Galilee account (2:1—3:6) and late in the Temple (11:27—12:37). These two series of scenes consistently follow or adapt a simple pattern whereby Jesus answers a question with a question in return, and the answer of his respondents—or their inability to contest his point—provides or leads to his answer. In other words, he sets them up to answer their own question. A classic example is the story in which Jesus is asked whether to pay the imperial tax or not (12:13–17). Jesus' question in return, "Whose is this image?" produces their answer, "Caesar's," to which he answers, "Give Caesar what is Caesar's and God what is God's," reserving what is made in God's image for God.

The first series of scenes (2:1—3:6) begins when Jesus forgives the paralytic and the scribes object, "Who can forgive sins but one, God?" to which Jesus responds with his question, "Which is easier . . . ," to forgive or to heal? The answer to his rhetorical question is obvious, and Jesus says to the paralytic, "Get up, take your pallet and go home"—*a forteriori*, the mortal can forgive. Second, Jesus' disciples are asked, "How is it he eats with tax collectors and sinners?" Jesus puts his responding question as a proverb, "The healthy don't need a doctor but the sick do," and when they cannot contest it, he responds, "I come . . . to call sinners." To the question about his disciples not fasting, Jesus responds in a proverb that takes a question form, "The groom's friends can't fast when the groom is with them, can they?" The answer can only be "No," so his disciples cannot fast at the present time, which is met with a concluding answer promising later fasting when the time is right, as well as with other proverbs about appropriate action from sewing patches and storing wine, which lead to a second conclusion, "New wine for new skins."

The final two stories in this sequence concern the Sabbath. Jesus meets their question about why his disciples glean on the Sabbath with a question, "Haven't you read what David did . . . , how he entered God's house . . . and ate the bread offering . . . and gave it to those who were with him?" mocking those who can read for not seeing the analogy. When they cannot answer this charge, Jesus responds, "The Sabbath is for people not people for the Sabbath, so the mortal is master even of the Sabbath." This sequence of controversy scenes ends as it began, with a healing. The question to Jesus is put without words, "And they were observing him to see if he would heal on the Sabbath so they could charge him." In response he asks them, "Is it allowed on the Sabbath to do good or to do evil, to save life or to kill?" There can be only one answer, although "they were silent," and, in turn, Jesus heals the man. In a move that is not part of this interchange but an apparent response to all the scenes above, his questioners hold council on how to destroy him.

By the end of the gospel the controversy is broader, the stakes are higher, and the scenes are more elaborate, but the common pattern remains: question, question, answer, answer (11:27—12:27). In the first instance Jesus is asked, "By what authority do you do these things? Or who gave you the authority to do them?" Jesus says he will answer them when they answer his question, "Was John's baptism from heaven or from mortals?" When they will not affirm John and yet cannot deny him in face of the crowd's support, they say they do not know, and Jesus refuses to answer their question. But he tells them about John, with implications for himself, in the parable of the vineyard tenants who killed the owner's loved son, a parable ending in two questions. He asks the first, "What will the vineyard owner do?" and he lets the parable answer for them, "he will dismiss the tenants," and then puts his corresponding answer as a second rhetorical question, "Haven't you read this Scripture, 'The stone the builders rejected has become the cornerstone . . . ?,'" leaving them seeking to seize him, "for they knew he spoke the parable against them."

The scene on paying the tax was introduced above: Jesus claims that those made in God's image are God's. To the Sadducees' question about the much married woman, "at the resurrection, when they are raised, whose wife is she?" he asks in return, "Are you not deceived about this, knowing neither the Scriptures nor God's power?" They have no answer and he responds that the risen do not marry or get married off but are like angels in heaven. And about resurrection, he asks another question that introduces his answer as an interpretation of Scripture, "Have you not read in the book of Moses how God spoke to him at the bush saying, 'I am the God of Abraham and the God of Isaac and the God of Jacob'? He is not God of the dead but of the living. You are much deceived." Apparently when he can answer from the Scripture they read, he takes this as their answer, to which he responds.

A scribe then asks, "What is the first commandment of all?" (12:28–34). Jesus hears this as a straight question and answers with the

Shema.[2] It seems that a controversy scene does not develop when the initial question is not parried with a question. The man responds by reflecting the Shema again yet more strongly, at which Jesus commends him as one not far from God's kingdom. The closing "no one dared ask him another question," is taken as Jesus' victory in the controversy, in this case not because he shamed an opponent but by teaching and being taught. In a further scene Jesus becomes the interrogator of the scribes, asking how they can teach that the Messiah is David's son when the Psalm contradicts it (12:35–37). That there is no counter question either demonstrates that the scribes have no response, or that they have slipped away—and now it is the crowd who are hearing him gladly.

I suggest that the quite complex meanings woven into the simply patterned scenes above could be shaped and carried by traditional tellers because of the clear polarity in the question/question answer/answer mold. This pattern reflects the participatory and agonistic character of oral controversies and of stories that continue controversies by retelling them.[3] There are several recurring and reverberating elements that I hear in these controversy scenes as I try to pick up what a traditional audience might hear.

First, those who question Jesus are all people of authority and learning, yet they represent different groups and are concerned about different aspects of Jesus practice. The scenes are not amalgamated, though the tellers' closings speak of groups conspiring against him (3:6) and a crowd hearing him gladly (12:37b).

Second, until the scribe's final question, it is explicit that each questioner is testing Jesus or seeking to trap him. Therefore each story involves tension about how Jesus will be able to put the ball back in their court. His repeated success builds up force.

Third, the appeal to stories from Scripture in three different scenes with the prefix, "Haven't you read . . . ?" is a sharp rebuke to those who can read but do not get the point. This claims the Scripture for those who do not read but hear it and do it.

---

2. This commandment from Deut 6:5 was recited in rabbinical Judaism at set times of day and was referred to as "taking on oneself the yoke of the kingdom of heaven": "Hear, O Israel: the Lord our God, the Lord is One, and you shall love the Lord your God with all your heart and with all your life and with all your means" (*b. Berakhot* 61b; see excerpt in chapter 11).

3. See Dewey, "Gospel of Mark as an Oral-Aural Event."

Fourth, Jesus' defense of his conduct and convictions presents a consistent picture of what he stands for, although this is never summarized and for the traditional audience need not be. We hear in the first series of scenes that people have the right to forgive and be forgiven, the marginal have a right to be included, the disabled to be healed, the hungry to eat, and mortals to give and receive good on the Sabbath (2:1—3:5). The second series of scenes claim God's right to send messengers that are welcomed and heard, to receive allegiance from those made in God's image, to give life even to the dead, and to be loved with all the heart, life, mind, and strength by those, paradoxically, who love others as they love themselves.

The controversy scenes shape and carry the content of this teaching in a dramatic and polemical account of memorable events that evoke the presence of the one who spoke. The final interchange with the scribe, in which a straight question receives a straight answer, breaks the pattern of question met by question and it acknowledges a person in authority as near to God's kingdom. At the same time, the closing scene in which Jesus puts the absent scribes down with his twist on David's son, his attack on scribal practice, and his defense of widows (12:35–44) returns hearers to the primary polemic.

## Healing Scenes

In addition to exorcism and controversy scenes, Mark features repeated healings. I call these "demand" scenes, because suppliants claim Jesus' help.[4] There is usually a description of the affliction, the request is made and the request is met, but the *sine qua non* is the central voicing of the demand, an element that does not occur in exorcism or food-provision stories. Demand stories in Mark take up a traditional pattern of a suppliant pressing for healing that is already present in the prophetic narratives about Elijah and Elisha, which were apparently much told in popular circles (1 Kgs 17:18; 2 Kgs 4:1, 22–28; Luke 4:25–27; Jas 5:17; *Lives of the Prophets* 10; 21; 22).[5]

---

4. Wire, "Structures of the Gospel Miracle Stories," 99–108; Wire, *Holy Lives*, 124–42.

5. Wire, *Holy Lives*, 66–73; 185–88. For collections of rabbinic Elijah and Elisha stories, see Ben-Amos, "Narrative Forms in the Haggadah," 213–17; Ginzberg, *Legends of the Jews*, 4:195–246; 6:316–48; Lindbeck, *Elijah and the Rabbis*, 171–94.

In Markan healing stories the demand is accentuated in two primary ways. On the one hand, the stories describe obstructions that threaten the suppliants' access to Jesus, yet their remarkable persistence, identified as "trust," allows for healing. The crowds often bar people from approaching. When four people let the paralytic down through the roof, Jesus, "seeing their trust," heals him. The bleeding woman presses through the crowd to touch Jesus' clothing and is healed before he knows it, so that he concludes, "Your trust has healed you." This healing obstructs Jesus' progress to the synagogue leader's house and his daughter dies, but Jesus says to him, "Don't be afraid, keep trusting," and she lives again. Blind Bartimaeus cries out to Jesus all the more when he is silenced by the crowd and Jesus says to him, "Go, your trust has healed you" (2:5; 5:34, 36; 10:52; cf. 4:40; 9:23).

Other stories show Jesus himself obstructing the demand. When Jesus' rejects the Syrophoenecian woman's appeal for her daughter's healing with a proverb that features her as a dog, she trumps it in the same idiom, and he concedes the case (7:24–30). More often, it is the story about a healing that Jesus himself obstructs, a pattern that becomes programmatic in Mark. The accounts seem to stress this obstruction in order to show how it is defied. So the leper, who is told to say nothing to anyone but the priest, proclaims the news so widely that Jesus could no long teach in a town (1:44–45). The synagogue leader and his wife, though told strongly not to tell others about their daughter's healing, have no choice with a funeral in full swing (5:43). The deaf man's story ends, "He commanded them to tell no one, but the more he commanded, the more excessively they proclaimed it" (7:36). In each case, it is the persons who pressed for the healing who tell the story of their success. Not only will they not be denied, but the gospel speaker becomes an eager accomplice in this telling despite Jesus' orders against it. By using the same verb here, "to proclaim," as used in reference to proclaiming the gospel by the John the Baptist, Jesus, the disciples, and future believers, the men and women who tell this gospel present these stories as the same good news of God's presence that Jesus proclaimed (1:4, 14, 38; 3:14; 13:10; 14:9).

What then of the charge that the scenes in Mark are accounts of recent events and not the stuff of tradition? We have found simple but deeply traditional patterns of storytelling in the exorcism, healing, and controversy accounts that give each kind of story a particular meaning.

Jesus questions and expels life-threatening spirits and leaves people in their right minds. Jesus returns questions and returns answers until his opponents give up controversies with him. Jesus lives among people in need and responds to their demand to be healed. Would not one of each kind of story, thoroughly analyzed and comprehended, be a more effective way to get the meaning across?

Yet meaning in a performance tradition is not an abstract summary of a method but a telling of enough concrete events to show what has happened, that is, to present and represent what such events mean in this tradition. Not only do the number of stories complicate the patterns but one kind of story may overlap with another and bleed meanings, as in the exorcism of the boy that is also the story of a father's demand for healing (9:14–27) or the paralytic's story in which the trust of his four bearers is rewarded by a healing that consummates a controversy (2:1–12). The tradition cannot, apparently, be cut into neat squares of meaning. When we further recall that Mark is only one performance of a living and shifting oral tradition that represents only one of many gospel streams that tells one of many ways people at the time spoke of rediscovering trust in God after the Temple's destruction, we can understand why scholars prefer to study Mark as a single man's text written for a single context.

# 11

## Scenes of Vision: A Voice from Heaven and the Mortal Coming on the Clouds

Another kind of scene in Mark is the heavenly vision, not common in modern storytelling but pivotal in this narrative. A past vision is told of a voice coming from heaven and a future vision of a mortal coming on the clouds. These vision scenes signify points of divine initiative in blessing or judging human affairs.

### The Vision of a Voice From Heaven

A vision of a bright light and a voice from heaven is told twice in Mark, at the first appearance of Jesus in the Jordan River and again at a mid-way turning point in Jesus' story on a high mountain (1:9–11; 9:2–8). Our clues for understanding these scenes will come from asking two questions: Who has the vision and what impact has it on them? And how do those who hear the story draw on a tradition that interprets what the vision means? I begin with the first question about both stories of a heavenly voice. Whose vision is it, and with what impact?

No doubt it is Jesus who sees the vision and hears the words addressed to him as he receives John's baptism of repentance for the forgiving of sins. "Right when coming up from the water he saw the heavens split open and the Spirit coming down into him like a dove and there was a voice from the heavens 'You are my beloved son. I delight in you!'" (1:10–11). This is told, not as a public investiture with a royal title, but as this man's vision of being claimed by God and receiving God's Spirit. This Spirit casts him out into the desert for forty days of testing.

And when John is seized by Herod Antipas, Jesus comes into Herod's territory of Galilee proclaiming the good news that God's kingdom is arriving. This puts into motion all the action that follows in Mark.

The contrast with the second story of a vision from heaven is striking because the outline is so similar: in a special place certain people see the heavens open or blinding light and hear a voice from above naming Jesus God's loved son (9:2–8). In this case, it is the three disciples whom Jesus has brought up the mountain who receive the vision. They see Jesus in blinding white talking with Elijah and Moses and are told, "This is my son, the beloved. Listen to him!" But already within the vision account something goes awry and Peter responds with the plan to stay there and build shelters for everyone, "for he did not know how to respond because they were afraid" (9:6). Other signs of an aborted impact on them follow: Jesus says not to tell anyone what they saw, Jesus identifies John the Baptist as Elijah whose suffering prefigures his own, and Jesus, finally, tells his disciples that they lack the prayer that can heal (9:9–29). It is even possible that there were tellings of Mark that took the disciples' vision of Elijah and Moses as their own projections, which suddenly vanish when Jesus rejects their account and says that Elijah has already come and gone. In any case the voice from the cloud, "Listen to him!" refers back in Mark's context to Jesus' just previous prediction of his death and resurrection and his teaching that each must lose life to find it (8:31—9:1), an instruction of the disciples' task that is not realized within the performance of Mark.

And how would those who hear these two vision scenes in Mark draw on a wider and deeper tradition? The pattern of telling visions of a voice from heaven (*bat kol*, literally, daughter of a voice) appears in rabbinic cases as a means to determine judicial decisions.[1] A more primary use seems to be to acclaim some person as intimate with God so as to receive God's blessing and protection.

> In the hour that they took Rabbi Akiba out to kill him
> It was the time to recite the Shema.
> And it happened that they were combing his flesh with iron combs
> and he was taking on himself the yoke of the kingdom of heaven
>     [reciting the Shema].

1. *y. Yevamot* 1.6 and *b. Berakhot* 52a; *y. Mo'ed Qatan* 3.1 and *b. Bava Metzi'a* 58b–59a,

His students said to him, "Our Rabbi, must it go this far?"
He said to them
"All the days of my life I have been troubled by this passage:
'[Love the Lord your God] with all your life—'
even if he takes your breath.
I said, 'When will it come in reach and I do it?'
And now it comes in reach, will I not do it?"
He was prolonging [his voice] with "One"
until his breath went out with "One."
. . . A voice from heaven went out and said
"Blessed are you, Rabbi Akiba,
that your breath went out with 'One'. . . ."
(*b Berakhot* 61b., cf. *b. Avodah Zarah* 18a).

A second voice then summons him into life in the world to come. Perhaps closer to Jesus' vision in Mark is the story attributed to Judah the Patriarch about a first century Galilean miracle-working rabbi Hanina ben Dosa whom God calls his son. This story of God multiplying Sabbath bread for Hanina's wife is introduced by these words:

Day after day a voice from heaven goes out and says
"All the whole world is fed on account of Hanina ben Dosa
And Hanina my son satisfies himself with a pan of carob pods
From a Sabbath evening to a Sabbath evening!"
(*b. Taanit* 24b, cf. *b. Berakhot* 17b)[2]

Hearers of Jesus' story in this tradition will take the voice from heaven at his baptism as a sounding of this kind of exceptional intimacy with God that gives Jesus the care, power, and direction of God's Spirit so that he can empower and guide others, hence "Listen to him!" The disciples' inability to receive their vision on the mountain nor to accept the direction in which Jesus leads threatens the arrival of God's kingdom in this gospel—although later predictions that his followers will give witness before governors and speak with God's Spirit project a possibility beyond the story that is told (13:9–13).

Many of Israel's other long-standing traditions—of beloved sons, of Moses and Elijah, of transforming visions—are implicated here and

2. My translations from *Holy Lives*, 362–63, and 113. See another such story in chapter 15.

also demand attention.[3] Although the accounts in Mark of visionary events in Jesus lifetime were quite new, what they were claiming and how and why they claimed it seems to be an integral part of a rich and still leavening tradition.

## The Vision of the Mortal Coming on the Clouds

A second kind of vision scene in Mark appears, not in telling past events, but in predicting a vision to come. Three times Jesus projects a future vision of a mortal[4] who comes in power, on the clouds, or with angels. The key locations of these scenes in Mark indicate their significance: at the climax of Jesus' first passion teaching, at the high point of his discourse on the future, and just before he is condemned by the Sanhedrin.

> Whoever is ashamed of me and my words in this adulterous and sinful generation,
>
> the mortal will be ashamed of when he comes in the Father's glory with the holy angels.
>
> And he said to them,
>
> "I tell you for a fact that there are some standing here who will not taste death
>
> until they see God's kingdom having come in power." (8:38—9:1)

> But in those days after that affliction
>
> the sun will become dark
>
> and the moon will not give its light
>
> and the stars will be falling from heaven
>
> and the powers in the heavens will be shaken.
>
> And then they will see the mortal coming in clouds with great power and glory.

3. See Levenson, *Death and Resurrection*; Najman, *Seconding Sinai*; Horsley, *Hearing the Whole Story*, 99–108, 231–43; Chilton et al., *Comparative Handbook*, 71–75.

4. As noted above, the usual English translation of this term as "the Son of Man" reflects the literal Greek rendering of a common Aramaic and Hebrew term for the generic human being, used both for the human species among other animals species (Dan 7:13) and for the mortal *vis a vis* the immortal God (Ezek 2:1, 3, 6, 8, et al.). Because the comparison of humans to God is featured in Mark while the human species among other animals is not, I translate "the mortal."

And then he will send the angels out
and he will gather up his elect from the four winds,
from the ends of earth to the ends of heaven. (13:24–27)

The high priest questioned him again and said to him,
"Are you the Christ, the son of the Blessed?"
But Jesus said, [You say that] I am,[5]
and you will see the mortal seated at the right hand of power
and coming with the clouds of heaven." (14:61b–62)

This prediction of a coming vision of a mortal in heaven is well documented more than two centuries earlier in Daniel 7:13, perhaps one century earlier in the *1 Enoch* 45–51, and broadly in the first century CE (Matt 24:30; 25:31; 26:64; Luke 21:27; 22:69; Rev 1:7, 13; 14:14). Because renditions of it in Mark vary considerably and no written sources are mentioned, oral reception of the tradition is likely.[6] In any case, what this narrative uses of the tradition can only be drawn from this gospel. In the three Markan passages quoted above, each scene has three major components: 1.) there are people ("whoever," "they," "you") to whom the sight, vision or time will come; 2.) there is the mortal or human being who is coming with or in the clouds of heaven; and 3.) there is God who seats the mortal in glory on the right hand as God's kingdom comes.

The people to whom this vision will come are depicted in two ways in these accounts and the narrative that links them. On the one side are those "in this adulterous and sinful generation" who find Jesus shameful. They will see "the mortal coming in the clouds" to their shock and regret. Rather than going to their deaths in peace and honor, "this generation will not pass away until all these things happen" (13:30). In

---

5. The bracketed words are not in the earliest Greek manuscripts and yet may be the earlier reading because they appear in the early third century scholar Origen, in the oldest Syriac translation, in a ninth century Greek codex, and in a number of early minuscules, including family 13. Although they could be a rough scribal harmonizing with Matthew, the *de* that precedes—which in Mark is usually adversative—speaks against that, as does the scribal tendency to extend rather than to curtail affirmations about Jesus. It would also be surprising if a strong affirmation in this tradition had no effect on other gospels.

6. It is possible that the fact Daniel 7 is an Aramaic text reflects and/or contributed to oral circulation of this tradition.

Mark, not only are the Pharisees addressed as this generation, "I tell you for a fact, no sign will be given to this generation," but also Jesus' disciples, "O distrusting generation . . . how much longer will I put up with you?" Hence it applies to "whoever is ashamed of me in this adulterous and sinful generation" (8:12; 9:19; 8:38). The coming of the mortal one in a world set in its own ways signifies its judgment.

On the other hand, these predictions of a heavenly vision do not dramatize this judgment. There are no tirades against the nations or laments over the waywardness of God's people. No punishments are mentioned.[7] In spite of its location in a story of suspicion, betrayal, and execution, the scene of the coming mortal is adorned in the most positive images. The mortal comes "with the clouds of heaven," "with great power," "in his Father's glory" (14:62; 13:26; 8:38). Even the angels are not sent out to gather the sinners for judgment but to gather "his elect from the four winds, from the ends of earth to the ends of heaven" (13:27). It is a victory of enthronement to the right hand of God (14:62), a time for joyful celebration and festive drinking: "I will not drink from the fruit of the vine again until that day when I drink it new in God's kingdom" (14:25). Jesus tells the crowd and his followers that "Some of those standing here will not taste death until they see God's kingdom having come in power" (9:1). Even the judgment, when the mortal will be ashamed of those now ashamed of Jesus' words, signals not so much their destruction as their implied remorse.

The language of clouds, angels, and cosmic changes could signify an expected end to the natural and historical order and those at home in it. But the more pervasive images of God's kingdom—the gathering of scattered peoples and the feasting with new wine—suggest rather a reversal of the world's power relations, as in Jesus' proverb about Satan: the strong man is bound so that his house can be plundered and his goods seized (3:27). What interests the traditional audience for whom this gospel is told is clearly the benefit of this reversal for God's scattered people, not the exposure of those ashamed of Jesus. Though addressed once to the high priest in what may be words of judgment, "You will see the mortal seated at the right hand of power," the story of the coming vision in Mark is largely directed to those who receive it as their hope.

---

7. Reichardt, *Endgericht durch den Menschensohn?*

The role of the mortal in this scene has been widely interpreted as royal, "seated at the right hand of power," and judicial, "the mortal will be ashamed" of "whoever is ashamed of me." These are important aspects of the wider tradition as can be seen in Daniel 7:14: "I saw one like a mortal coming in the clouds of heaven . . . To him was given dominion and glory and kingship, that all peoples nations and languages should serve him." It appears also in *1 Enoch* 46:4–5: "This mortal . . . shall push the kings off their thrones and from their kingdoms." But the stress in Mark is put instead on the vindication of this mortal and of the others that he represents: "He will gather up his elect" (13:27), a motif also prominent in other parts of this tradition: "The holy ones of the Most High will receive the kingdom . . . Their kingdom shall be an everlasting kingdom" (Dan 7:18, 27); and "He will become a staff for the righteous ones in order that they may lean on him and not fall. He is the light of the gentiles and he will become the hope of those who are sick in their hearts" (*1 Enoch* 48:4).

Can this role of the mortal in the scene of the coming with God's glory provide a basis for interpreting what is meant by "the mortal" in Mark as a whole? This seems unlikely in the two controversy stories reviewed above that claim for the mortal under attack the right to forgive sins on earth and to be blessed by the Sabbath. The question there is what people may do on earth, not in glory. And in the other Markan references to the mortal, Jesus is speaking of himself in his passion: This mortal one "must suffer many things" and "be dismissed as nothing" (8:31; 9:12), "be handed over" (9:31; 10:33; 14:41), "go as it is written of him" (9:12), "give his life as a ransom for many captives" (10:45), and no one can be told the story "unless the mortal one rises from the dead" (9:9). But if the mortal refers to the human being generically, as it does in Hebrew and Aramaic, and is therefore applied by Jesus to himself, a composite picture is possible. Jesus could then represent in the controversy stories the right of mortals to forgive on earth and eat on the Sabbath (Mark 2) and represent in his passion the mortal's present fate of shame and death (8:27—14:42). But in the vision of God's glory when the mortal vindicates the just it is not clear if Jesus is to be the mortal vindicator coming on the clouds or if the mortal's coming will vindicate him against those ashamed of him so that he can drink with his followers in the celebration of God's glory (8:38—9:1; 13:24-27; 14:25, 61–62).

The images of God's glory appearing in the clouds evoke God's manifestation to Moses on Sinai, also the celebration of God's glory in the Psalms and the prophets' visions of God's final triumph.[8] In the Markan predictions of this vision, God's glory can also be referred to as God's kingdom or rule (8:38—9:1; cf. 14:25), which means that the vision scene cannot be interpreted in isolation from the kingdom that Jesus proclaims. Yet it would seem that royal images of God seating the mortal on the right hand of power are undercut by Jesus' teaching that God's kingdom is like a mustard seed and belongs to children. On the one hand, this may be understandable from the different functions of the parable and the vision, namely, to reveal the daily truth and to affirm the ultimate truth. And a certain poetic license must be granted to visionary speech that reaches beyond the known world.

On the other hand, this gospel is keenly aware of the dangers of visionary speech. When the disciples concede to Jesus that they have been arguing over who will sit on his right and left in glory, Jesus asks whether they can be baptized with the baptism he undergoes, a proleptic reference to his death where one will be hanging on his right and one on his left (10:35–40; 15:27). If the hearers of the coming vision are thinking of themselves as the elect to be gathered from the four winds to see God's glory, the gospel story makes them face his words to Peter, "Get behind me, Satan," and to the scribe in the Temple, "You are not far from the kingdom of God" (8:33; 12:34). It seems that God's glory is no one's possession. Perhaps this is why the vision of future vindication is expressed in this gospel only *in extremis* when Jesus demands that they lose life to find it, when he tells them how bad things will get, and when the high priest tries to goad him into blasphemy (8:34—9:1; 13:14–27; 14:55–64).

Returning to the question of whether the scenes in Mark—here specifically the visions—are recent news rather than weighty tradition, the answer must be that these recent visions have taken on weighted ways. The voice from a torn open heaven that endows Jesus with the Spirit to declare the arrival of God's kingdom is told in the idiom of a *bat kol*, giving it an authority that cannot be gainsaid. Even the disciples' vision of Jesus transfigured with Moses and Elijah, which they do not understand, leaves reverberating the words, "This is my beloved

8. Exod 24:16–18; Pss 8:5; 24:10; Isa 40:3–5; Zech 2:5; Ezek 1:26–28; Dan 7:9–14; *1 Enoch* 14; Newman, "Glory, Glorify."

son, listen to him," which in turn echo the words of Moses on how to receive a prophet, "listen to him" (Deut 18:15). And they are followed by Jesus' explanation that Elijah has come and prepared the mortal's way. The coming time is predicted in the equally authoritative language of apocalyptic visions. This coming vision offers at the mortal's point of no return a highly dramatized assertion of the ultimate vindication and fulfillment of life for all God's scattered peoples. Each telling of these visions becomes for traditional hearers a kind of proxy vision of God's delight and glory that frame a mortal's life.

# 12

## The Story Pattern of Mark
## as Performance Tradition[1]

The major challenge in making the case for Mark's composition in performance is to show that the story as a whole has been shaped in the telling. Readers and scholars alike will concede that language choices and scenes in Mark were traditional, but few will accept that the gospel as a whole was composed in traditional performance. We ourselves tell stories, but not of such length, and when we sit down to write we use these stories, but in service to our own statements, and we expect the same in ancient texts. In part, our misunderstanding is caused by the great changes since that time in composition practices and writing techniques. These changes have allowed us to compose and write simultaneously, whereas they composed as they spoke (or as they practiced a speech in advance), and writing required a scribe, or, for the few rich enough to have learned to write but poor enough to lack a scribe, writing required a long block of time to say it again slowly.

I will begin with some other factors that have blocked our recognition of oral storytelling patterns in whole gospel construction. Then I will review positive contributions to hearing Mark as a whole coming from literary study of Mark's genre, then contributions from study of oral story patterns generally, and finally contributions from recent research on Mark as a whole gospel composed in performance. My own

1. This and the following chapters develop further my argument on Mark's story pattern that appeared in Wire, "Mark: News as Tradition," in *The Interface of Orality to Written Text: Speaking, Seeing, Writing in the Shaping of New Genres*, edited by Annette Weissenrieder and Robert B. Coote (Tübingen: Mohr/Siebeck, 2010) 52–70. Used with permission.

analysis will come in the following two chapters where I present the story pattern of Mark as a conflict in process and as an account of a prophet's sign.

## Obstructions to Perceiving the Story Pattern of Mark

Perhaps the main factor that has hindered recognizing oral patterns in whole gospels has been the long-standing assumption that the gospels were written by individual authors. From this perspective some explanation was required for why the gospels were so episodic, as if they were made up of stories strung together like beads on a string. The answer given was that each story about Jesus (including the passion story) had for years circulated independently, except where some were gathered into homogenous collections of sayings or healings or controversies.[2] This scenario left the writer's hand most visible in the ordering, linking, and adapting of separate units or collections. The focus here on the writer's creative work was a reaction to the form critics' focus on recovering what Jesus had said and done. The form critics held that each original story and saying was shaped in a single setting—whether of Christian mission to the world, teaching converts, or preaching to believers—and that these units simply coalesced into gospels. This thesis allowed them to peel off the predictable shaping of the unit for church use in hopes of recovering the original sayings or events.

In contrast to both form criticism and redaction criticism, the thesis of composition in performance projects neither originals shaped by uniform social conventions into gospels, nor a galaxy of free-floating units and unit-groups at the disposal of inspired authors. With attention shifted from original events on the one hand, and authors' interpretations of neutral accounts on the other hand, performance composition claims that tradition is always told as a meaningful whole narrative, flexible in size and detail, and yet functioning recognizably as an integrated story.

A second obstacle to understanding storytelling practices in Second Temple and post-destruction Judaism has been the minimal research that has been done on the communication practices of the

---

2. These were seen in chains of miracle stories in both John and Mark and in the sayings collections of "Q" and the *Gospel of Thomas.*

great majority of people who did not read and write. Although there are some studies of rumor and storytelling in the Roman East[3] and some collecting of early Jewish stories,[4] the great weight of research has focused on the less than ten percent of families with some literacy including their oral interpretive practices.[5] Few take up the challenge of sifting from documents and artifacts the stories and narrative practices of the society at large.

Third, those who do investigate an individual figure who is not known to be a writer of documents in this period, such as Rabbi Ḥanina ben Dosa or Jesus, tend to focus on this individual in contrast to others and claim historical results without enough attention to their social context or the aims of our source documents.[6]

Finally, the oral-formulaic school that has been so fruitful in its studies of formulas and themes in traditional literatures has not been as comprehensive in its study of whole story patterns. Albert Lord's programmatic study, *The Singer of Tales*, mentions the many kinds of story patterns in the South Slavic songs Milman Parry collected, but concedes that Parry recorded more return songs that other kinds due to their parallels in the Odyssey.[7] Lord proposes that return songs are part of a wider rescue cycle pattern with the following elements: tale of capture, shouting in prison and release on condition of return to prison, return home in disguise and recognition, return to prison to rescue or be rescued, and a possible wedding in conclusion. Within this broad sequence each song in the tradition, though separate, is yet inseparable from others. This shows how illuminating the parallel is between certain South Slavic and Homeric stories, but it also shows how specific these findings are, even within the two traditions, so that similarly in-

---

3. Ahn, "Transmitters of the Jesus-Event"; Botha, "Social Dynamics"; Hearon, "Storytelling"; Hearon and Maloney, "Listen to the Voices of the Women." On rumor more broadly, see Shibutani, *Improvised News*; Kapferer, *Rumor*; Gary Fine, "Rumor, Trust and Civil Society."

4. Ginsberg, *Legends of the Jews*; Nadich, *Jewish Legends of the Second Commonwealth*; Ben-Amos, "Narrative Forms"; Wire, *Holy Lives*.

5. See Alexander, *Transmitting Mishnah*; Jaffee, *Torah in the Mouth*; Carr, *Writing on the Tablet of the Heart*.

6. See the critique in the preface of Neusner's *Building Blocks of the Rabbinic Tradition*. In light of such critique, Neusner had rewritten his *A Life of Yohanan ben Zakkai* and produced *Development of a Legend*.

7. Lord, *Singer of Tales*, 120–21.

tensive and inductive work within other traditions' story patters will be required to get such results.

Later Lord speaks of story patterns evolving from myths about gods that are subsequently applied to heroes, characterized by a sequence of absence, devastation, arrival, and restoration, or evolving from basic social problems in a sequence of conflict, advocacy, and resolution.[8] But these patterns are so abstract as to be hardly useful for distinguishing between stories. And when Lord speaks of the gospels specifically, he applies the cross-cultural life-of-hero myth, stretching from birth, precocious childhood, growth, marriage, investiture, deeds, to death of a substitute person, and death.[9] Yet Mark lacks the entire first half of these steps, and Mark's exorcisms, healings, controversies, and disciple trainings are not mythic. If the coherence of Mark is to be seen in terms of an oral story pattern, it cannot be borrowed from elsewhere or derived from abstractions. Rather it will need to be found in this gospel as read in the context of Israel's first century traditions.

## Contributions from Study of Mark's Literary Genre

In seeking the story pattern that gives unity to Mark's gospel as an oral composition, we do not at all begin from scratch. The question of the genre of the gospels as literary documents has occupied scholars for more than a century. This research not only makes it difficult to conceive of Mark as an oral composition, but it can also make positive contributions.

The form critics of the mid-twentieth century may have contributed the most, with two basic insights: that the gospels were announcements of good news and that they were shaped in community contexts. In New Testament texts the word "gospel" always means a welcome oral proclamation. The only question is what it refers to. Under the influence of Karl Barth, form critics understood the gospel narrowly as the news of salvation through Jesus' death and resurrection, whereas in Mark it incorporates the entire story of Jesus proclaiming and enacting God's kingdom against all opposition which brings on his death and vindication. The form critics also saw that this proclaiming was communal in

8. Lord, *The Singer Resumes*, 12–13.

9. Lord, "Gospels," 133–91.

that it generated a common life that embodied and transmitted this news.

Yet it was also visualized narrowly with miracle stories seen as mission propaganda, Jesus' sayings as catechesis for new believers, and Jesus' death and rising as preaching to the church. This narrowing of the meaning of gospel to one saving death and the narrowing of community to church also meant that the Markan tellers and hearers were not seen as integral to Israel nor were they seen as Gentiles attracted to God. By projecting back our modern experience of Judaism and Christianity as two religions, these critics saw gospel communities claiming Jesus over against Israel, distorting the interpretation of Jesus' conflicts with authorities and the meaning of his death and vindication. It is in this context that they adopted Karl Schmidt's understanding of the gospel genre as being *sui generis*, without precedent. Nonetheless, all understanding requires some framework, and they could only sustain this view by making broad concessions that the gospels incorporated familiar prophetic sayings and healings and were analogous to accounts of the death of Israel's righteous.

Today most biblical scholars hold that the genre of the gospels is some form of biography, the story of a life told to edify and inspire others.[10] The proposal of a biography genre makes the contribution of including the whole of Jesus' story that a gospel tells. The proposal can also encompass other figures in so far as their lives shape and are shaped by his. But nothing is said in Mark about Jesus' birth, heritage, or education, and little is said about Jesus as a model of human character, all standard elements of Greco-Roman biography. If we keep in mind the contributions of form criticism that the gospel is oral proclamation in a communal setting, then analogous biographies will not in any case be the literary creations of a Diogenes Laertius or a Suetonius but popular accounts with a likely oral history, such as the Life of Aesop or the accounts of Daniel or Tobit. In content, parallels are closest with the biographies of the prophets, especially the stories of Elijah and Elisha and parts of Jeremiah. Klaus Baltzer has identified elements common in stories of prophets' lives: the prophet is chosen as God's instrument, does wonders demonstrating God's power, intervenes on behalf of victims, renews polluted cults, gives God's word to rulers, prophesies

10. For example: Aune, *The New Testament in Its Literary Environment*; Aune, ed., *Greco-Roman Literature and the New Testament*.

political events, and receives divine favor at his death.[11] A number of these characteristics are present in later biblical and pseudepigraphal texts such as *1 Enoch* 71; *Testament of Levi* 8; and *Lives of the Prophets*.[12] Many of these elements appear in Mark and suggest that the coherence of Mark's story may come from expectations about a prophet. Interest in a prophet's leadership may hold people's attention on a series of otherwise unrelated episodes.

Nonetheless, the stories of prophets may be better understood as history rather than biography, since surviving records often chronicle more than one figure in a particular historical context.[13] Adela Yarbro Collins has recently argued that Mark's gospel, as a recitation and interpretation of recent events, is less a life of Jesus than a history of the eschatological events that come to a head in him.[14] She compares the way Mark combines teachings, healing accounts, and stories of saving death to the Deuteronomistic history that incorporates the stories of Elijah and Elisha within a much broader story of Israel spanning northern Mosaic and southern Davidic traditions.[15] History in this sense is not interpreted in terms of the critical intentions of a Thucydides, but is seen more to have the wide sweep of a Herodotus, who readily incorporated legendary accounts as the stories of a people. Collins also recognizes an apocalyptic interest of Mark in impending events as seen in Daniel, and she calls Mark "an eschatological historical monograph."[16] "Monograph" indicates an author writing according to a genre readers of his time will anticipate, whereas a composing performer embodies in him or herself the tradition people are waiting to hear. This is not the same phenomenon. Yet there is a decided contribution here toward our sighting of the Markan story pattern. What holds Mark together is not only oral and communal and grounded in the prophetic role. Mark claims the broadest canvas for its news of a historical reversal of this world's power structure coming by repentance and trust in God's rule.

11. Baltzer, *Biographie der Propheten*, 181–89.

12. These pseudepigraphical texts are available in Charlesworth, ed., *Old Testament Pseudepigrapha*, 2 vols.

13. Collins, *Mark*, 29–30.

14. Ibid., 42–44.

15. Ibid., 37–42.

16. Ibid., 42–44.

## Contributions from Study of Oral Tradition

I turn now to what help is available from those who have analyzed story patterns in oral tradition. One approach is motif analysis, pioneered by Antii Aarne and represented in Stith Thompson's six-volume *Motif Index of Folk-Literature.*[17] It catalogues stories according to narrative motifs. At best, this is very concrete. For example, a man who gives only half a carpet to cover his old father finds that his own son is keeping the other half to cover him when he is old. But the effort to locate parallels means that more stories are classified generally, as in "wise child exposes father." And tracing story transmission from such classifications becomes questionable. Also, longer stories tend to be classified piecemeal by several motifs rather than by an overall story pattern.

A second approach of folklore analysis has distinguished different broad genres by story content: myths are about divine figures establishing the cosmos, tall tales are about fiction and fantasy, and legends are about great leaders of the past.[18] In these categories, our stories are best called legends, although I avoid the term because it has come to mean fabrications, whereas folklore legends are always told as stories about real, albeit extraordinary, events. But the chief problem with these categories is that they tell too little about the structure of the stories. Ben-Amos is right when he argues that analysis within folklore types needs to be culture-specific and time-specific, an *oikotype* as he calls it.[19] Yet his descriptions of the *oikotype* of haggadic stories follow broad structuralist lines rather than culture-specific divisions.

A third approach by structuralists has pressed the analysis of story patterns in more detail. To oversimplify, the French school, following Claude Levi-Strauss, has analyzed stories synchronically, that is, looking for overall patterns that are sustained in the whole piece.[20] They stress patterns of tension and resolution within a story, tension between forces such as the natural and the cultivated, the one and the many, living and dying. When using the language found within the story to

17. Stith Thompson, *Motif-Index of Folk-Literature.*

18. Jolles, *Einfache Formen*; Bascom, "Forms of Folklore."

19. Ben-Amos, "Analytic Categories and Ethnic Genres"; and Ben-Amos, "Concept of Genre in Folklore."

20. Levi-Strauss, *The Raw and the Cooked*; Greimas, *Structural Semantics*; Greimas, *On Meaning*

identify multiple interacting oppositions, this analysis can be very illuminating. The Russian formalists, on the other hand, often analyzed stories diachronically, tracing patterns of sequence in the narrative line. Vladimir Propp located up to thirty-one "motifemes" in Russian folk-tales which always appear in the same order, though elements may be omitted.[21] Others speak more generally of actions in which a donor tests a hero, the hero responds to the test, and the donor rewards the hero.[22] This analysis of sequence was the method adapted to identify the return song pattern in both the Homeric and Slavic epics.[23]

Some scholars of oral tradition have objected to structural analysis in general, arguing that traditional storytelling does not maintain a firm structure, not of patterns of opposition nor of patterns of sequence, because the structure is in the tradition rather than any single enactment of it. Lauri and Anneli Honko report that a South Indian performer of the Siri epic spoke of "knots," "joints," or "halting places" in telling a story, suggesting the tradition is a network with points where a choice must be made before continuing on one path or another, or a journey with landmarks where one stretch has been covered and others remain ahead.[24] Even the much repeated parts of a performance that Lauri Honko calls "multiforms" are seen to vary considerably in "thickness of texture."[25] This has been interpreted, on the one hand, to mean that "a folklore work . . . exists only potentially; it is only a complex of established norms and stimuli; it is a skeleton of actual traditions which the implementers embellish."[26] If so, the tradition is something like the lowest common denominator of all its performances.

On the other hand, John Miles Foley suggests that the tradition's pathways are myriad and that the phrase or scene that is performed in an act of "immanent art" represents *pars pro toto* this unspeakably complex traditional network. With him, I take the tradition as the ultimate whole, in the sense of the full length and breadth and depth of a people's memory—the "story horde," as Foley puts it, that holds the

21. Propp, *Morphology of the Folktale*, 25–65.
22. Jason, "Model for Narrative Structure in Oral Literature."
23. Lord, *Singer of Tales*, 120–24.
24. Honko and Honko, "Multiforms in Epic Composition," 69–71.
25. Honko, "Text as Process and Practice."
26. Jakobson and Begatyrev, "On the Boundary between Studies of Folklore and Literature," 91–92.

connections between all piecemeal meanings.[27] Yet until it is told, it is an unbounded maze of pathways fading off at the edges of human sight, a strictly potential reality. Once told, however, a traditional story is the whole story in the actual and bounded sense, the work of traditional art. Therefore, I take the story of Mark that we have as an adequate basis to identify a story pattern, even though this telling in script is only one instance of the Markan tradition.

Is there any substantive distinction, then, between a study of the story pattern of this gospel as an artistic performance and a study of the genre of Mark as an author's text? Without denying how much can be learned from studies of Mark as one person's creative writing, the differences are great. To mention only a few: sources drawn on are not other documents but oral accounts; story patterns will be coming from oral storytelling; multiple favored tellers must be assumed over decades; tellers are probably not literate and may represent a wide range of people; transmission is through sound and rhythm; the pressing interests of the hearers are engaged in the context of their own past; and they know the tradition and their lives and will reject interpretations that violate either.

## Contributions from Study of Mark Composed in Performance

Turning in recent research to the story pattern of Mark composed in performance, I find specific proposals hard to come by. Scholars who have recognized Mark as an oral tradition stress different aspects of the coherence of this performance but seldom focus on the coherence of the whole story. Karl Ludwig Schmidt found that popular folk traditions about monks, saints, and hasidim were the best analogues for the gospels: "These 'authors' had no choice but to restrain themselves (indeed, they more or less *wanted* to restrain themselves), because they were carried along by a tradition."[28] James D. G. Dunn says that "The gospel of Mark can readily be seen as a written example of an oral performance of the Jesus tradition." He stresses the flexible "living tradition" of remembering Jesus through telling his story, which began

27. Foley, *Immanent Art*; and Foley, *How to Read*, 109–24.

28. Schmidt, *Place of the Gospels*, 62.

already in Jesus' lifetime and continued through and after the gospels.[29] But neither Schmidt nor Dunn delineate an overall structure of this oral tradition.

Yet it seems that one kind of analysis of Mark's story pattern stresses more the sequence of events. Joanna Dewey speaks of Mark being shaped in a process of one performance building upon another performance, "in an oral tradition that had already created a continuous, more-or-less coherent narrative" based on the framework of Jesus' ministry, death and resurrection.[30] She particularly notes acoustic echoes within stories, in groups of stories, and in the whole narrative that hold it together in the style of an oral composition, but without identifying any specific echoes that are essential to its coherence. In his proposal of Mark as oral tradition, Pieter Botha also calls the process of transmission an art of recomposition, and he sees the tradition functioning as a unified system that generates oral compositions in performance by means of formulas and themes.[31] He is convinced that the story will not have been told as a whole for the first time fifty years after the events but must have been shaped by itinerants like Peter whose accounts became known and were finally dictated for preservation as spoken in public performance.[32] Botha concludes that the story pattern about a martyred and vindicated hero is told in the context of mythic narrative patterns from Israel and the broader Near East, but at the same time it is the story of a suffering mortal who draws others toward his own faith in God for whom all things are possible.[33]

Since Martin Kähler identified the gospels as "passion narratives with an extended introduction,"[34] the practice has been to read Mark's structure from back to front. The passion story itself is broadly taken as a cohesive unit, and in 1980 George Nickelsburg proposed that a pre-Markan passion account shares in a genre of Jewish literature called Persecution and Vindication Stories.[35] He finds in these stories twenty-

29. Dunn, "Living Tradition."

30. Dewey, "Survival of Mark's Gospel," 503, 495–96. See also Dewey, "Oral Methods."

31. Botha, "Mark's Story as Oral Traditional Literature," 304–31.

32. Ibid., 322–31.

33. Botha, "*ouk estin hōde*," 202.

34. Kähler, *The So-called Historical Jesus*, 80 n. 11.

35. He identifies as "Persecution and Vindication Stories": Genesis 37ff, the

one components, among them provocation, accusation, ordeal, and vindication. Though he wants to draw conclusions about a literary genre of the passion story, he has to concede that these components reflect "a generic type of narrative that was a conventional medium for telling stories about . . . persecuted righteous persons."[36] Nickelsburg sees two other themes, namely those of Messiahship and Temple, that are also necessary to comprehend the genre of Mark as a whole. In response, however, Thomas Haverly suggests that, since Jesus' assertive behavior brings on threats to destroy him already in Mark's third chapter, the single pattern of provocation, ordeal, and vindication could integrate the entire oral gospel.[37] Haverly himself says little else on Mark's story pattern since he takes oral tradition to be largely identified by the formulas and themes that make up its stable skeleton presented as a true story, the form of which varies according to the personal style of the teller or the social practices of the hearers.[38]

A second promising mode of analyzing the Markan story pattern follows more the French than the Russian structuralist bent, looking for dynamic polarities rather than a sequence leading up to a climax. Oppositions are seen to underlie the story at each key point. In the American context, this has been developed in light of conflict theory in sociological analysis. Richard Horsley sees the conflict between the rulers and the ruled in all aspects of Mark.[39] He insists that the tradition did not function in fragments of stories or sayings but focused on figures who were leading the resistance to rulers. Mark is evidence of the oral *Kleinliteratur* of the people who interpreted Jesus in light of Moses the liberator and Elijah the restorer as God's instrument in the present struggle against the allied economic and political power of the Jerusalem elite, the Herodians, and the Roman occupiers.

---

story of Ahikar, Esther, Daniel 3 and 6, Susanna, and Wisdom of Solomon 2 and 4–5. Nickelsburg, "Genre and Function of the Markan Passion Narrative," especially 155–63.

36. Ibid., 163.

37. Haverly, "Oral Traditional Literature," 313.

38. Ibid, 37–44.

39. Horsley, "A Prophet Like Moses and Elijah," 178–83, 188–92; and Horsley, *Hearing the Whole Story.*

Botha sees truth-telling peasants standing against the urban elite who seek to deceive them.[40] Whereas a modern mentality assumes an unfinished universe with broad human opportunities, Botha says this gospel assumes a universe determined by possessing powers or spirits, representing either the power of God who wills human health and mutual care or the power of Satan who wills human occupation and destruction. In this world, Jesus demonstrates faith in God by which a person can do all things and announces God's kingdom as the reversal of all existing power relations.

David Watson has specified this analysis by proposing that the Markan Jesus reverses the honor-shame values of his culture by modeling service and resisting ascriptions of honor, cultivating a new family among the culturally shamed where honor is established by acts of humility and compassion.[41] Although Jesus is not consistent in silencing those who would extend his honor, Watson argues that the theme is much repeated, which is sufficient to make the point in an oral context.

The influence of apocalyptic in Mark's gospel is usually seen in the arrival of God's kingdom at the coming of the mortal in glory, but the apocalyptic in Mark is equally important for understanding the conflict between God and evil. This is one way of speaking of the biblical drama which comes to a head in prophecy and apocalyptic. Schmidt concedes that Jewish apocalyptic "may be the literary germ of the gospels"[42] but that the traditions are much more various. Yet the Markan gospel sees at every turn that the powers of evil dominate life and threaten to bring death and destruction. Only when the strong man is bound, as Ched Myers has highlighted, is the stronger one able to plunder his wealth (3:27; 1:7).[43] Fernando Belo brings the French structuralist and political approaches together to powerful effect in a running analysis of Mark in terms of pollution and cleansing, debt and gift, passion and resurrection.[44] In her recent commentary Adela Yarbro Collins treats the apocalyptic aspects of the narrative at length. Yet she interprets them

40. Botha, "Mark's Story of Jesus and the Search for Virtue."

41. Watson, "The 'Messianic Secret.'"

42. Schmidt, *Place of the Gospels,* 26.

43. Myers, *Binding the Strong Man.*

44. Belo, *Materialist Reading of the Gospel of Mark,* 98–232.

primarily in terms of long-standing traditions of a sequence of ages before the end rather than by stressing God's conflict with evil powers that remains in process as the gospel is being performed.[45]

45. Collins, *Mark*, 42–69, 591–619.

# 13

## The Story Pattern as Conflict in Process

I propose two ways the story pattern of Mark can be described: synchronically as a narrative tension and diachronically as a narrative sequence, the latter being developed in the next chapter. I see my double-talk here as a way to cover more adequately the complexities of the gospel. But also it is a sign that I know I have not exhausted the field, and that the unity in this performance of Mark has multiple facets.

### Story Pattern as Agōn

Analysis of Markan tradition as a conflict suits the oral composition thesis particularly well. Agonistic scenes encourage heroic and demonic characterizations, heighten the drama, and draw the audience into identification with one side against the other. This story pattern could be called the agōn or contest in the most basic, even mythic sense, whether it is told in the idiom of the oppressor as destruction and counter-destruction, or in the subversive or comic vein to expose the weakness of those who are so sure they rule.[1] Each episode in such a narrative tells the whole story—the threat dispelled, the hunger gone—and any scene told well can stand for them all. It is indicative of this point that I can remember only one episode of many Appalachian stories of this kind that were told me about the landlord and the Bryan boys. This time they lure the landlord's sheep down to the creek and take one each spring for the Bryan table, while he complains about how his herd doesn't grow

1. Ong, *Fighting for Life*; Davis, "Agon and Gnomon"; Wills, *Quest of the Historical Gospel*, 35–50, 181–215.

under their care. Similarly, but in urban California, Mrs. Irvine had stories about her sons and the San Anselmo police. In one of these stories as I remember, each son is pulled over for speeding on Bolinas Avenue until the last son lets on that the speed limit sign was washed away in the winter flood and the cops have to tear up all the tickets. In this kind of conflict narrative, one story can stand for the entire repertoire or can trigger another story until they build into a crescendo. The storyteller highlights the contrast between the contending parties, develops suspense through repetition and rhythmic patterns, and above all flouts established authority and celebrates the local heroes.

The fact that the story of Mark is not consistently heroic, in that Jesus evades adulation, eats with outcasts, and welcomes children, may only highlight another characteristic of oral storytelling, namely the freedom of the hero from conventional bounds. This is paralleled in folktale heroes such as Tale in Balkan Moslem stories, the Pelt Kid in Panamanian Zuni lore,[2] and Aesop in the *Life of Aesop*.[3] The stark contrast in Mark between Jesus walking on water and crying out on a cross could also reflect the different voices that go into the process of oral story construction over decades, since tellers seldom bleach out one dramatic scene just because another is quite different, apparently finding the extremes of life neither unlikely nor incompatible.

## Jesus versus the Legal Authorities

Several tensions sustained throughout Mark hold it together as one statement. Perhaps the most prominent tension in Mark is between Jesus and the legal authorities, often called the scribes and/or Pharisees. Both Jesus and they are attributed authority, explain what God requires, and interpret the meaning of Scripture; but each questions the other's conduct and considers the other to be misleading the people. The scribes accuse Jesus of expelling demons by the power of the ruler of demons, and Jesus accuses Pharisees and scribes of nullifying God's commands with their traditions (3:22; 7:8, 13). The scribes and Pharisees are shown to be established and defending their practices as traditions of the elders, whereas Jesus is depicted speaking from a heav-

2. Foley, *Singer of Tales in Performance*, 30–41.
3. See Wills' translation of *Life of Aesop* in *The Quest*, 181–215.

enly calling and defending his authority in the prophetic tradition of John the Baptist (1:2–11; 9:11–13; 11:27–33). The conflict is dramatized in concrete stories about fasting, eating, divorce, and cleansing rather than as general principles, though we hear an occasional concluding summary: "the Sabbath is for people, not people for the Sabbath," or "declaring all foods clean" (2:27; 7:19).

## God versus Satan

On the cosmic level the tension is drawn up between God and Satan. After a kind of title, the story begins with the first person speech of God attributed to Isaiah announcing, "I will send my messenger ahead of you." And God speaks again when the Spirit comes down on Jesus, "You are my beloved son. I delight in you!" (1:2, 11). This divine initiative continues as the Spirit drives Jesus out into the desert to face Satan, and Jesus returns to Galilee to announce God's kingdom or rule.

This kingdom is not presented as an established condition but as something coming into a hostile environment. Jesus' first act of power is to silence and cast out an unclean spirit who exposes him as God's holy one (1:24). When accused of casting out demons by Beelzebul, Jesus identifies the accusations as blasphemy against God's Spirit (3:22–30). Three other times Jesus expels life-threatening spirits: from the fishers on the sea, from the man living among the graves, and from the boy with seizures (4:35–41; 5:1–20; 9:14–27). The graveyard story clearly implicates Rome in the unclean spirit's name, Legion, in its not wanting to be sent out of the country, and arguably in the massive Gentile food supply represented by the herd of swine (5:1–20). Because such exorcism stories are marginalized in Matthew and Luke and disappear in John, this aspect of Mark is only now being recognized for its significance.[4] In a world that is Satan's, held captive to the one who looks out from the tribute coinage, God is seen arriving to reclaim the people, who are made in God's image and created for partnership and for love of God and neighbor (12:13–17, 27; 10:2–9; 12:28–34).

---

4. Myers, *Binding the Strong Man*, 190–94; Botha, "Mark's Story of Jesus," 170–84; Horsley, *Hearing the Whole Story*, 121–48.

## Trust versus Fear

A third level of tension takes place in the people. Faced with the challenge God's Spirit makes to Satan's rule, they are torn between trust and fear. Four fishers and eight others, "many tax collectors," and "many women" follow Jesus (1:16–20; 2:15; 3:16–19; 15:41), yet their trust is mercurial and their conduct is increasingly ruled by fear of hunger or shame or death. It is those from the crowd, people in the most desperate straits, who become the models of trust, whether by Jesus' challenge to them—"Don't be afraid. Just keep trusting." "All things are possible for the one who trusts!"—or by their own initiative—"I trust! Help my distrust!" "Your trust has made you well." (5:36; 9:23; 5:34; 9:24; 10:52).

One can also speak of an overall tension in Mark between Jesus' trust in God's coming rule that allows God's power to work through him and other people's fear of loss that makes them subject to Satan's present power structures. The entire drama of Mark can be seen as an intensifying struggle between unclean spirits and God's holy Spirit. As has been shown in the exorcism stories above, the Romans with their legions who will not leave the country are implicated as unclean spirits, and the scribes from Jerusalem who accuse Jesus of exorcizing by Satan's power are accused in return of blaspheming against the holy Spirit (5:1–20; 3:22–30). Even Jesus' family is seen to oppose doing God's will (3:21, 31–35). Though Jesus' disciples are taught his way, even to the point of teaching sessions in a house apart from others where they receive "the mystery of God's kingdom" (4:10–13, 34 passim), yet they seem to understand less and less and finally betray and deny him (8:17–21, 32–33; 9:33–37; 10:32; 14:10–11, 43–46, 66–72), leaving only the weak and desperate with the trust to which Jesus credits their healings (5:34; 7:29; 10:52).

It is evident in these conflicts that the storyteller does not take a neutral position. The whole weight of the story banks on the coming of God's kingdom, which is described in process of expelling destroying spirits, exposing empty authorities, and displacing fear with trust. This is the news it is telling. At the same time, there is a heavy counterweight of reality, seen from the start in the Spirit's driving Jesus out to be tested by Satan. Satan possesses—or Rome occupies—the present time and the story's space, the legal authorities keep the pressure on Jesus, and the disciples' fear is the order of the day. This realism is the

126

default setting, never in doubt, though it is challenged frontally by the announcement of God's overriding power that gives Jesus "authority . . . not like the scribes" (1:22) and elicits the trust that heals and saves. The storytellers who make this challenge are apparently taking on the powers of the world and rejoicing in each thrust and parry in their struggle against established structures.

The outcome of the story is ambiguous. On the one hand many are healed and the women hear from the young man in the tomb that Jesus is raised, in a passive tense that indicates this is God's action. Yet they fear rather than trust, and the message that Jesus goes ahead of them to Galilee is not told to the disciples. The tellers of this tradition are now defying Jesus' repeated instructions not to tell and ignoring the final report that the women who were told to tell did not. This makes Mark both an account of failure to trust God and, in each telling, an overriding demonstration of trust. The performance of Mark sustains the conflict.

# 14

## The Story Pattern as Report of a Prophet's Sign

The pattern of the whole Markan story can also be considered diachronically as a sequence of functions in the way Propp analyzed the Russian folktale and Lord described the return song. But can Mark's loose construction of one scene after another be grasped as an integrated narrative line? And can a pattern be found in this story that is analogous to other reports of the time, that is, an oral storytelling pattern that is readily available for speaking and hearing? These are the key questions.

### Five Elements of the Report of a Prophet's Sign

The introductory scene in Mark is clearly the arrival of a prophet in a time of crisis (1:1–15). The opening of the gospel culminates in Jesus' first public appearance in Galilee, but it begins with the prophet John. John appears according to earlier prophecy and announces the sign of baptism for deliverance of those who repent, apparently so they can escape some sign of destruction he has announced against their ruler Herod Antipas for taking his brother's wife (6:17; Josephus *Jewish Antiquities* 18.109–19). Herod's taxes, raised in order to build new cities, weighed heavily on the land, but this egregious act must have been considered beyond all bounds and it brings opposition to a head. When John appears at the Jordan, crowds come from everywhere to be baptized. Herod's arrest of John is quickly told, but the end of John's story is delayed until the sixth chapter when a flashback recounts the banquet where Herod serves John's head on a platter. At that time John

128

is vindicated by Herod's declaration that John has been raised from the dead in Jesus (6:14–16).[1]

The five elements in this telling of John's story—appearance in crisis, giving of a sign, crowds, suppression, and vindication—are reflected in many early Jewish stories about prophets who give a sign of something that will take place, in John's case the sign that the baptized will be delivered when Herod meets his judgment.[2] These stories show their popular origins in the signs that promise the people's deliverance and the rulers' downfall, in the great crowds that come out, in the rulers' stark violence against the people, and in the ultimate vindication of the prophet. It is evident that the movements described cannot have taken place without such stories in which people spread word of the signs, of the crowds one could join, and of God's sure vindication when rulers block the fulfillment of the signs. Many of these stories are preserved in the histories of Josephus, heavily colored by his view that those who claim to be prophets are frauds.

> And even the nation of Samaritans did not escape disruption. A certain man who had no qualms about lying and devised everything for the pleasure of the crowd gathered the Samaritans, commanding them to come with him onto Mt. Gerizim, which is taken by them to be the holiest of mountains. And he maintained that he would show to those who arrived the holy vessels buried there where Moses deposited them. The men in arms held his word to be persuasive and, camping in a certain town called Tirathana, they took on those who continued to collect so as to make the ascent into the mountain in a great multitude. But Pilate anticipated their ascent, occupying it in advance with an escort of cavalry and heavy-armed infantry. They engaged those who had first gathered in the village, formed a battle line and killed some, while others ran off in flight. They took many captive and Pilate killed the prominent leaders and the most able-bodied men among those who fled.
>
> When the disturbance was put down, the council of the Samaritans went to Vitellius, a man of consular rank who was

---

1. Note that when Josephus tells John's story, the vindication is described differently: "The opinion among the Jews was that destruction came on [Herod's] army in vindication of John, since God chose to afflict Herod" (Josephus *Jewish Antiquities* 18.116, 119); Wire, *Holy Lives*, 206–9.

2. On these prophets see Gray, *Prophetic Figures*; Horsley, *Jesus and the Spiral of Violence*; Riedo-Emmenegger, *Prophetisch-messianische Provokateure der Pax Romana*.

governor of Syria, and accused Pilate of the slaughter of those that perished. For they had gone to Tirathana not for revolt against the Romans but for escape from the outrages of Pilate. And Vitellius sent out Marcellus, one of his friends, to take charge of the Jews and commanded Pilate to go back to Rome to inform the emperor about the things the Samaritans were charging. (Josephus *Jewish Antiquities* 18.85–89).[3]

Here the story pattern is clear: the Samaritan appears in Tirathana when Pilate has outraged the people, he announces the sign of finding holy vessels buried by Moses, the crowds gather, Pilate intervenes to suppress the action, and the Samaritans are vindicated when Pilate is replaced and sent home to give an account of himself.

## Jesus' Story as an Account of a Prophet's Sign

The question is whether the same sequence of appearance in crisis, giving of sign, crowds, suppression, and vindication can provide the story pattern for the Markan story of Jesus. Having been baptized by John who predicted a stronger one coming to baptize with God's Spirit and having been driven by that Spirit into a time and place of testing, Jesus appears in Galilee at the crisis point in John's repentance movement, "when John was handed over" (1:14). In the heart of Herod's territory, Jesus announces God's kingdom. This is a sign of an event about to happen, as is the Samaritan's sign that they will find the holy vessels that Moses buried so they can rebuild their temple. Similar signs are told in other stories of the prophet Theudas' sign that the Jordan River will part and the Egyptian prophet's sign that the walls of Jerusalem will fall down (Josephus *Jewish Antiquities* 20.94–98, 167–72). Each sign is a threat to those who reject it but the hope of deliverance and blessing for those who receive it. Though all the stories tell how the prophet is suppressed before the sign can be fulfilled, the hope continues to be told, as can be seen when Paul is described arriving in Jerusalem and is mistaken for the Egyptian expected to return (Acts 21:38; Josephus *Jewish War* 2.261–63; *Jewish Antiquities* 20.167–72).

3. My translation from the Loeb Greek edition: *Holy Lives*, 259–60. See twenty-four stories about prophets living from 150 BCE to 150 CE who give signs and sixteen new stories from this period about Hebrew Bible prophets giving such signs in *Holy Lives*, 181–277.

The end of the Markan story of Jesus that tells his suppression and vindication also follows the pattern found in the stories of prophets' signs. Jesus is persistent in his challenge to power, neither evading the pilgrimage city at the time of Passover nor compromising with authorities once betrayed to them there. His vindication comes in the words to the women at the tomb, brief as they are, announcing that he is alive—at large—and has gone ahead to meet his followers in Galilee.

Between the opening appearance when the sign is announced and the closing suppression and vindication of the prophet, the story about the prophet's sign has only one intermediate element, the gathering of the crowds. Can this single factor adequately comprehend the long and complex narrative of Mark? Though interpreters have favored readings of Mark that stress Jesus' role, the stories are in fact at least as much about how he is and is not received. On the one hand, people follow this prophet in great numbers, making the movement and its power, and, on the other hand, his popular following mobilizes the authorities to eliminate him. After he announces God's rule, fishermen follow instantly when called, people in the synagogue marvel at his "new teaching with authority," "and right away his reputation goes out everywhere into the whole region of Galilee" (1:18, 20, 27–28). Jesus' exorcisms and healings are crucial in drawing the crowds so that soon "the whole town is gathered at his door," and before the end of the first chapter, "he was no longer able to enter a town publicly but would be out in deserted places and they would come to him from everywhere" (1:33, 45).

When the paralytic's stretcher is let down to Jesus through the roof "on account of the crowd" (2:4), the legal authorities begin to question him for forgiving the man's sins, then for eating with tax collectors "since they were many and they followed him," for having his disciples not fast but glean grain on the Sabbath, and for himself healing on the Sabbath, until they hold council with the Herodians about how to destroy him" (2:1—3:6). This would seem to be enough about this prophet to show his touch with the crowds and his offense to their leaders, but Mark continues six times this long with more elaborate stories, stronger accusations, and crowds of thousands, all in spite of the fact that Jesus forbids the unclean spirits, those he heals, and his disciples to speak about him. Meanwhile, he continues to provoke the legal authorities by accusing them of canceling out God's word with their purity traditions, and he tells the crowd that it is not what goes in but what comes out of

131

people that pollutes them. He begins to heal Gentiles and at Passover he leads his disciples toward Jerusalem, teaching them that he will be killed there.

## Jesus' Second Sign in Mark

In Jerusalem there may be a second beginning of the prophet's sign story. He appears mounted on a colt and hailed by crowds, as if for the first time, and he gives a very different sign by throwing those who are buying and selling out of the Temple, overturning the moneychangers' tables and the pigeon-sellers' seats, and not letting anyone carry a vessel through the Temple. Such correcting of worship practices was not foreign to prophets' behavior,[4] but in this account it provokes debate and opposition from Temple authorities and, in spite of crowd support, he is betrayed by a disciple, swiftly tried by the legal and imperial courts, and crucified the following morning. This second sign in Jerusalem seems to be taken by the storyteller some forty years later as a sign of destruction against the Temple, framed as it is with the story of a fig tree cursed for not bearing fruit (11:12–23).[5] When this account is told after the Temple's destruction in 70 CE, the fulfillment of this sign of destruction in the Romans' burning of the Temple could reassert the credibility of Jesus' initial sign of deliverance in the coming of God's kingdom, a sign that remains outstanding but discredited after hopes of deliverance from Rome have been dashed. If the destruction foreseen by sign has taken place, can the deliverance foreseen by sign be far behind?

But what is this kingdom of God? Although Mark is a gospel of action rather than interpretation, Jesus twice sits down to teach, and in each case he reinterprets a sign. First God's coming kingdom is interpreted in parable as a sure and full harvest in spite of multiple bad soils, no productive work, and the smallest of seeds (4:1–34). This shifts the wartime focus on God's kingdom as Rome's expulsion from Jerusalem toward a broader vision of God's triumph when good news that is spread to all peoples finally produces its fruit. In Jesus' second speech, the sign of destruction in overturning the tables of power is

4. Chilton, *Pure Kingdom*, 115–33.

5. For further stories of prophets' signs of destruction from this period, see Wire, *Holy Lives*, 183–223.

interpreted to point beyond Jerusalem and its Temple toward a global reversal at the arrival of the mortal "after this tribulation" (13:1–37). In Mark, the harvest and the transformation of power are yet to come. This means that the sequence of events from the prophet's arrival, the sign, and the crowds through suppression and toward vindication is still in process, not only in its conclusion, but from beginning to end. The prophet's task continues and is passed down to Jesus' followers because God's judgment and deliverance are not over. This is particularly evident in the second half of the gospel. Each prediction of Jesus' passion introduces a passion teaching to his disciples (8:31—9:1; 9:31–37; 10:32–45). Not only are John the Baptist and Jesus "delivered over," but so will be his followers (1:14; 9:31; 10:33; 13:9–13; 14:18–21, 41–43). As crowds gather, Jesus' repeated instruction to his followers is "watch out," "stay alert" (13:33–37; 14:34–38).

## Story Pattern as Conflict and as Prophet's Sign

When the story pattern of Mark is seen in two ways, synchronically as agōn or conflict story and diachronically as story of a prophet's sign, there should be greater depth of vision than either approach can provide alone. The conflict stories need not be relegated to a subordinate role as mere sword-carriers or crowd-gatherers between the sign's announcement and its suppression. Since oral stories survive only when told, we can assume they must have been told continually from their beginnings, each able to function as the whole story about Jesus in the synchronic sense of the crisis overcome or the challenge met.[6] But in spreading news of this prophet's sign, his execution and his going ahead to Galilee, tellers would be favored who could bring the stories of God's controversy, Jesus' feats, and the disciples' struggles into the account of the sign they were watching for. This in turn intensified the conflict stories within a sequenced plot. And the listeners who favored one teller over others became the guardians of the tradition by cheering a fine account and curbing any telling that played loose with the stories they knew and the news that bound the stories together.

What both approaches to Mark's story pattern show in different ways, and intensify when taken together, is the unfinished nature of

6. Wire, "The Miracle Story as the Whole Story."

Mark's story, its character as news of something in process. Each account of God facing down Satan, Jesus taking on the authorities, and human trust overcoming fear assumes the domination of the powers that be. At the same time, each telling of the prophet's sign is a claim that the suppressed and vindicated prophet was right and his sign of God's kingdom will be fulfilled. This coming of the new order is focused on the present process of telling the story that makes trust out of fear and mobilizes people toward the new reality. In this process it is not evident that the tellers or hearers sensed any contradiction between accounts of the bold feats that gathered the crowds and the suppression that followed, knowing as they did how empires handle such threats, and relying as they did on the women's news that the story was not over.

The problem with the story pattern of Mark, it turns out, is not lack of cohesion. In at least two ways—as a polemical drama of relentless conflict and as a prophet's sign challenging given structures with God's coming kingdom—Mark never lacks position or direction. Although any scene would seem able to stand for the whole, Mark comes to us as a succession of scenes or lections that only gain strength by their accumulation. And for those who hear it as Scripture, the story begins again when it ends by setting off its own retelling in new contexts.

# PART 3

# Soundings in Mark

This third part of the case for Mark as a performance composition is a series of soundings in the gospel as a whole. Their purpose is to test how an understanding of Mark being composed by a number of tellers opens up possible solutions to several problems that have plagued Markan interpretation.

The first problem I tackle is the tension between the gospel's apparent focus on the question of Jesus' identity—"Who is this that the wind and the sea obey him?" (4:41)—and the reticence of this gospel to supply any clear answer to the question it poses. Whereas the Fourth Gospel in its first chapter makes eight different titular affirmations of Jesus' identity, Mark begins with the events of John the Baptist's sign of deliverance through baptism and Jesus' sign of the good news of God's kingdom. Granted that both are identified by God's voice (1:2, 11), the effect is to designate John and Jesus for the task at hand. From there the account says more about what Jesus does than who he is. Only the unclean spirits and the authorities claim they know him while his followers say little or, in Peter's case, are told to tell no one. Hearing Mark as the story of oral performers, how does this help us understand why Jesus' identity is handled so ambiguously?

A second conundrum in understanding Mark rises from the central place in this story of the announcement of God's kingdom arriving. The problem is that the kingdom Jesus announces does not arrive at the climax or in the conclusion of the story. This sets up a tension which is normally alleviated by downplaying the significance of the opening announcement or by reinterpreting God's kingdom as an expectation fulfilled in the communal life of Jesus with his followers or in the church as a result of his resurrection. Yet the community of the disciples is hardly an ideal as depicted in Mark, and the church is prefigured only in descriptions of persecutions to come (13:9–13). This leaves the question in the air whether Jesus was wrong in his prediction or whether we have not understood what God's kingdom meant. Can hearing Mark as a gospel shaped in a process of tellers speaking to traditional listeners help explain what Mark signifies with this sign of God's kingdom arriving?

Finally a third *crux criticorum* is presented by the end of the gospel. The manuscripts offer three distinct endings, and even if we settle for what seems to be the earliest end at 16:8, we are faced with several intractable problems. Jesus' disciples are not present to witness the brief resurrection story. Jesus himself does not appear. And the women who provide the only witness are described saying "nothing to anyone, for they were afraid" (16:8). Can a reading of Mark composed by a series of tellers help to make this ending not only tolerable but positively meaningful?

One approach to unraveling these knots in understanding Mark through an oral composition thesis would be to identify conflicting aspects of the gospel with successive tellers. For example, a teller favored early in the history of this gospel may stress the sign of God's kingdom in an apocalyptic sense whereas a later teller, though retaining the opening scenes, interprets it as eternal life given by God to the just, leaving a tension in the story. This assumes that each teller is something like an independent author who does with the story what she or he will.

However, in traditional transmission the tellers pride themselves on passing on the story as they have received it. Nonetheless, they will have told it in new times and to new listeners, and hence in ways that could be heard at that point. A study of inconsistencies between the tellings of various persons might then rather provide a window into different contexts of telling over what, in this case, is a very turbulent first century in the life of these communities. This would be instructive, if very difficult, since we do not know how many tellers in which major contexts had the early shaping roles in Mark.

Here I will take a different approach, not delegating the two sides of what appears to be an inconsistency to various tellers or to various situations of telling. Rather, I have found it most stimulating to ask how the people who told Mark might not only have tolerated but even have cultivated what we consider to be tensions in the story. Therefore I will be approaching the three problematic areas mentioned above through careful review of the relevant parts of Mark, on the one hand, to highlight the problem we have in each case, and, on the other, to discover new ways of hearing the stories that are compatible with—or, better, that directly point to—characteristics, interests, or perspectives of those who are likely to be telling the Markan story.

I name the following chapters with phrases from Mark that can represent for us the problems we have in comprehending it, or should I say, in receiving what we think we comprehend. I ask first about Jesus, "Who is this?" (4:41). Then I ask about Jesus' sign and its fulfillment, "God's kingdom is arriving!" (1:15). Last I come to the women at Jesus' tomb, "And they said nothing to anyone" (16:8). In each case I want to know how that which we find difficult in understanding Mark can turn out to help us better understand the people who are composing Jesus' story in Mark.

# 15

## "Who Is This?"[1]

After Jesus' first public action, the teller of Mark reports, "All the people were astounded and began saying to each other, 'What is this? A new teaching with authority! He commands even the unclean spirits and they submit to him!'" (1:27). And after Jesus expels the unclean spirits from the sea, the teller speaks for his disciples, "Who is this, that even the wind and the sea obey him?" (4:41). It is Jesus' authoritative words and powerful actions that make the tellers of Mark voice the people's wonder, "What is this? . . . Who is this?" The teller's talk about Jesus broadens when we hear Herod claim that Jesus is John the Baptist resurrected (6:14–16), while others say he is Elijah or one of the prophets, and Peter calls him the anointed, the messiah (8:27–28). Jesus responds by saying that the mortal must suffer and die and be raised. And when Peter objects, Jesus calls Peter Satan for tempting him: "for you are not thinking the way God does but the way humans do" (8:31–33). In this sequence of voices, those who tell the story do not focus on who chooses the right title for Jesus—whether prophetic, messianic or divine—but on where people stand in the basic conflict structuring the synchronic story pattern of Mark between Satan's rule and God's rule, between thinking the way humans do and thinking the way God does.

When the storyteller expresses again the question of who Jesus is, it is in another conflict scene after Jesus overturns the tables in the

---

1. This and the following chapter further develop the argument of my article: Wire, "The God of Jesus in the Gospel of Mark," in *To Break Every Yoke: Essays in Honor of Marvin L. Chaney*, edited by Robert B. Coote and Norman K. Gottwald, Social World of Biblical Antiquity 2/3 (Sheffield: Sheffield Phoenix 2007) 292–310. Used with permission.

Temple courtyard, and here the question of Jesus' underlying authority is explicit. The teller speaks first as the high priests, scribes and elders, "By what authority are you doing these things?" (11:28), and then as Jesus, "Was John's baptism from heaven or from humans?" This sets up the leaders to answer their own question about Jesus. But they will not acknowledge John's authority from God and cannot publicly deny it, so they plead ignorance—and Jesus, through the teller, has made his point. In these arguments Jesus claims authority from God, thinks the way God does, and expects in this world dominated by human power to take the consequences as John has before him. Jesus refers in these passages to his resurrection (8:31; 9:9; also 9:31; 10:34), confident in his vindication and God's coming kingdom. Yet it is not made clear what resurrection means. Is it being raised in another prophet as Herod says of John (6:14–16), or in a communal body as suggested later by Jesus' "I will not drink again from the fruit of the vine until that day when I drink it new in God's kingdom" (14:25)?[2]

## God's Son

Although the focus throughout the telling of Mark is on the authority with which Jesus acts, not on a proper title, several names are used to express his authority in conflict with that of others. Seven times voices with some authority call Jesus God's son or an equivalent phrase.[3] In five cases these are words of Jesus' violent opponents who are attacking or mocking him. Unclean spirits call him "holy one of God," "the son of God," and "son of the most high God" (1:24; 3:11; 5:7), and Jesus expels them. The high priest charges him, "Are you the Christ, the son of the Blessed?" (14:61) And the centurion who has executed him says, "This man was a son of God" (15:39). The tellers do not take these speakers as character witnesses to define Jesus' identity. Rather, they credit the world of spirits, even when unclean and opposing God's kingdom, and

2. On communal resurrection see Levenson, *Resurrection and the Restoration of Israel*, 156–65.

3. I do not include the words "son of God" in the gospel's first verse that are missing in Origen and the first hand of the Sinaiticus manuscript among others and were probably added later to strengthen the opening line. This is the conclusion of a number of text critics: Greeven, *Textkritik des Markusevangeliums*, 41–46; Collins, "Establishing the Text"; Ehrman, *Orthodox Corruption*, 72–75; Parker, *Living Text*, 145.

they credit the appointed priests and executioners, even when arbitrary and violent, with having what it takes to recognize the threat Jesus presents to their authority.

The only other two times in Mark that Jesus is called God's son occur in visions as a voice from heaven (1:11; 9:7).[4] The second of these I mention first, the disciples' vision on the mountain. Its credibility is compromised by Peter's inappropriate building project, by Jesus' instruction not to tell what they have seen, and by Jesus' correction that Elijah has already come and gone (9:5–13). Yet because the voice that they hear echoes the "my son" of the first vision and adds the demand, "Listen to him!" it does reveal to Jesus' followers his authority and demands their attention to his instruction, perhaps especially the teachings at the center of the gospel about losing life to find it, learning to be last, and serving as he serves (8:34–37; 9:35–37; and 10:42–45). The tellers of this vision identify Jesus as a prophet whom God will raise up for Israel, of whom Moses said, "Listen to him!" (Deut 18:15–19).

The meaning of Jesus as God's son as told in Mark depends on the first vision story, the vision Jesus has at his baptism (1:9–15). He sees the heavens torn open and the Spirit coming down on him like a dove, and a voice from heaven addresses him, "You are my son, my beloved. In you I delight!" Although this kind of story about a voice from heaven, a *bat kol* or literally "daughter of a voice," can appear in rabbinical texts to decide a case of law or to punish and reward conduct,[5] the telling here is closest to other stories about first century figures who are simply declared to be intimate with God:

> One time the sages gathered in the upper room of the house of Gorjo in Jericho. A voice came out from heaven and spoke to them: "There is a person here among you who is chosen for the holy Spirit and his generation is not worthy of him. At this they directed their eyes toward Hillel the Elder. When he died they said, O the humble one, O the devout one, the student of Esra! (*t. Sotah* 13.3–4)

> Rabbi Jehudah said that Rab said, "Day after day a voice from heaven comes out and says, 'All the whole world is fed on ac-

---

4. See the analysis of vision scenes in chapter 11.

5. Kuhn, *Offenbarungsstimmen im Antiken Judentum*; Kuhn, *Die Offenbarungsstimme in der rabbinischen Literatur*; and Marx, "Bat Kol—A Divine Voice."

count of Hanina ben Dosa, and Hanina my son satisfies himself
with a pan of carob pods from a Sabbath evening to a Sabbath
evening!" (*b. Ta'anit* 24b; cf. *b. Berakhot* 17b)[6]

Though Hillel is the most revered teacher among first century rabbis and
Hanina a rural Galilean miracle worker, the voice from heaven honors
both as God's unique intimates. In Hillel's case his great wisdom is expressed in his being "chosen for the holy Spirit" in such a way that "his
generation is not worthy of him;" in Hanina's case his miracle-working
power is recognized in his being called "my son" "for whom the whole
world is fed." Yet both are described as the most humble of people.[7]
When the performers of Jesus story in Mark tell Jesus baptismal vision
and the voice or *bat kol* blessing him as God's son, we can gather from
these other stories that they consider him uniquely intimate with God.
He will have every kind of wisdom and power needed for the task God
gives him, yet he will be the most humble of people.

Jesus' baptismal vision in Mark draws not only from *bat kol* storytelling but also from traditions known in the Hebrew prophets, especially Ezekiel's visions—much elaborated by the rabbis—and Isaiah's
servant song in its Aramaic form: "Behold my servant, I will bring him
near, my chosen in whom my Memra is pleased; I will put my Holy
Spirit upon him; he will reveal my judgment to the peoples" (*y. Hagigah*
2.77a; *Targum Isaiah* 42:1).[8] My point is not that the tellers are reading the prophets and quoting texts, but, as the Aramaic here indicates,
that these visions and stories are known from public readings, popular
tales, and festival songs and offer the tellers many options to express the
profound events heard in stories about Jesus.

To know what the tellers of Mark mean by this vision of Jesus
being called "my son," we must hear it not only within the world of
the other stories above but also in the context of the whole story being

6. See the continuing story translated in Wire, *Holy Lives*, 113.

7. Similar stories of the heavenly voice honor others such as Samuel the Small who
receives the Spirit, and Honi the Circle Drawer is described as a son of God (*t. Sotah*
13.3–4; *m. Ta'anit* 3:8); Chilton et al., *Comparative Handbook*, 68–76. Honi's story is
translated and discussed in Wire, *Holy Lives*, 124–29; and now in Jaffee, "Honi the
Circler in Manuscript and Memory."

8. Chilton et al., *Comparative Handbook*, 73–74. On the heavens opening and the
Spirit or angel descending, see *Aseneth* 14:1–8; *Testament of Judah* 24:2–3; *Testament
of Levi* 18:6–8.

told in Mark, that is, as it functions in the tellers' story pattern in both its synchronic and diachronic aspects.[9] Synchronic analysis attends to the conflict already in focus above between God and Satan or deliverance and destruction; diachronic analysis sets the vision in the story of this prophet's task and his fate. After the heaven is split open and the Spirit comes down on Jesus with God's voice calling him "my son" and "delight," this Spirit of God immediately casts him into testing so that when John is "handed over," Jesus announces God's good news of the kingdom arriving. The baptismal vision is therefore best identified as Jesus' calling to this task of announcing God's kingdom, and in Mark this task shapes his life and his death. All this happens by the initiative of God's Spirit.

And it is significant that God's Spirit as shown in the telling of Mark is not restricted to the loved son. John the Baptist predicts a mighty one coming after him baptizing with holy Spirit (1:8), and though we don't see Jesus baptizing in Mark, we hear Jesus' voice through the teller saying his followers will be baptized with the baptism with which he is baptized (10:38). This is explained in terms of drinking his cup, that is, bearing witness in the face of death. And he assures them that they need not worry how they will hold up at that time, because when they are handed over and led away the holy Spirit will tell them what to say (13:11).

## King and the Christ

Royal titles for Jesus appear toward the end of Mark, but they are not given positive development. After Jesus is hailed as Son of David by a blind beggar in Jericho (10:47–48) and is welcomed into Jerusalem by crowds shouting, "Blessed be the coming kingdom of our father David!" (11:9), Jesus in the Temple argues from David's psalm that the Christ cannot be David's son (12:35–37; Ps 110:1). Similarly, what might have been told as royal acclamation in the soldiers' taunt, "Hail, King of the Jews" (15:2), in the title over the cross, "King of the Jews" (15:26), and in the high priests' words, "Let the Christ the King of Israel come down from the cross so we might see and trust" (15:32), are told as vicious

---

9. See chapters 13 and 14.

mockings. Even Jesus' triumph in entering Jerusalem on a colt is highly ironic (11:1–11).

The word "Christ" appears five times in Mark, but two of these are given without a definite article as though the word is used for Jesus' name (9:41) or the name of his message, "The beginning of the good news of Jesus Christ" (1:1). But three times in the telling of Mark Jesus is called "the Christ," a Greek translation of Aramaic for "the Messiah," signifying the anointed one. When Peter identifies Jesus, "You are the Christ," the messianic meaning is explicit (8:29–33). Jesus immediately forbids his disciples to speak to anyone about him and insists that "the mortal must suffer many things. And when Peter rejects this assertion, Jesus calls him Satan. Finally, at Jesus' trial the high priest asks, "Are you the Christ, the son of the Blessed?" Jesus accepts this only as qualified, "[You say that] I am,[10] and you will see the mortal seated on the right hand of power" (14:61–62), the mortal he has earlier announced will vindicate him (8:38). Finally, when the high priests and scribes mock Jesus, "Let the Christ, the King of Israel, come down now from the cross so we can see and trust," what follows is darkness, a cry, and death (15:32).

Thus each of the three times Jesus is called the Messiah he contradicts the designation or strongly qualifies it by referring instead to "the mortal" or by demonstrating his own mortality. The royal language is simply not acceptable to the storytellers, probably because God's kingdom allowed no claims such as those made by King Herod the Great and his sons. In the way Mark is told, Jesus calls himself "the mortal" and uses no other term for himself,[11] so we are left with this name as our best clue to the role he takes in Mark.

---

10. Some manuscripts read 14:62 simply as "I am." This assumes that the longer variant comes from a scribe harmonizing Mark with Matthew or Luke. But it is unlikely that harmonization would be used to make Jesus' answer equivocal. And if Mark is an earlier tradition known to Matthew and/or Luke, have the other gospels preferred the equivocal answer? The longer reading is more probable. See chapter 11, n. 5.

11. It is possible to read the reference to the "beloved son" in the parable of the vineyard as Jesus' speaking of himself, but in the context of the continuing argument about the authority of John the Baptist, a reference to his death seems more probable (12:6). When Jesus is said to claim that only the father and "not the son" knows "that day or the hour" when the mortal will come on the clouds (13:32), he seems to be accepting the family relation given in his baptism, but here he declines knowledge others attribute to him, rather than claims authority for himself from it.

## The Mortal

There is a growing consensus that the Greek and English phrase, "Son of Man," is a literal translation of the Aramaic and Hebrew phrase for generic humanity.[12] I note that it can be conceived in contrast to other animal species as the human being, or in contrast to God as the mortal creature. Although Mark clearly draws on Daniel's vision where a human being is contrasted with four animals representing successive empires that have occupied Israel (13:26–27; Dan 7:13), the comparison of kingdoms to animals is dropped in Mark. By contrast, human desires and abilities are repeatedly contrasted with God's desires and abilities (7:8; 8:33; 10:27; 11:30; 14:36). This makes the translation "mortal" more appropriate than the translation "human being" in this telling, as it is also appropriate when translating the same phrase in the Ezekiel vision accounts where God consistently addresses Ezekiel as "mortal" (Ezekiel 2—47).

At three points in Mark, there is a clear reference to the mortal in Jewish visionary tradition of Daniel 7 and *1 Enoch* 46–48, 61–62.[13] Jesus' warns the disciples at the end of the first passion teaching, "Whoever is ashamed of me and my words in this adulterous and sinful generation, the mortal will be ashamed of him when he comes in his Father's glory with the holy angels" (8:38). Likewise at the end of Jesus' statement on last things, "Then they will see the mortal coming on the clouds with all power and glory . . . and he will send the angels and gather the elect" (13:26–27). And finally to the high priest's question, "Are you the Christ, the son of the Blessed?" Jesus says, "[You say that] I am. And you will see the mortal seated on the right hand of power and coming with the clouds of heaven" (14:61–62). There is nothing in these texts or their immediate contexts to require that Jesus is speaking of himself. Each one promises the transfer of power that will replace rapacious human kings with a mortal vindicator of the just.

However, the reference to the mortal is quite different in other parts of Mark. In the first two places the mortal appears, the reference appears to be strictly generic. When Jesus says the paralytic's sins are forgiven, the scribes charge, "He blasphemes. Who can forgive sins except one, God?" (2:7). Jesus then demonstrates that the mortal has

---

12. Chilton et al., *Comparative Handbook*, 533–42; Collins, *Mark*, 187–88.

13. On these passages see chapter 11.

authority to forgive sins on earth *kal vakhomer* (*a forteriori*) by doing the more difficult thing of healing the person. Jesus is not claiming for himself alone this human authority to forgive on earth, because he later insists that his disciples forgive others on earth so God will forgive them in heaven (6:12; 11:25). The Sabbath claim is even more explicitly made on behalf of all mortals, "The Sabbath was made for people, not people for the Sabbath, so the mortal is master even of the Sabbath" (2:27–28). He says this to justify his disciples' Sabbath gleaning; it applies only secondarily to his own Sabbath healing that follows. He may speak of the mortal rather than a person here because the question is whether forgiveness and getting food on the Sabbath are prerogatives reserved for the immortal God or not. So in the early stories of Mark, Jesus claims for the mortal generically the right and responsibility to forgive others and to do good on the Sabbath.

The remaining nine uses of "the mortal" in Mark speak of the harsh life of human suffering in which rising up comes only after going down to rejection and death. This starts with the first passion prediction, "And he began to teach them that the mortal has to suffer many things . . ." (8:31). Granted that he begins here to indicate his own specific journey, he does not thereby cease to speak of humanity at large but takes for himself the common fate of mortals—humiliation and death, as the way to life—"in this adulterous and sinful generation" (8:38). Jesus faces his death, reinterpreting what could be a royal anointing by the woman as a preparation for burial (14:3–9), and consenting to death against his own will: "Not what I want, but what you want" (14:36). Why God allows this death is not of primary interest to the storyteller and only two hints suggest the reason, that God's life-giving power can work through one person's death for many others—and can overcome death: "The mortal came to give his life to free many captives"; and "This is the blood of the covenant poured out for many" (10:45; 14:24). At the same time, following each of the three passion predictions, he teaches this path to his disciples (8:34—9:1; 9:33–37; 10:35–45). Toleration of hardship is presented here, not as an ascetic turn toward martyrdom, but as facing an evil for which mortals are responsible (14:21, 41), and doing a service that gives life for others according to scriptural warrant (9:12; 10:45; 14:21, 49).

The challenge in the second half of Mark is to understand how the mortal that Jesus identifies himself with in his suffering is being related to the mortal who will come in God's glory. Does the fact that Jesus takes on himself the generic human role in the former case imply the same in the latter? This cannot be assumed in Mark because of the sharp way certain things are reserved for God alone, such as knowledge, goodness, divinity, authority and judgment: "Concerning that hour only God knows;" "Only God is good;" "The Lord our God, the Lord is one;" "You shall love the Lord your God from your whole heart;" "To sit at my right or my left isn't mine to give but goes to those for whom it is prepared" (13:32; 10:18, 29–30, 40). In a recent essay, Bruce Chilton speaks of Jesus as a visionary making a poetic juxtaposition or claiming a parabolic intimacy of the mortal on earth and the mortal in heaven.[14] I see that the third person speech which the performers attribute to Jesus here provides in each case a careful reservation. The mortal on earth does not substitute for others in their suffering but belongs among them and may represent them. The mortal on the clouds remains the one whom God will appoint in that day to gather and vindicate those who have trusted God. Again, authority is reserved for God. In this way the storytellers consistently present Jesus as the humble one before God to whom God is therefore able to give whatever truth-telling and life-giving power is needed for mortal life.

## Authority Belongs to God

The minimal Christology of this gospel on several fronts has been a challenge to recent Christian interpreters. Some historical critics argue that it reflects Jesus' own stance soon overlaid with confessions.[15] Recently a literary critic, Elizabeth Struthers Malbon, has proposed that it is the author who has created a tension between the character Jesus who insists on pointing to God alone, and the narrator who presents Jesus as Christ in the opening line and in characters' recurring acclamations.[16] In this way, she says, the narrator can call the hearers to be devoted to this Jesus Christ who is devoted to God alone.

14. Chilton et al., *Comparative Handbook*, Appendix 2, 554–60. On visionary rhetoric see also Schüssler Fiorenza, "The Followers of the Lamb."

15. Bultmann, *Jesus and the Word*; Perrin, "The Christology of Mark"; Fredriksen, *From Jesus to Christ*; Mack, *Myth of Innocence*; Crossan, *The Historical Jesus*.

16. Malbon, *Mark's Jesus*, 231–58.

But is this simply a narrative tension? The storytellers have dramatized repeatedly the way Jesus has turned back various acclamations of his status with exorcisms (1:25; 3:12; 4:39; 5:8, 13; 9:25), others with rebukes (8:33; 9:9; 10:18), and still others with corrections in terms of himself as the mortal on earth or in terms of the mortal in heaven (8:38; 10:45; 14:62). Must this not be heard as a strong rejection of acclamations that confuse earth with heaven and mortals with God? To ignore or finesse this not only misses the insight it might give us into the social location and basic religious convictions of the story composers but also of the Jesus their voices present. These—the tellers and Jesus himself— are people who reject all the claims to royal status and divine glory that have been used to exploit them and look in confidence to the coming of God's kingdom.

When we recognize Mark as a storytellers' composition over decades in a congealing performance tradition, at least it is clear that its meaning cannot be reduced either to events in Jesus' life with the historians or to a creative author forty years later with the literary critics. What we hear in the gospel is what mattered to a number of favored gospel tellers who shaped this story about Jesus in their zeal to keep announcing God's kingdom that Jesus had lived out. Here the divine and royal titles that appear in the cries of the demonized and the mockings of rulers to dramatic effect are sharply undercut by words and actions attributed to Jesus. One might try to distinguish different tellers and writers of this tradition and their distinct emphases to explain tensions in the Christology, but the short time frame and the relative consistency in the way the scenes are told makes this unproductive. Throughout all the tellings of Mark the focus is sustained on the conflict set off by Jesus' news of God's kingdom arriving. There are the defensive reactions of Satan vis-à-vis God, the parrying of the legal authorities with Jesus, and the bouts of human fear in face of the challenge to trust the good news. All these draw the crowds, which in turn leads toward the ruler's violent intervention.

The question "Who is this?" is dramatized most effectively in the scene where Jesus is accused of exorcizing by the power of Satan. He responds that any mortal's blasphemy against him can be forgiven, but to blaspheme what God's Spirit is doing to release people from destruction is an eternal sin (3:22–30). This makes the question "Who is this?" not a matter of what title suits Jesus best but of what side is he on, by what authority he acts. Does he exorcize by the power of Satan or by the power of God when he claims God's Spirit is realizing God's kingdom and will not be thwarted? If Mark is heard strictly from these performers and this writer and not from other New Testament traditions, then its message—or I should say its strategy—is to get out the news of this prophet's sign of God's kingdom to all people in full confidence that their turning to God in repentance and trust will be met by the coming of God's kingdom among them. Jesus is the one bent on doing this. Those who tell his story re-present him.

# 16

## "God's Kingdom Is Arriving"[1]

If the story of Jesus in Mark's gospel is told as an account of this prophet's sign of God's kingdom arriving, it is crucial to understand what this sign means. The background is not obscure. First century Palestine suffered under the increasingly arbitrary, exploitative and violent rule of local Herodians and imperial procurators. And the people of Israel had a long and well-cultivated tradition about God's delivering them from oppression and opening a way toward their living in the land in peace. So Jesus' sign of God's kingdom, like the signs of dry river crossings and falling city walls announced by other contemporary prophets, raised the hope for a present deliverance, recovery of the land, relief from taxation and restoration of a rightful and just kingdom. It was in this setting that stories were circulating about prophets giving signs. But what exactly this prophet in Mark was announcing, what the crowd came to expect, and what later tellers and writers of this story were affirming is neither obvious nor necessarily uniform, and it is this broad and probably moving target at which I aim. Fortunately, due to the tenacity of the tradition, there is primary evidence in this narrative called Mark. Yet, unfortunately, the different voices are not distinct but make up an overlapping and shifting whole.

Seeking a better grasp of God's kingdom as it functions within this gospel, I take up four major points in Mark where God's kingdom is central: Jesus announces God's kingdom, Jesus explains God's kingdom in parables, Jesus teaches how to enter God's kingdom, and Jesus proj-

---

1. The present chapter builds on the analysis of stories of prophet's signs in chapter 9.

ects a vision of God's kingdom arriving. I confess to a double purpose, not only to hear the message or strategy described as God's kingdom in this composition in performance, but also to discover from this hearing, if possible, something about the process in which this composition was shaped and about its performers. All of this should help me deal with what remains an underlying human question of whether past experience of deliverance and future visions of vindication can sustain a continuing present effort to expect what Jesus here calls God's kingdom to be realized in a human world.

## God's Kingdom Announced

The announcement of God's kingdom comes at the programmatic opening of Jesus' preaching in Galilee "after John was handed over" (1:14–15). John's arrest was a crisis not only for Jesus but for all those John had baptized to be forgiven and to escape God's judgment coming upon their ruler Herod Antipas' egregious sins (6:18). We are not surprised that a ruler has eliminated a prophet from the stage before his signs of destruction and deliverance have been accomplished. Yet at John's arrest Jesus paradoxically announces "the good news of God . . . : The time has come and God's kingdom is arriving! Repent and trust the good news!" (1:15).

"God's kingdom," here a simple declarative announcement, defies translation. I see three options: stick with a transliteration of the Greek, *basileia*, an empty term for us until filled;[2] cut loose and go after the function of kingdom in that time, a grant of land that provided an independent and productive living—I once translated "inheritance";[3] or keep the traditional God's kingdom or rule as inescapable and struggle to hear it in its full context. I've take the last option here. The verb in the sentence I do not translate literally—"God's kingdom is drawing near," but I say "is arriving," because the parallel phrase in the perfect tense, "the time has come," indicates not just anticipation but virtual arrival.[4]

---

2. Schüssler Fiorenza, *In Memory of Her*, 118–30.

3. Wire, "God of Jesus in the Gospels' Saying Source," 281–82.

4. In *An Aramaic Approach to the Gospels and Acts*, Matthew Black proposes a possible Aramaic root being translated here that signifies in the perfect tense arrival or at the least arriving (*qrb*), preferring that choice to *meta* (Hebrew *naga*ʿ) because the prepositional phrase that should follow *meta* is lacking.

The following challenge to repent continues John's demand for a total reorientation of life, now specified positively in "trust the good news."

God functions here as the sponsor of a new order becoming visible in the repentance and trust of the crowds. The announcement of a prophet in an oral culture has performative character. As with a blessing or curse, the announcement not only predicts, but achieves what it says by the agency of God and its report by the storyteller sustains that performative power. God's agency is explicit in the words attributed to God and recited as if addressed to Jesus in the opening quote, "Look, I am sending my messenger before your face who will prepare your way" (1:2). It is through the prophets, though John, through Jesus, and though the tellers of this story that the agency of God—also called the Spirit in the baptismal vision account—challenges people to repent and trust the good news of God's kingdom arriving. At the same time, the hearers' response and participation is taken as essential to the project. Jesus immediately calls four disciples, and they in turn become people-fishers (1:16–20). Soon he chooses twelve, apparently representing all Israel's tribes, and sends them out to the towns and homes to call for repentance and to cast out destroying spirits (3:13–19; 6:7–13, 30).

The announcement of God's kingdom is best characterized by the two demands that it generates: repent and trust. Why repentance is necessary is shown when Jesus and his followers meet rejection and Jesus begins to compare people and God. First it is God's will or orientation that is contrasted with people's own will. When Jesus is told that his mother and brothers have come to take him home, he ignores them and says, "Whoever does God's will is my brother and sister and mother" (3:20–21, 31–34). To those who come from Jerusalem, he says, "You let God's commands go and hold to the traditions of people" (7:8). And when Peter rejects Jesus' prediction that he will suffer, he says, "Get behind me, Satan, for you do not think the way God does but the way people do" (8:33). What his family, his critics, and his disciples want is contrasted with what God wants, hence the call to repent.

This contrast between people and God shifts in the second half of the gospel from desire to ability, from will to power. When his disciples ask who can be saved if not the rich, he says, "With people it is impossible, but not with God, for all things are possible with God" (10:27; cf. 14:36). When the Temple leaders ask the source of his authority, he asks them, "Was John's baptism from heaven or from people?" (11:30). And when he leaves the coin with Caesar's image to Caesar, he reserves what is in God's image for God (12:17). God has power and gives authority and identity that the rich, the Temple authorities and Caesar cannot touch. And Jesus himself, after great struggle, concedes, "Not what I want, but what you want" (14:36).

This sharp distinction between what people and God want and can do shows why the arrival of God's kingdom requires repentance. The reorientation needed could not be more radical. What makes it possible? This appears in the second imperative: "Trust the good news" (1:15). I translate the verb here not "believe" but "trust" because it is not assent to a proposition but risking commitment. In Mark it is trust in God that bridges the gap between people and God. Those who seek healing are repeatedly described as persons who trust: Jesus heals the paralytic when he sees the trust of those who let him down through the roof (2:5); he encourages Jairus, "Don't be afraid, just trust" (5:36); he says to the hemorrhaging woman and blind Bartimaeus, "Your trust made you well" (5:34; 10:52). This consistent reference to trust—or distrust in Nazareth where Jesus cannot heal—shows that the performers recognize and dramatize across many stories that the power to repent and act in a new way comes from trust in God's arriving rule.

Then is this a challenge to trust in miracles? It seems that way when Jesus says, "Whatever you pray for and ask, trusting you have received, it will happen for you" (11:24). Yet this is not spoken to challenge someone wanting healing but to challenge his disciples' reverence for the Temple Mount when he says, "Trust in God. I tell you the truth, if anyone says to this mountain [Zion], 'Be taken up and thrown into the sea,' and . . . trusts that what he says happens, it will happen for that person" (11:22–23). Elsewhere in Mark, credulousness is critiqued: "If someone says, 'Look, here is Christ! Look there!' Don't trust [it]" (13:21, 5).

Nor can it be said that Jesus calls for trust in himself in this gospel. Only three times in Mark does trusting appear with a direct object, and it is not Jesus who is trusted but the good news, God, and John the Baptist (1:15; 11:22, 31). Jesus attributes several healings to persons who claim them rather than to himself: "I take your point, go, the demon has gone out of your daughter" (7:29; cf. 5:34; 10:52). When the demon-possessed boy's father begs, "If you are able, help us," Jesus responds, "If you are able? All things are possible for the one who trusts!" (9:22–23).

This could be heard as a call to trust in Jesus' power, but the man does not hear it that way and accepts the challenge himself, "I trust. Help my distrust!" (9:24). Power is not indigenous to humans but comes from their trust in God for whom all things are possible (10:27; 14:36). By trusting the good news that God's kingdom is arriving, people are able to repent of their desires that are contrary to God's desires and be open to God's power for themselves and for others.

## God's Kingdom in Parable

Although Jesus has been shown early in the story as a skillful interlocutor by returning the questions of the scribes with questions and proverbs (2:1—3:6),[5] he only sits down to teach when with the crowds. Here we are told that the people press on him so he sits in a boat and tells stories (4:1–34). Our question is: Does Jesus speak in parables here in order to make his announcement of God's kingdom clear, or does he speak this way in order to conceal a mystery from outsiders that he explains privately to his followers? Modern interpreters tend to answer by finding a tension between the author of Mark and his sources. A recent literary analysis of Philip Sellew, followed by Adela Yarbro Collins, proposes that Mark had two sources here, an oral collection of Jesus' parables taught "as the people were able to hear," and a written dialogue in which Jesus answers questions about the mystery of his parables by explaining each element in his story of the sower.[6] Mark then puts the two together as best he can in order to show his own view—evident in the gospel as a whole—that the crowds "hear Jesus gladly," the officials contest what they hear, and the disciples require constant in-house teaching to no avail.

Yet the presence of tabular explanations in dream and vision writings need not mean that that the explanation of the sower parable comes from a literary source. In his study *Parables in Midrash*, David Stern points out that Mark's sower and vineyard parables share a pattern of parable followed by interpretation (*mashal* by *nimshal*) that appears in

---

5. See chapter 10 on the controversy scenes.

6. Sellew, "Oral and Written Sources in Mark 4:1–34"; Collins, *Mark*, 239–40. They build on Klauck's thesis in *Allegorie und Allegorese in synoptischen Gleichnistexte*, 67–91.

Jewish popular speaking as a way to praise or blame someone who is present. This is already happening, Stern says, at a time when parables are told in many forms but are not generally considered literate enough to use in writing.[7] Markan storytellers would know and could project these oral dynamics, and in their storytelling accomplish again just this praise and blame. Listening as we are for traditions being performed, we can best focus on how tellers set up who is hearing Jesus' stories to their praise or blame.

In Mark, the parables of what God's kingdom is like can be heard on three levels, suggesting, if not a three-stage development of the tradition, at least three different kinds of ears that are hearing. On the first, almost literal level, the stories tell God's bounty, as do the tales in Talmudic and apocalyptic texts of giant peaches in Israel and thousand-grape clusters in the world to come (*y. Peah* 8.4 [20ab]; *2 Bar* 29:5; 74:1). There must be some humor—and pathos—when peasants hear all the ways their marginal land manages to thwart them, but this story's sower makes it all up and more with a wild yield where land is good. The same wild yield appears in the story of the farmer whose seed grows on its own to harvest, as well as in the account of the discarded mustard seed that becomes a shelter for birds. This must be the parable of God's kingdom heard by peasants who dry-farm small holdings or by day laborers pushed off their land through debt and fraud. In each parable, the bounty is attributed to the earth on which the seed in sown: "others fell on the good earth and bore fruit" (4:8), "from itself the earth bears fruit" (4:28), "when it is scattered on the earth, this least of all the seeds . . . becomes greater than all the plants (4:31–32)." This focus on fruitful earth suggests that the gift of God's kingdom could be heard as a land grant, in the way that Rome's client kingdoms were grants from the emperor, only in this cultural context heard as God's restoration of ancestral lands to the poor. The great majority of the crowds would hear exactly this "good earth" in "to you is given . . . the Kingdom of God" (4:11). And the imperial occupation might also hear this, since it is fear of revolt and loss of the land, not any metaphor, which motivates the Roman execution of Jesus.

At a second stage or with a second audience these parables of the kingdom become a challenge to spread the good news, the seed being

7. Stern, *Parables in Midrash*, 185–206.

heard as the word that is told, the earth as its hearers, the growth or harvest as God's gift that multiplies the seed for more telling (4:14-20). It would be heard this way by people who receive with repentance the mystery of God's kingdom and begin an infectious new life. This interpretation of the seed as a word seeking good ears would also trip up the scoffers when they realize that the problem is not the seed but the quality of the earth, not the message but their hearing. Because most parables attributed to Jesus are exposés of this kind, this may have been an early meaning of the story.[8]

If the first literal hearing of the parables is picked up by the peasant majority at one end of the social map and by the few—had they been listening—who occupied their land on the other, and the second hearing of the seed as word is picked up by Jesus' followers in their enthusiasm and by their detractors in their distain, it is the third hearing about those who refuse to hear that is central in the telling that has come down to us. Apparently at this stage the teller is dealing less with the conflict between God and Caesar over the land, or even the conflict between gospel proclaimers and gospel detractors, than with the conflict between trust and fear in Jesus' followers. The sower's seed falls on one bad soil after another (4:16–20), just as the tenants kill all the messengers and even the son (12:8). Jesus' speech that carries the parables is focused on this anomaly of good news rejected:

> And when they were alone, those around him with the twelve asked him the parables. And he was saying to them, "To you the mystery of God's kingdom is given, but to those outside all things are in parables 'so that they look and look and don't see, and hear and hear and don't understand, lest they might turn and it be forgiven them'" [Isa 6:9–13]. And he said to them, "You do not understand this parable? And how will you come to know all the parables?" (Mark 4:10–13)

Many proposals have been made to cancel out the offense of these words that suggest God's kingdom is the possession of Jesus' followers to the exclusion of "those outside" who hear only parables that they do not understand. Since the disciples' question at the start and Jesus' answer at the end fit together better than the piece does as a whole, some suggest that the words about the mystery and the quotation have

---

8. Chilton et al., *Comparative Handbook*, 165; Wire, *The Parable is a Mirror*.

been added by the writer to give an esoteric aspect to the book, and, if done earlier, added by a teller to the performance. Or Jesus' statement, including the quotation from Isaiah, could be read in Greek as a question: "Has the mystery of God's kingdom been given to you while everything is in parables for those outside 'so that they look and look and don't see . . . lest they turn and be forgiven?'" But references later in Mark to special explanations for the disciples suggest that this sentence is at least no longer to be taken as a question (4:34; 9:28–29; 10:10–12). Or, as Bruce Chilton argues, Mark follows the Isaiah tradition of the Aramaic Targum that speaks of people who behave in such a way *that* they do not see lest they repent and be forgiven, not people who are given parables *in order* that they not seek forgiveness.[9]

But another explanation may be able to incorporate the offense in the Isaiah text and yet not understand an esoteric gospel. If many—or rather most—rejected Jesus' good news, he may be shown defending his calling from God by quoting Isaiah's defense of his own prophetic calling. Isaiah says God told him to make the people hear so often that they have shut their eyes and ears and refuse to repent. Isaiah goes on to ask, "How long, O Lord?" and God says it will last until they are exiled and their land burned down to a tree stump, to which the teller of Isaiah's story adds, "The holy seed is its stump." Looking back from exile, Isaiah claims the people's rejection of God as his successful mission, and the teller of Isaiah's story claims his rejected mission as the holy seed of God's restoring work. Although the mystery of God's kingdom could have been told in the Markan tradition as the "holy seed" for the restoration of all Israel, in the form we receive it, Jesus, in the face of rejection, says the parables were his way of stopping the ears of those who did not want good news that required turning and receiving forgiveness. The parables have hid from some what they revealed to others.

Yet this remains an esoteric message unless it is heard in the context of the disciples' question before and Jesus' answer afterwards, which are themselves set in the context of Jesus' speech—not to the legal or political authorities—but to the crowd, and here specifically to "those around

9. Chilton, et al., *Comparative Handbook*, 163, 166. This is supported by the fact that the Targum of Isa 6:9–10 ends the Isaiah quote with people not being "forgiven" as does Mark, whereas the major Hebrew and Greek texts (MT and LXX) both speak them of not being "healed."

him with the twelve" (4:4, 10). Jesus' question to them asking how they are going to receive all the parables if they do not understand this parable does not take those who are "outside" as a contrasting group. These who are given the mystery are also given the parable that carries it, and the danger is that they themselves will look without seeing and hear without listening so as not to turn and be forgiven. The explanation of the seed parable that follows is aimed here less at exposing those who reject the gospel outright than those whose commitment lacks maturity with the result that they fall away in persecution or are lured off by distraction or desires.[10]

The following parable of the lamp puts to rest any thought of exclusive knowledge: "A lamp is not lit in order to be put under a basin or under a bed, is it? Isn't it lit to be put on the lamp stand? For nothing is hidden except in order to be revealed, nor is it covered except to come to light! Let whoever has ears hear!" (4:21–23). When the prophetic critique against those who look without seeing and hear without listening recurs in Mark, it is in Jesus' blast of seven rhetorical questions directed at his disciples for their blindness (8:17–21).

The speech ends with the comment that the parables are told to the people "as they were able to hear" and yet, because they did not, "he unraveled everything for his own disciples" (4:33–34). As with jokes that need explaining, much is lost. Yet nothing could be more inclusive than the repeated, "Let the one who has ears hear" (4:9, 23).

When Mark is received as a performance composition, we can hear it at several levels. We can take the first quite literal hearing of the seed parables as basic without dismissing other ways that the stories were spoken and heard. This is possible because no one stage of the tradition has the exclusive authority that a literary reading attributes to the author, and no one teller has a single audience. Although the voice of the performer—for us the performing writer—shapes what is heard at any one time, it is the weight of the accumulated tradition that makes people listen, and different people hear differently, even at one time. Nor was there an original story before there were tellers that could serve as its standard, since the tradition was shaped in the telling. God's kingdom can then be harvest for the peasant, a word that bears fruit

---

10. Mary Ann Tolbert, *Sowing the Gospel*, sees how the disciples are included here, but her taking the parable as a schematic outline for the different groups who reject Jesus in Mark assumes her literary approach and limits the multivalence of the parable.

for its sowers, an exposé of those who refuse to hear, and a warning for those who think they have the mystery in hand because of special instruction.

## Entering God's Kingdom

When Jesus speaks about God's kingdom in Mark again, it is not a time of transformation nor a mystery given to hearers, but a place of welcome. Jesus' disciples are arguing about which of them is greatest. So he picks up a child and says, "Whoever welcomes this child in my name welcomes me, and whoever welcomes me, welcomes not me, but the one who sent me (9:37). A disciple wants to prevent a stranger from casting out demons in Jesus' name, but Jesus says, "Whoever is not against us is for us" (9:40). The default setting is apparently inclusion, "whoever." But if it is the child grasping to be picked up that represents Jesus who represents God, the situation on the ground is not good. "Whoever offends one of these little trusting ones,[11] better a millstone . . ." (9:42), and "If your eye offend you, cut it out, better that you enter God's kingdom one-eyed . . ." (9:47). When Jesus' disciples turn away children brought to him, he says, "God's kingdom belongs to their kind . . . Whoever doesn't receive God's kingdom as a child will never enter it" (10:14–15).

The trusting child is finally contrasted with the rich man who wants to inherit eternal life in order to supplement his virtue and wealth. But he will not give away what he owns and be at home in God's kingdom. When Jesus exclaims it is harder for a camel to step through a needle's eye than for the rich to enter God's kingdom, the disciples gape and ask, "Who can be saved?" and Jesus admits, "For humans it is impossible, but not for God, because everything is possible for God" (10:26–27). Entering God's kingdom is equated here with having eternal life, having ones treasure in heaven, and being saved—all traditional ways of speaking of life in the world to come. But the force of the argument is that the rich who cannot let go of their security in goods have already lost the security of God's kingdom where the children are at home.

---

11. The words "in me" are absent in Sinaiticus, Ephraemi, Bezae and most of the Old Latin manuscripts. They were likely brought in here from Matt 18:6 (Vouga, "'Habt Glauben an Gott,'" 98, n. 20; Dunn, *Jesus Remembered*, 500, n. 55).

Yet a scribe is "not far from God's kingdom" and a respected council member is "waiting for God's kingdom" (12:34; 15:43), so one never knows—which returns us to "whoever." Here the performers show their hand again against any narrowing of the circle. This "whoever" echoes in another idiom the previous refrain, "Let the one who has ears hear."

## The Arrival of God's Kingdom

As the story of Mark moves toward its climax in Jerusalem, Jesus begins to speak of a time when God's kingdom will come in power (8:38—9:1; 13:26-27; 14:25, 61-62). He says that people will see the mortal coming on the clouds with God's glory, and the angels will gather God's people from the four winds. This mortal seated on God's right hand will be ashamed of those who have been ashamed of Jesus and his words. And Jesus will drink wine and celebrate with his followers in God's kingdom.[12] What do these images tell about the arrival of God's kingdom? Caution is necessary not to mistake visionary language as literal and yet to hear it with full seriousness.

First, these predictions of future visions indicate that God's kingdom is not fully realized in Jesus' lifetime. Second, an event is expected thereafter when it will arrive in power. Only God knows the day and hour (13:32), but twice Jesus says it is to be within his generation (9:1; 13:30). Yet "this adulterous and sinful generation" may mean the present time of blatant sin which demands judgment rather than an exact number of years. God's kingdom is not to be confused with the present or recent wartime trauma (13:7-8). Rather, it is associated with God's action through a quotation of Isaiah that speaks of cosmic changes of sun, moon and stars (Isa 13:10; 34:4; Mark 13:23-25).

Third, the arrival of God's kingdom will reverse the structures of power so that God's glory will be evident to all, and those who find Jesus shameful will be ashamed. This is apparently the consequence of the mortal's being "seated on the right hand of power" in Jesus response to the high priest (14:62). Fourth, it will unite God's people who have been scattered, and they will drink and celebrate together (13:27; 14:25). Fifth, the consummation of the kingdom is not said to come from the people's repentance and trust, from their hearing the mystery,

12. See parts of chapter 11 and 15.

or from their entering God's kingdom. Rather their trust, their hearing and their entering are a result of the kingdom's arriving. What is not possible for people is possible for God (9:23; 10:27; 14:36).

Nonetheless, sixth, people are enlisted in hearing and spreading the word of this kingdom arriving and in welcoming those who bring the good news of peace to their homes (1:17; 4:14; 5:19; 6:7–13). When those who speak and welcome the news are rejected, this is taken, not as evidence against its coming, but as evidence for its coming by revealing the threat that God's kingdom presents to those who claim the rule for themselves. These points about the kingdom reflect a consistent stance of the tellers of Mark that is not compromised by their different emphases in different contexts.

In spite of these strong affirmations of a coming arrival of God's kingdom, the harsh reality on the ground is also starkly presented. Jesus' repeated efforts to prepare his disciples for what will happen in Jerusalem comes to nothing—he is betrayed, denied, and deserted by them, turned against by the crowds, condemned by the Sanhedrin, delivered up by Pilate, reviled by those crucified with him, and, in his own words, abandoned by God as he dies. At Mark's end, this leaves the good news of the kingdom hanging on the thread of a rumor among women that a young man at the tomb said Jesus was raised and went ahead of them to Galilee. How this can be enough to reverse the bitter end of the story is not evident, but it seems to be so understood. Does the fact that the gospel is being told show that some followers went to Galilee and found him, so the speaker is confident that others can as well? But there is no story of someone finding Jesus, which signals for us that God's kingdom has not yet come in power and remains threatened by human fear. Yet a way ahead has been pointed, not by Jesus' own trust, which in this story gives way to despair on the cross, but by God's act of raising and sending him ahead.

The risk here is extreme, as these storytellers make plain. If one death was not enough, how many will be enough? Who can demonstrate that Jesus was not deluded up until the end when he discovered that God would not rescue him? Is this the sacrifice of Isaac without the ram (Gen 22:13)? These are questions that the passage of time could only intensify. Today some will reject any vision of the world as God's struggle with evil, choosing to see nature as neutral and humans able to live within it in life and in death. But the experience of those who tell

Mark may not allow this. Their country is occupied by an imperial system geared for maximum exploitation, their chief leaders are corrupt, their people are possessed by fear. They have to confront the reality they know. And they do it, to their credit, not with simplistic formulas of comfort, but with the account of a man who trusted God and died for it—whose story did not end there. The story stimulates tellers and hearers who continue to spread it. This is the work of following Jesus, which involves great risks. Forerunners go ahead, but in anticipation of this kingdom the following is always new, a process of shaping the story while being shaped by it.

# 17

## "And They Said Nothing to Anyone"

What does a resurrection story mean that has no certain ending, no disciples as witnesses, no appearance of Jesus, and no telling of the story? Can hearing Mark as a tellers' composition help deal with this major conundrum in interpreting the gospel?

### Where Mark Ends

The presence of three distinct endings of Mark (and other endings that combine or elaborate these) is visible in most translations: the short ending at 16:8 with the women fleeing and telling no one; the intermediate ending of two sentences assuring hearers that the disciples get the message and tell the story; and the long ending in 16:9–20 with its several appearances of Jesus, disciples' responses, and Jesus' ascension.[1] Although no Greek manuscript of Mark's end survives from before the fourth century, at that time both the prime Vaticanus and Sinaiticus manuscripts have only the short ending at 16:8, and this ending is supported by the patristic writers Eusebius and Jerome, who identify the long ending that extends to 16:20 as an addition to Mark.[2] Yet because the long ending is attested already in the late second century by Tatian and Irenaeus, appears in Codex Bezae in the early fifth century, and becomes the dominant reading in the medieval church, modern

---

1. I follow Parker's way of distinguishing the different endings as short, intermediate, and long. See his clear exposition of the issues raised by Mark's ending in *Living Text*, 121–47.

2. Ibid., 133–34.

translations include it with only footnote qualification. The intermediate ending that completes the gospel in one Old Latin manuscript appears between the short and long endings in some later manuscripts and translations, producing the grotesque effect of a story with three endings. But the very fact of two independent efforts to solve the problems of the short ending supports its priority, as does the fact that the other gospels diverge sharply from each other after the common scene of women finding the open tomb.

Here we need a new multidimensional format to present this gospel in at least three different stages of its development, the short ending in our earlier text, and each longer ending in separate second century renditions of the gospel. The question remains how the extensions were added. They could be forgeries by scribes, either to harmonize the four gospels when they were being copied together, or to address new issues at that time as has been proposed for the longer ending by James Kelhoffer.[3] But if the gospels were shaped in performance, storytelling would continue after writing and a difficult ending might well generate various adaptations. In the case of the intermediate ending, oral composition is suggested by the fact that the story of the empty tomb is itself being much revised in the telling to include an eclipse and an ascension of Jesus, and to omit the women's not telling. The long ending suggests oral provenance by the way pieces have been added to the short ending seriatim, first brief reports of some appearances of Jesus told in other gospels, then Jesus' rebuke of the disciples for not believing, his instruction to preach, his promise of miracles, and finally a report of proclamation and Jesus' ascension.

The oral composition thesis can honor both later endings as evolutions of Mark in different second century contexts, but this must be done in some format which does not obscure the difficult ending at 16:8 that apparently preceded and provoked them.[4] The added endings have

3. Kelhoffer's *Miracle and Mission* investigates the second century context and the meaning of the long ending. He does not develop an oral composition option but takes the long ending as an individual's forgery.

4. John Miles Foley's Pathways Project is developing the software for multidimensional display of oral and oral-derived texts that change over time; online: http://oral tradition.org. David Parker reviews electronic New Testament editions now in process in *Introduction to the New Testament Manuscripts and Their Texts*, 200–202, 216–23.

no business being included in the text in editions that attempt to print the earliest available text.[5]

Once the added material is recognized as such, some interpreters evade the difficult 16:8 ending by saying the first writing was unfinished or the original ending was lost. An unfinished book is conceivable, but the idea that an author should be terminally interrupted or even die at his narrative's climax stretches probabilities too far. And a performer so cut off in the telling would do no damage to the tradition that many people would know and complete. The lost ending thesis has had broader support.[6] Yet Kurt Aland argues that it would have to be the autograph—the original papyrus—that lost its final page for this page to leave no trace. That would be a proposal of last resort to a form critic. Both Kurt Aland and David Parker reject it, leaving us with a Mark that ends at 16:8.[7] Although second century telling continues creatively, it is this short ending that survives in the fourth century parchments which is our clue to the early formation of Mark.

## No Disciple Witness

We know that we must pursue the meaning of this earliest ending of Mark at 16:8, but the three problems it presents seem intractable: the resurrection story contains no disciple witness, no appearance of Jesus, and no telling of the women's story. This gospel stresses from the beginning that Jesus chooses twelve disciples and trains them in order to extend his work of announcing God's kingdom and healing the people. He warns them repeatedly that he will be killed and will rise on the third day, yet they misunderstand, betray, and deny him, flee when he is arrested, and do not come back to bury him, even though John the

5. If we think that text criticism is no longer contested ground, consider the fate of the original printing of the RSV New Testament in 1946 and the Bible in 1952, which put the intermediate and longer endings in the footnotes where they belong. The press was threatened with boycotts. Editions since then, including the NRSV, have included these endings in the text with only a footnote to say that they are not in "some of the most ancient authorities," then adding that they appear in "most manuscripts," deceiving the novice who does not know that most manuscripts are Medieval.

6. Bultmann, *History of the Synoptic Tradition*, 285, n. 2, 441–42; Metzger, *Textual Commentary on the Greek New Testament*, 126 n. 7; Elliott, "Mark 1.1–3—A Later Addition to the Gospel?" 586–87.

7. Kurt Aland, "Der Schluss," 460–61; Parker, *Living Text*, 143.

Baptist's disciples had retrieved and buried his headless corpse (6:29). The Markan characterization of Jesus' disciples is consistent and indicates a failure of major proportions in Jesus' work. Women from his company do observe his death and burial, yet "from far off" and without access to the tomb.

What are we to make of these women?[8] Do they become the witnesses? They are introduced in the gospel only after Jesus' death (15:40–41), yet they are said to be not just three but many, not bystanders but people who have been following and serving him in Galilee and have come with him to Jerusalem, and not anonymous but named at the death, at the burial, and again at the tomb. They surface for us the issue of social power in a world before even the theory of human equality was recognized. Theirs is a world securely bifurcated between those who are served and those who serve. Most blatant in these scenes is the dichotomy between agents of imperial power and the ones they execute for threatening that power. This dichotomy overlaps another one between the Greek and/or Latin speaking urban elite and the native rural laborers who supply their physical needs. This is sharpened in turn by a further dichotomy between those who are trained in a skill, perhaps even literacy, and the great majority who receive orders from others. I mention one further dichotomy—passing over the well and the sick, the free and the slave—namely, there are male householders and female care-givers. The anomaly here is this group of non-literate rural care-givers who follow a just-executed man, present in the story all along we are told, but now suddenly appearing on center stage. Many women's stories have been told in Mark, but these are the first women who are primary actors, upon whose witness depends the climax of the tellers' story. The low status of these women on so many indicators does not lead to any explanations or apologies, suggesting that the early tellers may come from the same social milieu.

The women are shown taking care of business in their anointing the dead, first buying spices on Sabbath eve, then coming at dawn,

8. On the women's resurrection witness in Mark, see: Schottroff, "Maria Magdalena und die Frauen am Grabe Jesu"; Sawicki, *Seeing the Lord*; Fisher, "The Empty Tomb Story in Mark"; D'Angelo, "Re-Reading Resurrection"; Mitchell, *Beyond Fear and Silence*; Hooker, *Endings*, 4–30; Gaventa and Miller, eds., *Ending of Mark and The Ends of God*; Upton, *Hearing Mark's Ending*; Bauckham, "Eyewitnesses in the Gospel of Mark."

discussing how to get in the tomb. They find it open, step in, and are shocked by a youth in bright clothing seated on the right. He speaks, first to calm them and to acknowledge that they have come to find Jesus who was crucified, second to give them the news that Jesus has been raised and is not there, pointing to the place he lay, and third to give them a task. In the Codex Bezae of the early fifth century, the message he gives them is addressed strictly to the disciples in direct discourse: "Tell them, 'I am going ahead . . . there you will see me.'" But in the earlier tradition, the youth speaks in indirect discourse, including the women invisibly in the instruction, "Go tell the disciples and Peter that he is going ahead of you into Galilee. There you will see him as he told you." They are to tell, to follow Jesus, and to see him.

A tradition of women as the initial witnesses of the resurrection echoes in other New Testament accounts of Jesus' resurrection, yet in ways that subordinate the women's witness to that of the twelve. Matthew and John not only say that women come first to the tomb, but also that Jesus himself appears to them there. Yet in Matthew the message that the angel and then Jesus gives the women reaches its fulfillment only when Jesus commissions the eleven on the mountain in Galilee (Matt 28:7, 10, 16–20). And in the Fourth Gospel, Mary Magdalene sees the stone gone and tells Peter and the loved disciple, who find the tomb empty, and this "other disciple . . . saw and believed"—all before she sees Jesus, hears him speak, and tells the disciples: "I have seen the Lord" (John 20:1–18). In Luke, the first to see Jesus are the couple on the road to Emmaus. Of the two, only Cleopas is named, although Luke prefers two male witnesses or messengers, perhaps because the second here is taken to be a woman. Yet their witness is trumped by a single sentence that follows, reporting a previous appearance to Peter (Luke 24:34). Paul names Peter and the twelve in his list of resurrection witnesses, then a group of five hundred, then James and the disciples, but he does not stress who was first in the same way he says that he himself was "last of all" (1 Cor 15:5–8). He apparently wants wide agreement to his formulation from those who favor Peter's witness and James' witness and the witness of the women that he has folded into the five hundred.

In regard to Peter's witness to Jesus' resurrection, the traditions vary greatly. He is called Simon, Simon Peter, Cephas, and Peter, and there is no narrative of an appearance to him alone in the New Testament sources (Matt 28:16; Luke 24:33–34; John 20:2–10, 19–26; 21:2–23; 1

Cor 15:5; Mark 16:14). This suggests that Peter's priority may be a concept coming from Peter's status rather than a story from an event. The Markan account stands out by not subordinating the women's witness to that of the disciples. Although the disciples and specifically Peter are supposed to be reminded to go to Galilee, as they had been told earlier (14:28), no story of their going to Galilee appears. In the Markan telling, the women are the resurrection witnesses.

In so far as the Christian gospel is conceived as a witness to Jesus' resurrection, this closing could be proposed as a covert signature of a female author.[9] But there is no reference here to writing, and women at this time were very seldom literate. However, if the gospel was composed in performance by favored tellers, the key role of resurrection witness given to women may be a trace of women as early shapers of the story.

## No Appearance of Jesus

The gospel ending at 16:8 tells no appearance of Jesus. The other gospels and Paul all tell of Jesus appearing to specific people, programming us to expect something similar being at least projected in this gospel. Yet the many different stories about who saw Jesus and what happened make clear that there was no single early resurrection story.[10] Each account must be heard independently, so also the account of the performers of Mark.

First, it is possible that the Markan tradition takes the story of the youth in the tomb telling that Jesus is raised and where he is going as

9. Martin Hengel ("Das Begräbnis Jesu bei Paulus," 181) did write, "Dass die Frauen ewig geschwiegen hätten meint Markus gewiss nicht—es sei denn, man macht feministisch-progressiv, eine der drei Frauen zur Autorin des Evangeliums, die sich hier damit zum ersten Mal 'outet.' Aber das hat m. W. bisher selbst keine der Vorkämpferinnen der feministischen Exegese behauptet."

10. C. H. Dodd proposed in 1955 that the early oral resurrection traditions were "worn down" by much telling into a concise statement of the situation, appearance, greeting, recognition, and command, while later stories became more elaborated and distinctive. But these formulaic patterns can often be traced to specific uses of the stories to prove Jesus' resurrection when contested or to provide a foundation for Christian mission, interests reflecting the defensive posture of an inside group, whereas the more free-form stories may reflect the variety of experiences typical in early accounts of a shocking event. Dodd, "Appearances of the Risen Christ."

a sufficient demonstration of Jesus' resurrection. Matthew takes a very similar account of the angel's message to the women as a resurrection story introduced with an earthquake and concluded with Jesus' message to the women. The story is heightened but not lost. When Matthew goes on to tell a second appearance to the disciples in Galilee, we expect the same in Mark, but no second appearance is told. What then is the gospel of Mark pointing to with the youth's instruction to follow Jesus to Galilee and see him there?

Two options suggest themselves when reading this in light of the whole Markan story of Jesus. A gospel teller may be stressing Jesus' preceding them to Galilee in order to signal persistence in the task Jesus shared with his disciples in Galilee of proclaiming God's kingdom. Earlier in this account of his last week, Jesus had predicted that the shepherd would be struck and the sheep scattered, concluding "But after I am raised I will precede you to Galilee" (14:28). Yet this sentence is not strong evidence for a restored Galilee ministry because it is such a mirror image of the message at the tomb and fits so loosely in its own context that it may have been added to supply a referent for the youth's final words "as he told you."

Nonetheless Jesus preceding them to Galilee could indicate following him in the prophetic practice in which Jesus trained them, leaving home and losing life to find it (8:35; 10:29), gaining the rewards of new family at the cost of persecutions and trials (13:9–13; 10:30; 3:35) until the good news reaches all peoples (13:10; 14:9). This might reflect the life of the Markan tellers who continue this proclamation. The disciples and the women would then see Jesus in Galilee, much as they did on the road to Jerusalem when he preceded and they were "alarmed and afraid" and yet followed him (10:32). We might say they would see him only the way Moses saw God when hidden in the cleft of the rock—not face to face as in other resurrection stories, but from behind as a mortal being followed (Exod 33:20–22).

Alternately the stress in the resurrection story in Mark may fall on going to Galilee after Jesus in order to see him. But does Jesus expect a reunion in Galilee? At his last meal, Jesus makes clear that he will share no banquet with them until God's kingdom has arrived (14:25).[11] Seeing Jesus may then point back to what Jesus predicted three times in this gospel about the coming vision of the mortal—"you will see the

11. Park, "Problem of the ΑΠΟΥΣΙΑ of Jesus."

mortal one seated at the right hand of power coming with the clouds of heaven" (14:62); "they will see the mortal one coming in clouds with all power and glory" (13:26); "some of those standing here will not taste death until they see the mortal one having come in power" (9:1). The youth's words, "there you will see him," echo the same verb spoken in these crucially placed predictions—the first at the end of Jesus' second passion teaching, the second at the climax of his discourse on last things, and the third in his answer to the High Priest's final question about whether he is the Christ.

This way of understanding the youth's message, developed by Lohmeyer and Lightfoot and later reframed by Marxsen and Schottroff, takes Jesus' resurrection on the third day reported by the youth as an anticipation of the coming of the mortal one to consummate God's rule.[12] The cosmic signs of sun darkening and moon falling need not imply the end of the world, since they can be used to describe God's deliverance in Israel's struggles (13:24; Exod 14:45; Judg 5:20; *Biblical Antiquities* 31:1–2). Under imperial occupation, images of the elect being gathered and a victory banquet being served are surely drawn from historical memories and raise historical hopes. Our hesitancy to read the youth's message as an historical transformation may come less from hearing Mark than from our historical hindsight, knowing the darkness that came with the Temple's destruction. The tellers of Mark before that time may well expect Jesus' vindication momentarily, but afterward take wartime hopes as deception and tell Jesus' action in the Temple as his sign of destruction against it, the fulfillment of which then confirms Jesus' original sign of God's kingdom arriving.[13]

These two options for understanding the youth's message either as a call to Galilee proclamation or as a promise of God's kingdom yet coming in power are not mutually exclusive. In this gospel it is the coming of God's kingdom that provokes the call to repentance and trust in the first place, and an immediate expectation should only add urgency to that call.[14] Although we might think that Jesus could not both be

---

12. Lohmeyer, *Galiläa und Jerusalem*, 26–36; Lightfoot, *Locality and Doctrine in the Gospels*, 24–48; Marxsen, *Mark the Evangelist*, 83–95; Schottroff, "Maria Magdalena."

13. See chapter 14.

14. Schottroff writes, "Es ist der Eigenart dieser Eschatologie nicht ganz gerecht, das 'Sehen' des Auferstanden in Galiläa *entweder* als Parousie *oder* Epiphanie im Sinne von 1 Kor 15,3ff verstehen zu wollen, denn beides hängt für Markus eng zusammen.

followed in Galilee and then come with the clouds as God's victorious mortal, more than one image may be active in this kind of performance. Or an integration of both options can be communicated by tone or gesture. Possibly the tellers show Jesus claiming vindication by another mortal after he leads them in Galilee proclamation, or they show that the followers' anticipation of Jesus' return as the mortal drives them toward proclaiming God's arriving kingdom. In any case, Lohmeyer's glorification of Galilee as the holy land of Jesus' ministry in contrast to Jerusalem as the place of his rejection and death is not necessary to explain why the consummation is visualized outside Jerusalem.[15] The political context of the Galileans is sufficient grounds why they would not expect God's kingdom to appear in Jerusalem, whether the story is being told soon after the crucifixion of Jesus or later after the Temple was destroyed.

## No Telling

The final and most difficult problem with the ending of this gospel is the categorical statement in its last verse: "And they said nothing to anyone because they were afraid" (16:8). How then have we just heard the story? And why does the gospel put final stress on this statement?

The first question of how the story nonetheless became known is not the most difficult. The fear may be temporary. They are awestruck, in a state of shock, and later recount their fear as they pass on the message. Or the women do not tell the disciples as instructed, having lost confidence in them and knowing that the disciples would not believe what they were told. Or the women say "nothing to anyone" referring to the people they were told to tell, yet they told other women. Or the disciples went to Galilee as Jesus had told them earlier (14:28) and met him there, only later hearing the women's story about the empty tomb.

But these solutions are not adequate because the problem is not historical but rhetorical. It is clear that the narrative becomes known, however that happens, since we are hearing it. The question is why the

Jesu Auferstehung ist das entscheidende weltverändernde eschatologische Geschehen, ein Beginn, der bald an das umfassende Ziel der Erscheinung des Menschensohnes auf den Wolken führen wird." "Maria Magdalena," 21–22.

15. Lohmeyer, *Galiläa und Jerusalem*, 28–36.

171

gospel ends on this strange note. Here the literary interpreter has the advantage, because she or he has only to consider why an author in some particular time chose to end the story this way. For example, the author may be promoting the flight of Jesus' followers from Jerusalem in wartime by introducing for the first time a story about an angelic message to the disciples saying that Jesus would precede them to Galilee. But if the story is composed in performance by favored tellers over decades, the eventual scribe would never get away with such a radical change of ending. The meaning of the ending could certainly shift as the context changed, and at some point an audience could hear in this story a reference to fleeing Jerusalem. But earlier meanings must also be considered. A traditional proposal was that the women's not telling served as a apology or defense of Jesus' resurrection. The resurrection story, they said, did not arise from women's rumors of angels which were silenced by fear but from apostolic witness to Jesus himself. Yet this is an inadequate interpretation of a gospel that ends without telling Jesus' appearances to anyone, women or men.

One favored explanation today is that the author sustains at the end a perspective consistent throughout the gospel that human beings are not willing to risk their lives to proclaim God's kingdom. Finally even the women, who stay nearby to care for Jesus' body, are not ready to receive a living Jesus. The gospel ends as do so many of the miracle stories and teachings of Jesus: people are struck dumb, marveling among themselves, wondering and afraid. Yet this explanation that the final failure of Jesus' followers is being told in order to challenge hearers to take their place is inadequate in itself. It explains only how their failure could be used by later tellers, not where the story might come from.

If we step back and begin again from Mark as a story of a prophet's sign, its telling is unmistakably aimed toward provoking people to take a stand for or against this man and God's kingdom that he has announced. Initially it calls for people to follow him, and at the end it announces that he is risen. He is at large. He precedes his followers who proclaim God's kingdom until they see him come in God's power to gather the elect and to eat and drink with them at God's table.

But at this key point, the eye of the hurricane we could say, the story ends with the women saying "nothing to anyone, for they were afraid" (16:8). We have been stopped short. What did we ignore? First, we ignored the violent political situation that is sufficient grounds for the women's fear of promoting a resurrected criminal. Second, we ignored their social status that provided them no channel for their message when the men had scattered and, if found, would not listen. Third, we ignored their homes and children that demanded they act with caution.

Fourth, we ignored a pattern of secrecy threaded through Mark that could provide a clue to their practices. If we recognize in Jesus' silencing of those he heals a strategy to keep the crowds small and avoid the attention of authorities, we see depicted in his lifetime a practice of laying low in order to clarify and deepen the news of God's kingdom in a circle of trust. If the women do not broadcast in the street that a crucified man is no longer dead but leading his followers back to Galilee, and if they do not search for the deserters who will say they are crazy, they will flee where they will be welcomed, either to inner rooms in some home in Jerusalem or Bethany, or back to Galilee. Nothing more is heard. The sudden ending honors that. But there are "many women" who followed Jesus to Jerusalem (15:40–41), and they were close to each other in critical times. The ending of this gospel could indicate a period when they lay low and began to cultivate Jesus' story. They may have watched for Jesus and for the mortal he spoke of coming on the clouds, but they apparently kept their focus by rehearsing his story. In the story, they do not deny the twelve primary place in Jesus' circle but they find their models elsewhere, and when the disciples are gone they must surface and tell their own witness to Jesus' death, burial, and resurrection. This includes their not telling, making the story in its early years an inside telling about not telling.

What reverses the "not telling" is also not told. It could be the intensity of the women's focus on telling Jesus' story that draws other women in—as in an earlier response to Jesus' reticence, "The more he commanded them [not to tell], the more they told" (7:36). Eventually the story could not be contained among women in Galilee. Such a time of secrecy would help to explain why Paul who twice visits the apostles in Jerusalem over a period of fourteen years (Gal 1:18—2:1) refers to none of the stories of Jesus' life in Galilee. Only decades later do other gospels combine these stories with the resurrection appearance accounts that Paul knew to make a composite view of Jesus.

The ending of Mark seen in this way goes through a number of interpretations as tellers speak it in new settings. But the tenacity of the tradition, once it was known in a group, could hardly be exaggerated. A fine witness to this is Kurt Aland's wonder when he marvels at how four centuries later the parchment codices of the New Testament still end the Gospel of Mark with the words "And they said nothing to anyone, for they were afraid."[16]

16. Kurt Aland, "Der Schluss," 437–38.

# PART 4

## Conclusion

# 18

## Who Is Telling? Two Scenarios

As I said in beginning, when we read we are looking not only for information about a topic or even for a broad understanding of the subject in its context. We listen for the perspective of the person who is addressing us and compare it to our own perspective. It is a voice that we want to hear, a person speaking from a certain vantage point with certain purposes that we can concede or question or contest. We seek a conversation.

Reading an ancient text is therefore difficult. Where an author makes himself known, we find it challenging to converse with someone in a distant time and place and an alien culture. Paul's voice speaking to the scribe as he writes his letters is strong and his point in any one argument is hard to miss, though we struggle to place why this point is so important to him.

### Listening for a Voice

The gospel narratives are yet more difficult since the speakers do not identify themselves and perspectives often seem to be general or, where clear, at cross-purposes with other voices in the text. Our problem has been eased by scholars who have reconstructed individual authors from the gospel writings, allowing us to compare them with each other and giving each voice definition. Among these writers, Mark has been the most difficult to recover, because redaction critics have not had sources with which to compare the author's editing, and because literary critics are hard pressed to identify which tendency in the text is the writer's own voice.

The thesis that Mark's composition developed over time in performance seems only to complicate this further. So many people contributed to the early telling of Mark as a story of conflict provoked by a prophet's sign. And those who became long-term oral tellers are hard to distinguish from each other and from the early scribes who contributed to the story in the copying of it. Even if success were achieved in isolating several layers of the story's development, this would not do justice to the tradition that takes its identity and authority, not from the specific voice speaking but from the past. Edgar Bakker contrasts the Greek historians who take readers back in the imperfect tense to witness the past with the performers of Homer who use the aorist tense to reactivate the glories of the past in the present.[1] This reactivation is what Auerbach calls an "external" or "foregrounded" mimesis.[2] How this is done by different performers will vary according to the way they engage an audience. However, what is understood to be met in this performance is not the storyteller's perspective. Rather, it is the stance of the characters in the epic past that are being performed, thanks to the inspiration of the Muses who see them. If biblical narrative is performed in this sense, we do best to listen, not for the particular perspective of the one who tells the story, but for the perspective or impact of those figures of the past that are presented by divine inspiration. To put this in other terms, we need to allow the tellers to be performers of the common ancestral story. Granted that they are telling it in a particular time and place, which produces interesting shifts in the locution, but we miss too much if we ignore the aim of their speaking to bring the story to life.

Yet there were tellers. And because Luke's narrative of apostolic preaching in Acts as the foundation of the early church has so strongly programmed our imaginations, it is valuable to reach beyond what can be proven—as Luke has done there—and project other possible scenarios for the early generation of the tradition. I turn now to two possible scenarios for visualizing early tellers of Mark, the first drawn largely from external evidence in early Christian sources and the second primarily from internal evidence in Mark. The two cannot easily be

---

1. Bakker, *Pointing at the Past*, 92–113.
2. Auerbach, *Mimesis*, 4–20.

integrated with each other and a third may replace them, but the point is to be looking in more likely places than the literary speeches of Acts for the people who shaped the story and their purposes.

## Told in the House of Mary of Jerusalem

The first scenario takes its clue from the title "according to Mark" given this gospel to distinguish it from others when several gospels were collected in the first half of the second century. Since the name Mark was not chosen from among the twelve to claim eyewitness authority, it was probably associated with this document because someone named Mark had been its scribe.[3]

Mark was a common name, but first consideration can be given to persons of that name known to be active Christians in the first century, granted that we cannot confirm the accuracy of our sources. Paul mentions a Mark who is his fellow worker with Demas and Luke when he writes Philemon (24), and in 2 Tim 4:11 "Paul" asks Timothy—since Demas has deserted and only Luke remains—to bring Mark "who is useful to me for ministering/serving (*diakonia*)." With this request comes a plea to bring "the parchments" and "the cloak left in Troas with Carpus." Is Mark thought to help with writing? With personal care? This coworker or assistant is likely the same Mark who appears in Acts, since the Pauline tradition and Acts both link him to Barnabas, here in a greeting the writer of Colossians transmits from "Mark the cousin of Barnabas" (Col 4:10).

Mark is first mentioned in Acts when Peter is released from a high-security imprisonment by an angel at night after James the disciple is killed, and Peter goes first "to the house of Mary, the mother of John who is called Mark" (Acts 12:12, 6–19). Note that she is named in terms of her son, which suggests she is a widow, but the house is called hers, so Mark is probably yet a young man. Although he is not mentioned again in the story about this night, it is significant that Peter goes to Mary's home when the angel abandons him, that he is so familiar there that Rhoda who hears the knock while others are praying recognizes his voice, and that when he gains entry, he says what happened, sends

---

3. For another effort to deal with Christian sources on Mark, see Collins' introduction on authorship of the gospel (*Mark*, 2–6).

word "to James and the brothers," and leaves "for another place"—and the next day for another city. This suggests that the writer thinks Peter could expect to be sought at Mary's house once found missing. If Peter lived there, he would have a significant, probably long-term association with Mary and her son Mark. Note also that Mary hosts a gathering where Peter, James and "the brothers" are not present.

As Mark's cousin, Barnabas is a key figure in the Acts account about Mark. Barnabas must be the son of Mary's (or her husband's) older sister or brother, being considerably older than Mark since in Laconia he was mistaken for Zeus whose statues are very distinguished (Acts 14:12). According to this account, Barnabas had lived in Jerusalem long enough to become respected by the apostles to whom he had donated money from the sale of land, with whom he had interceded for Paul after his conversion, and by whom he had been sent to Antioch when they were concerned about the preaching to Greeks (Acts 4:36–37; 9:27; 11:22). At the same time, Barnabas had supported Paul, not only at Paul's return to Jerusalem after his conversion, but perhaps by sending Paul back to Tarsus when Hellenists were trying to kill him (Acts 9:27, 30), because Barnabas is the one who goes to Tarsus to look for Paul and bring him to Antioch where they make a common base for extended work with Gentiles (Acts 11:25; 11:26—15:35). These references show that Mark was a junior member of a family well-established in the earliest Jerusalem churches and later in Antioch, probably, with Barnabas, of Levite stock (Acts 4:36). Paul speaks of Barnabas not accepting support from churches where he worked (1 Cor 9:6), and since no mention is made of his artisan skills, this may indicate, along with the land Barnabas sold and the home Mary owned, that this family had sufficient resources to have provided Mark an education. As a native of Cyprus (Acts 4:36), Barnabas could probably speak Greek, which suggests the same for Mary and Mark.

John called Mark appears again when Paul and Barnabas take him as a helper on their mission to Cyprus. Mark then returns to Jerusalem as they continue north (Acts 12:25; 13:5, 13). Later Paul and Barnabas plan a second mission. However, Paul refuses to take Mark who deserted them earlier—as Luke tells it—and after a rousing argument they split up, Barnabas taking Mark to Cyprus, their native area, while Paul and Silas visit Syria and Cilicia where Paul was raised (Acts 4:36; 15:36–41). It is significant that Paul tells a very different story about his break-up with Barnabas (Gal 2:1–13). Paul says that he and Barnabas had received recognition in Jerusalem for their mission to Gentiles, and that Peter had come to Antioch and joined in eating with Jews and Gentiles. But when other people came from James, Peter had left the common table because the new arrivals would not eat with Gentiles. And all the Jews including even Barnabas had joined what Paul condemns as their hypocrisy. This conflict was clearly an issue of theological principle for Paul, as well as for the people from James. But in the case of Peter and Barnabas, it may have been an issue of hospitality, acting first out of consideration for the Gentiles and then for the Jerusalem guests at the expense of the Gentiles. Or was it a local Jerusalem allegiance? or a matter of status? In any case, Barnabas is allied here with Peter, not Paul, and whether we take Luke's or Paul's story as the turning point—family allegiance or table fellowship as the issue—Paul appears to operate independently of Barnabas from this time, and Acts tells only Paul's story. We cannot trace Barnabas' later work other than to see that the writer of Colossians encourages the church to welcome Barnabas when it sends greetings to his cousin Mark (Col 4:10).

But the story of Mark's connection to Peter continues. If Mark was remembered as a coworker and occasional helper to Paul (Phlm 24; 2 Tim 4:11), in 1 Peter, he is called "my son" (5:13). What Eusebius in the fourth century quotes from Papias writing before the mid second century is often discounted as an effort to legitimate Mark by association with one of the twelve. However, it does not read that way:

> And the presbyter (John) would say this: Mark became Peter's interpreter and wrote accurately as much as he remembered, though not in order, the things either spoken or done by the Lord. For he did not hear nor follow the Lord, but later, as he said, Peter, who would give teachings as needed but did not make any orderly compilation of the Lord's sayings. So Mark committed no offense in writing single items as he remembered them. For he took care of one thing, to leave out none of the things he had heard and to say nothing false in them. (Eusebius *History of the Church* 3.39.15).

Eusebius says elsewhere, citing 1 Peter's "my son," that Mark wrote the gospel in Rome and that Peter learned of the gospel by the Spirit and ratified it for church use, a story Eusebius claims to have from Clement of Alexandria supported by Papias (*History of the Church* 2.15.1–2). But

181

this latter reference is in a lyrical passage about Peter in Rome perhaps spun from the 1 Peter words of endearment. Without further early evidence, the tradition that Mark tells Peter's story becomes accepted by Irenaeus' time (*Against Heresies* 3.1.1).

Yet there is no sign that stories about Jesus' life before his last meal are circulating in the churches of the Hellenistic cities that produce the New Testament letters. Where were the stories being told and shaped into this gospel? Mark's focus on conflict provoked by a prophet's sign suggests an origin, not in the Roman provinces that were considered pacified and ruled by the Senate such as Italy, Greece and Asia Minor, but in the East where local kings and the emperor's procurator-friends extracted all they could from the land. It may be that when Mark returns to Palestine to find his family in the war or post-war crisis he writes down this gospel. This might be the case if the story was cultivated over years in gatherings such as the one in Jerusalem who had heard Peter's stories in the 30s and 40s. Mark would have special reason to write down an account told by his mother Mary and continued by a Rhoda or another teller in that group now that the home was destroyed and the congregation scattered. Women leaders with less mobility than men and known for storytelling in the ancient world might have applied these gifts to cultivating such accounts. Although Mark's name gets associated with the writing, the tradition he records may already have been audible in Galilee and Syria due to the influence of the Jerusalem churches, so that other forms of the gospel which are transcribed later became shaped around it.

Can we say anything about the telling of Jesus' story that might have been taking place in Mary's house in the middle four decades of the first century? They had two quite different sources for their story. One was their own experience of the last week of Jesus' life, including perhaps word from the three women at Jesus' tomb. This gave them the climax of Jesus' story: the crowds welcoming what they hoped to be God's kingdom but the ruler intervenes before it is realized and Jesus is killed. Then three days later he is vindicated by resurrection according to the women's words—if they fled to Mary's home where others would believe their story. But the accounts of Jesus in Galilee they had to fill in by asking Peter, who seems to have lived there and told a good story, often on himself. Or perhaps the women from Galilee also told stories of women Jesus had healed and the crowds that had followed him.

There was no leisure at Mary's house to construct the story of Jesus because people came constantly to ask. So one of them might tell, beginning from John the Baptist, about Jesus receiving the spirit coming down on him like a dove, and then his calling fishers of people. And when her voice was tired another would take up the story with the wild man in the synagogue and Peter's mother in law and the leper. When the gathering was large, it may have fallen on Mary, whose house it was, to tell the story in an orderly way: about the prophet who appeared, his sign, the crowds, his death and his rising, highlighting the conflicts that cut across all that happened. But the people would not let her omit any of the stories. Living in Jerusalem in the final years of the war and fleeing before the Temple's burning, this household might tell Jesus' actions in the Temple as his sign portending its destruction, and then tell its end, which may have confirmed for them that God's kingdom, Jesus' sign of deliverance, could not be far behind.

## Told among Women in Galilee

A second scenario asks the gospel of Mark itself to answer the question of who told the story. There is no doubt but that Mark is oriented to Galilee. Jesus is depicted living strictly in Galilee except for forays north with his followers to escape the crowds, until his last tragic week in Jerusalem. This suggests Galilee as the obvious provenance for this tradition where some Jewish towns survived the turmoil of the first and second centuries and became a base for later rabbis. Stories about Jesus could have continued circulating within the accounts of this prophet once he was heard to be at large. The fact that the gospel takes place in the peasant and fishing villages rather than the cities could specify the location of their further cultivation. But who might take the story that everyone was telling and start to shape a tradition that formed Jesus' memory and anticipated drinking with him in God's kingdom? Who might yet have hope after what had happened?

The gospel ends with an instruction, first to the disciples and then to the women, to follow Jesus back to Galilee where they will see him (14:28; 16:7). There is no indication in Mark that the disciples remember this or go back to Galilee. The women, however, have a more striking experience. When they return to the tomb to anoint Jesus' body, they find not Jesus but a young man in white seated at the right who says Jesus is risen, reminds them that Jesus said he would precede them to Galilee, and tells them to tell his disciples. The women's vision at the tomb, like that of the disciples on the mountain, is too bright for them and they are afraid, telling nothing to anyone (16:5–8; 9:2–6). But the account later surfaces. This suggests a sustained experience of Jesus among Galilean women that became a composition site for this gospel.

Luke and Acts adhere strictly to a Jerusalem story of Jesus' resurrection and the church's birth, while Matthew and John integrate Jerusalem and Galilee resurrection stories, extending the story at the tomb with accounts of Jesus himself appearing to Galilean women/an (Matt 28:8–10; John 20:11–18). Only Paul omits all mention of women in his resurrection account, unless they are assumed to be among the five hundred who see Jesus at one time (1 Cor 15:5–8). And his letters tell no event from Jesus' life in Galilee, indicating how separately the stories about Jesus' lifetime were developing in the early years when Paul met with Peter, James and John (Gal 1:18—2:10). More than a decade may have gone by before others overheard the women's story and began to tell it in Galilee's villages, then in towns, and finally in cities there and elsewhere.

We lack the name of a favored teller of the Galilean tradition. John's gospel focuses on Mary of Magdala at the tomb, while the other gospels take pains to give the names of several witnesses (Matt 28:1; Mark 16:1; Luke 24:10). This suggests that Mark's gospel is the story of the many women who fled from Jerusalem (15:40–41). They will have met to share their fear and, in this tight circle shaped by their common trauma, they may have told each other the events that they had witnessed and the stories they had heard, drawing each other out as they sought a pattern in what Jesus had said and done. Joanna Dewey has noted how some stories in Mark see the event from the perspective of women who meet their own desperate needs and that of their children against great odds (5:25–35; 7:27–30).[4] A recent study by Elizabeth Minchin of women's storytelling in Greek epic has noted that the women who tell stories focus on the more intimate aspects of hu-

---

4. Dewey, "Women in the Synoptic Gospels," 56; Hearon and Maloney, "Listen to the Voices," 46–49; Hearon, *Mary Magdalene Tradition*, 19–42; Wire, *Holy Lives*, 385–88.

man action and reaction.[5] Women telling these stories often seek a mirror story from others in response, another story that can confirm that their point has been taken. In this way the women of Galilee could have composed Jesus' story, one story responding to another. Mark shows us the women of Galilee found a double pattern in Jesus' story. They told it as the story of a prophet's sign unfolding in a sequence of five events: Jesus' appearance in the crisis at the Baptist's death, Jesus' announcement of God's kingdom as their coming deliverance, the gathering of great crowds, the opposition that culminates in his execution by the ruler, and his vindication in resurrection. This sign of God's kingdom provoked a great conflict that became another pattern in their story, a conflict between God and Satan, between Jesus and the authorities, and between human trust and human fear, the fear that stunned them into silence.

And, when the story is finally overheard and told, why do those who tell it continue to give the final stress to the fear of the women that kept them from telling the story? Is the political danger still so great that fear remains the reality on the ground? Must it be explained why so much of Jesus' story has only now comes to light? Does secrecy add to the story's power, like the lamp in Jesus' parable, "not hidden except in order to be revealed" (4:22)? Or is this simply the last thing the women remembered, hence the way they chose to end their account, claiming nothing for themselves? And others telling their story had to respect that end.

There is a larger question about telling this story that comes from the emphasis in Mark on the gospel or good news. Could the story be presented as "good news" and be at the same time not told? Except in Jesus' announcement of the sign of God's kingdom (1:14–15), reference to this "gospel" or "good news" hangs loosely in Mark. Twice it seems to have been added to a phrase demanding commitment to Jesus: "whoever loses his life on account of me and the good news . . ."; and "whoever leaves home or brothers or sisters . . . on account of me and the good news . . ." (8:35; 10:29). Twice it adds to something quite different a call to tell everyone: "And first the good news must be proclaimed to all nations" and "Wherever the good news is preached in all

---

5. Minchin, "The Language of Heroes and the Language of Heroines," 33–34. She cites particularly Coates, *Women Talk*, 1996. On women's storytelling and group storytelling, see also Langelliur and Peterson, "Spinstorying."

the world, what she has done will be told in her memory" (13:10; 14:9). And finally it anchors the first line: "The beginning of the good news of Jesus Christ" (1:1)—where it later becomes the cause of certain books being called gospels. I suggest that all these provide a frame for Mark, built from Jesus' opening announcement of "the good news of God: . . . God's kingdom is arriving! Repent and trust the good news!" (1:14–15) Is the frame present or not yet present when the story is being told in its inner circle? Is the frame supplied by the wider circle of women who overhear the story and insist on telling it to others—yet they leave the end in respect for the story they overheard? Or is it someone later, even the one who transcribes the story, who frames it as "the good news of Jesus Christ," the mystery now revealed? Or, finally, is it the one who adds the long ending, including the words, "Go into all the world to proclaim the good news to every creature" (16:15)? I leave that open. What matters is to begin to hear Mark as a tradition, not of one man, but of those who tell it.

# 19

## Findings in the Case

In this study I have developed the evidence for Mark as a composition in performance by working backward from the Mark in our hands to the modern Greek edition, its early manuscripts, its transition into Greek, and the Aramaic story. This story is a report told in spoken but special language and carried in traditional scenes about a prophet's sign that sparked a great conflict, Jesus' news of God's kingdom arriving. To conclude the study I will run the film forward, so to speak, and summarize the findings at each stage, from the language and scenes and story patterns of this tradition to its Aramaic, Greek, manuscript, and present performances, in order to show the thesis that emerges if the evidence in this study is accepted.

## The Language[1]

In the beginning there is news, a rumor being told. It is spoken in short bursts of speech using the simplest words, phrases that follow each other in a fast and rough stream, linked if at all by "and," and telling what happened next. These are the "intonation units" that Wallace Chafe finds in his discourse analysis of how human speech is different from written language, and that Edgar Bakker says explain the distinct half-line units of the *Iliad*.[2] But as the *Iliad* shaped these into a "special speech" through traditional references and rhythms, the news in Galilee is shaped into "special speech" through the traditional references and

1. See chapters 6–8.
2. Bakker, *Poetry in Speech*, 35–53.

rhythms of its people. The reference to God's kingdom evokes Israel's monarchy, the prophet evokes Moses' promise to send one "from among your own people" (Deut 18:15), the sign evokes a whole history of God-given signs, and together they evoke God's anticipated deliverance of the people from their enemies. As for its traditional rhythm, the pattern in Israel is not metric but a doubling or parallelism, already echoed twice in the announcement being told, "The time has come, the kingdom is arriving, repent and trust the good news" (1:15), or as Bruce Chilton translates an Aramaic retroversion from the Greek, "Finished the time and near God's kingdom: Turn and confide in the report."[3] So from the first telling, before the story has half happened, this news takes the "special speech" of tradition.

## The Scenes[4]

Because the story is a whole report from the beginning, its development cannot be seen as a collecting of pieces until its gets its full size and identity. Rather, the story at any time is rich or simple depending on the context in which it is told. In Jesus' lifetime, his sign may already be confirmed with scenes of his exorcisms, controversies, or healings. These scenes highlight not only the crowds coming, who raise the threat of a ruler's suppression, but they also show how the announcement of God's kingdom provokes conflicts with unclean spirits, legal authorities, and people's fear that threatens their trust in the good news.

Telling these stories draws on traditions from many quarters— from the way other Jews are telling exorcism stories in an occupied province, from the practice of besting an opponent in controversy by asking the counter-question that offers the answer, and from revived stories about Elijah and Elisha. Nothing is told in a new way, since the polemics involved are long-standing and already on the table. The same applies concerning the visions of a voice from heaven and the vision of the mortal coming on the clouds. God is active again in ways heard before and expectations are high. Even the death of the prophet does not end the story, because he is vindicated and goes ahead of those who

---

3. Chilton et al., *Comparative Handbook*, 81–83.
4. See chapters 9–11.

follow. But there is a time of not telling that must not be forgotten, when fears overwhelmed and the account was heard in closed circles.

## The Story Pattern[5]

What focuses an account of so many parts and what keeps people telling it is the fact that the story is not over. God's kingdom is yet to come in power. But the conflict with destroying forces has been engaged, and there are indications everywhere of new life: "No one who left home or brothers or sisters or mother or father or children or lands . . . will not receive homes and brothers and sisters and mothers and children and lands with persecutions, and in the age to come eternal life" (10:29–30). Hardship is built in to the program, but also that big family with homes and lands, and enduring life. There is no question that trust in this good news continues to be tested, as the healing stories show. Everything depends on continued telling of the story, a telling that adopts the familiar oral five-step pattern about a prophet's sign: Jesus appears at the crisis in John's repentance movement, he announces the sign of God's kingdom arriving, he does feats that draw great crowds, the authorities become afraid and the ruler kills him, but God raises him up and sends him ahead. The story takes life and spreads through favored tellers who can speak with the voice of those who seek help, with the voice of Jesus in response, and with the voice of God who makes life from death.

## Told in Greek[6]

When the story is heard not only in the Aramaic-speaking villages and towns but also in the cities of Palestine and Syria, it enters a bilingual culture. Though many families speak Aramaic or another local language around home, they also speak Greek on the street and at the market. Linguists say that balanced bilinguality occurs only where cultural identification has become double, where many people in certain neighborhoods have two mother tongues.[7] It is such people that provide the bridge for the story of Jesus in Mark to become told in Greek.

---

5. See chapters 12–14.
6. See chapter 5.
7. Hamers and Blanc, *Bilinguality and Bilingualism*, 20–54.

When people who speak only Greek begin to appear in gatherings where Mark is being told, there will be tellings in Greek, retaining fewer and then fewer words in Aramaic that give contact with Jesus' spoken voice. This is not translation in the sense that books are translated but in the way that bilingual people can hear something in one language and speak it in another with the appropriate colloquial expressions and traditional allusions. This is possible because in these cities Israel's culture has already become bilingual, with kosher food sold in Greek and some synagogues that read the Torah in Greek. The Aramaic Mark will continue to be told, being replaced by the Greek telling only in those cities where Greek is taken as the cosmopolitan language appropriate for a tradition that aims to reach all people (11:17; 13:10; 14:9).

## Told in Writing[8]

Though some have projected that Mark is first written when a major change or crisis causes people to fear for its preservation, this is unlikely. In times of turmoil and mass movements of people, as occurred during the Jewish War from 66–73 CE, people are not buying long sheets of papyrus and vials of ink in order to spend weeks producing bulky scrolls to carry when fleeing the city or being sold into slavery. It is the oral story that is eminently portable, and it does spread as people scatter. Mark is more likely written down when communities who tell it in Greek gain literate participants who want to place Jesus' story in a case with their scroll of Isaiah or donate it to a benefactor. Or it is possible that skilled storytellers diminish as Israel's traditions become more distant and a script is sought to train the literate to speak it. Yet in the Roman East only 3 percent to at most 10 percent of the people are readers.[9] And they themselves seldom read to any extent, because Greek is written in lines of capital letters without any spacing between words or sentences and without headings or paragraphs, making comprehension of a new document impossible at first sight.[10] Therefore writing is not used for communication except where distance makes speech impossible, and

8. See chapters 3–4.

9. Harris, *Ancient Literacy*; Bar-Ilan, "Illiteracy in the Land of Israel," 35–38, 55–56; Hezser, *Jewish Literacy*, 34–36, 496.

10. Botha, "New Testament Texts," 627; Morrison, "Stabilizing the Text," 242–74.

such letters are composed in speech and delivered in speech after being practiced. But written texts have certain symbolic and pedagogical functions that do eventually lead to written copies of traditions that continue to be performed without consulting the script.[11]

And how can a performance like Mark become written? Writing cannot keep up the pace necessary to transcribe a live performance of Mark, and a teller has no reason to write down what people can better hear spoken.[12] It is possible that long-time hearers of the story take in mind to write it, claiming legitimacy by adhering as closely as possible to the tradition as told. Yet a writer will allow himself—and the literate were almost all men—to shape the story for those he expects to be hearing it read aloud, as the tellers before him have shaped it for their hearers. This means that the writer functions as a surrogate teller and his work is best called scribal re-performance.[13] Meanwhile performing continues, at first without recourse to the text but later in touch with it.

## Told in Copying[14]

The early manuscripts that survive from the scribes of Mark are very few. There is only one fragmentary papyrus from the third century ($P^{45}$), and each later papyrus is quite distinct from the others. The usual solution is to accept the text of Mark found in a full Bible manuscript from the fourth century (Vaticanus: B) as our best, because, in the case of Luke and John, a very similar third century papyrus has been found ($P^{75}$), suggesting a late second century source for both.[15] Our Greek editions and English translations are based on this Vaticanus text—an elegant parchment codex of the whole Bible apparently ordered by the Emperor Constantine from the church historian and bishop Eusebius, an artifact very far removed from a first century oral telling of Mark.

Recently it has been proposed by scholars in textual criticism that it would be more accurate to translate not one reconstruction of Mark

---

11. Nagy, *Poetry as Performance*, 107–14.

12. Lord, *Singer of Tales*, 126–29.

13. Doane, "Oral Texts," 80–82.

14. See chapter 2.

15. Martini, *Il problema*, 149; Parker, *Introduction*, 120–23; Barbara Aland, "Die Münsteraner Arbeit."

built largely on this text but four or five early manuscripts of Mark.[16] Then people who do not have access to the manuscripts could realize how different they are from each other and begin to ask where these differences come from. The story is still recognizable but especially at its beginning and end shows significant variations. The implication is that the differences are not all errors coming from faulty transmission of one original text but are different forms of Mark that developed as different tellings of Mark were written down, and as these in turn were copied for different readers. This means that interpretation must take into account the idea that Mark is not a single author's published text but a performance tradition, one that continues being performed by hand as well as by voice long after it is first transcribed. Performance survives as long as the story is being shaped for new audiences.

## Told Today[17]

This brings us to our own context. Because of the status of the biblical canon in the Christian church since the fourth century and because of the formative role of the Christian church in Western culture, any appeal to biblical texts takes on the weight of that tradition, both in the positive and negative sense of the term. In the twenty-first century on the west coast of the United States where the extremes of secularism and of conservative Christianity are both strident and not speaking to each other, this weight needs to be acknowledged. I argue that we do wrong either to petrify the text as a measure of unchanging truth or to discard it as irrelevant to the contemporary world. I propose instead that we have in Mark a tradition composed in the telling that should function today in a way appropriate for a performance text. It is in fact arguable that even in the more than a millennium and a half that Mark has been part of a closed canon, it has continued to be reconstructed—though in the guise of seeking the original text, and interpreted—though in the margins rather than the lines of that text. Ever since Mark was named a source of Matthew and Luke in the nineteenth century, it has been heavily studied with their sayings source "Q" in the search for the earliest Jesus traditions. More recently it has been read as a literary creation,

16. Parker, *Living Text*, 207–13.; Amphoux, "Une edition 'plurielle' de Marc."
17. See chapter 1.

and now is being performed on stage to recover the early experience of its oral delivery and reception. All along it has been interpreted in Christian communities as a guide for faith and practice. What more can be contributed by recognizing it, not chiefly as a source for earliest history, a canon for deducing theology, a literary gem or dud, or a drama for production, but as a story being shaped in the telling?

For one thing, we find an indispensable role for very different kinds of people in the telling and hearing of this text. Probably it was always the case that there are those tellers of Mark whose attention is on the preservation of the tradition and the forms that sustain it. Though they can err on the side of literalism, they do keep the tradition rooted in its deep past and nourished by those roots. Also, there were and are those tellers of Mark who make the new connections between the tradition and the present exigency, shaping its weight to bear down at the points of our greatest personal and social needs. Granted that a very different telling will appear under the evangelist's tent and in the French literary circles of Julia Kristeva. But as long as neither group leaves the telling of the story to the other, each of these Marks will be heard to our benefit. Were they to hear each other, tradition might recover direction and direction might recover tradition.

Second, Mark composed in performance speaks specifically to our increasingly inter-faith world. This is the gospel where Jesus says, "Only God is good," and, reciting the *Shema*, "The Lord our God, the Lord is One"; also "Everything is possible with God"; and, in Jesus' address to God, "Not what I want, but what you want." Yet we define ourselves by acclamations about Jesus that alienate others who believe in God and consider ourselves justified in doing this. Can Mark be told in a way that challenges Christians in a world we no longer dominate to follow Jesus in announcing God's kingdom?

Finally, scholars of oral tradition have long observed how the stories they study carry a society's ideals and values. Albert Lord goes one step further and says that these narratives hold clues how the problems the stories consider crucial for a people may be met and accepted if not solved.[18] The stories function in the people's task to envision where they need to go and how to get there through its narrative rhetoric. In a recent collection on the politics of orality, Nathalia King wrote an analysis of four variant tellings of the Mwindo epic from different po-

18. Lord, *The Singer Resumes*, 105–6.

litical regions in a contemporary small African society.[19] Each version of the story deals with their crucial social and political problem of how a tribal chief can arrange a peaceful succession that nevertheless does not allow an incompetent oldest son of his to take control. The stories all involve the chief's dealing with his wives and newborn children and present several quite different and dramatic scenarios. She argues that these are told in a communal context that allows the expression of the social contract between chief and people, but also allows for discussion and adaptations of that contract in the flexibility of the stories being told.

The question this puts to the Markan performance tradition is whether telling Mark is a way to express the social contract between the people who repeat it, and in turn whether the tradition is limber enough to allow for debating the modes and terms of this contract by different tellings of the story. Or can we hear the four canonical gospels dealing differently with some major *crux* for the communities engaged in following Jesus after the Jewish War—and potentially in times since? Where there is no social or political issue at stake, telling is strictly entertainment, and this is clearly not the case. But to what extent might gospel-telling today be realized as a mode of debate?

I asked at the start of chapter 16 if the process of telling Mark might help us address a broad human question: Could an affirmation that the world can be transformed in the present be sustained on the basis of a clear experience of this happening in the past and a sharp vision of its coming in the future? The performance tradition of Mark can be brought as evidence. The arrival of God's kingdom in power remains ahead, sustained by the projected vision of the mortal coming in God's glory to gather all those not ashamed of Jesus. There Jesus will drink again and celebrate with them. The story also brings vivid accounts from the past of Jesus' powerful acts on peoples' behalf and his constant interchange with the authorities by appeals to proverbial wisdom and Scripture. All this is told in ways drawn from the people's tradition, and each scene is shaped for the audience to whom the story is told. If it is not possible through such telling for people to repent their fears and to trust that the world can be transformed and God's kingdom arrive, how would it be possible?

19. King, "'Summoning Together All the People.'"

# Bibliography

Ahn, Byong-Mu. "The Transmitters of the Jesus-Event." *Christian Conference of Asia Bulletin of the Commission on Theological Concerns* 5.3 (1984) 30–39.

Aland, Barbara. "Die Münsteraner Arbeit am Text des Neuen Testments und ihr Beitrag für die frühe Überlieferung des 2. Jahrhunderts: Eine methodologische Betrachtung." In *Gospel Traditions in the Second Century: Origins, Recensions, Text, and Transmission*, edited by William L. Petersen, 61–67. Christianity and Judaism in Antiquity 3. Notre Dame: University of Notre Dame Press, 1990.

Aland, Kurt. "Der Schluss des Markusevangeliums." In *L'Évangile selon Marc: Tradition et Rédaction*, edited by M. Sabbe, 435–70. Rev. ed. BETL 34. Leuven: Leuven University Press, 1988.

Aland, Kurt, and Barbara Aland. *The Text of the New Testament: An Introduction to the Critical Editions and to the Theory and Practice of Modern Textual Criticism.* Translated by Erroll F. Rhodes. Leiden: Brill, 1987.

Alexander, Elizabeth Shanks. *Transmitting Mishnah: The Shaping Influence of Oral Tradition.* Cambridge: Cambridge University Press, 2006.

Amphoux, Christian-Bernard. "Une edition 'plurielle' de Marc." In *The New Testament Text in Early Christianity: Proceedings of the Lille Colloquium, July 2000*, edited by Christian-Bernard Amphoux and J. Keith Elliott, 69–80. Histoire du texte biblique 6. Lausanne: Zèbre, 2003.

———. "Evangile de Marc. Les types de texte dans les langues anciennes." *Mélanges de science religieuse* 62.2 (2005) 5–15.

———. "Schéma d'histoire du texte grec du Nouveau Testament." *New Testament Textual Research Update* 3 (1995) 41–46.

Assmann, Jan. *Religion and Cultural Memory: Ten Studies.* Translated by Rodney Livingstone. Cultural Memory in the Present. Stanford: Stanford University Press, 2006.

Auerbach, Eric. *Mimesis: The Representation of Reality in Western Literature.* Translated by Willard R. Trask. 1953. Reprinted, Garden City, NY: Doubleday, 1957.

Aune, David E., editor. *Greco-Roman Literature and the New Testament: Selected Forms and Genres.* Sources for Biblical Study 21. Atlanta: Scholars, 1988.

———. *The New Testament in Its Literary Environment.* Library of Early Christianity 8. Philadelphia: Westminster, 1987.

Bailey, Kenneth E. "Informal Controlled Oral Tradition and the Synoptic Gospels." *Asia Journal of Theology* 5 (1991) 34–54.

———. "Middle Eastern Oral Tradition and the Synoptic Gospels." *ExpTim* 106 (1995) 363–67.

# Bibliography

Bakker, Egbert J. "How Oral is Oral Composition?" In *Signs of Orality: The Oral Tradition and Its Influence in the Greek and Roman World*, edited by E. Anne MacKay, 29–47. Mnemosyne Supplements 188. Leiden: Brill, 1999.

———. *Poetry in Speech: Orality and Homeric Discourse*. Myth and Poetics. Ithaca, NY: Cornell University Press, 1997.

———. *Pointing at the Past: From Formula to Performance in Homeric Poetics*. Hellenic Studies 12. Washington DC: Center for Hellenistic Studies, 2005.

———. "The Study of Homeric Discourse." In *A New Companion to Homer*, edited by Ian Morris and Barry Powell, 284–304. Mnemosyne Supplements 163. Leiden: Brill, 1997.

Baltzer, Klaus. *Die Biographie der Propheten*. Neukirchen-Vluyn: Neukirchener, 1975.

Bar-Ilan, Meir. "Illiteracy in the Land of Israel in the First Centuries C.E." In *Essays in the Social Scientific Study of Judaism and Jewish Society*, edited by Simcha Fishbane and Stuart Schoenfeld, 2:46–61. Hoboken, NJ: Ktav, 1992.

Bascom, William. "The Forms of Folklore: Prose Narratives." *JAF* 78 (1965) 3–20.

Bateson, Gregory. *Steps to an Ecology of Mind*. New York: Ballantine, 1972.

Bauckham, Richard. "The Eyewitnesses in the Gospel of Mark," *Svensk Exegetisk Årsbok* 74 (2009) 19–39.

———. *Jesus and the Eyewitnesses: The Gospel as Eyewitness Testimony*. Grand Rapids: Eerdmans, 2006.

Baum, Armin D. *Der mündliche Faktor und seine Bedeutung für die synoptische Frage: Analogien aus der antiken Literatur, der Experimentalpsychologie, der Oral Poetry-Forschung und den rabbinischen Traditionswesen*. Texte und Arbeiten zum neutestamentlichen Zeitalter 49. Tübingen: Franke, 2008.

Baumann, Richard. *Verbal Art as Performance*. Rowley, MA: Newbury House, 1977.

Belo, Fernando. *A Materialist Reading of the Gospel of Mark*. Translated by Matthew J. O'Connell. Maryknoll, NY: Orbis, 1981.

Ben-Amos, Dan. "Analytic Categories and Ethnic Genres." In *Folklore in Context: Essays*, 38–64. New Delhi: South Asian Publishers, 1982.

———. "The Concept of Genre in Folklore." In *Folklore in Context: Essays*, 65–85. New Delhi: South Asian Publishers, 1982.

———. *Folklore in Context: Essays*. New Delhi: South Asian Publishers, 1982.

———. "Narrative Forms in the Haggadah: Structural Analysis." Ph.D. diss., Indiana University, 1976.

Ben-Amos, Dan, and Kenneth S. Goldstein, editors. *Folklore: Performance and Communication*. Approaches to Semiotics 40. The Hague: Mouton, 1975.

Bernstein, Basil. "Elaborated and Restricted Codes: Their Social Origins and Some Consequences." *American Anthropologist* 66/6 (1964) 55–69.

Black, Matthew. *An Aramaic Approach to the Gospels and Acts*. Oxford: Clarendon, 1967.

Botha, Pieter J. J. "Greco-Roman Literacy as Setting for New Testament Writings." *Neot* 26 (1992) 195–215.

———. "Mark's Story as Oral Traditional Literature: Rethinking the Transmission of Some Traditions about Jesus." *Hervormde Teologiese Studies* 47 (1991) 304–31.

———. "Mark's Story of Jesus and the Search for Virtue." In *The Rhetorical Analysis of Scripture: Essays from the 1995 London Conference*, edited by Stanley E. Porter and Thomas H. Olbricht, 156–84. JSNTSup 146. Sheffield: Sheffield Academic, 1997.

———. "New Testament Texts in the Context of Reading Practices of the Roman Period: The Role of Memory and Performance." *Scriptura* 90 (2005) 621–40.

———. "*ouk estin hōde* . . . Mark's Stories of Jesus' Tomb and History." *Neot* 23 (1989) 195–218.

———. "The Social Dynamics of the Early Transmission of the Jesus Tradition." *Neot* 27 (1993) 205–31.

Bultmann, Rudolf. *The History of the Synoptic Tradition.* Translated by John Marsh. New York: Harper & Row, 1968. German rev. ed., 1931.

———. *Jesus and the Word.* Translated by Louise Pettibone Smith and Erminie Huntress. New York: Scribner, 1934. Reprinted, 1989.

Byrskog, Samuel. *Story as History, History as Story: The Gospel Tradition in the Context of Ancient Oral History.* WUNT 123. Tübingen: Mohr/Siebeck, 2000.

Carr, David M. *Writing on the Tablet of the Heart: Origins of Scripture and Literature.* Oxford: Oxford University Press, 2005.

Chafe, Wallace. "The Deployment of Consciousness." In *Pear Stories: Cognative, Cultural and Linguistic Aspects of Narrative Production,* edited by Wallace Chafe, 9–50. Norwood, NJ: Ablex, 1980.

———. *Discourse, Consciousness and Time: The Flow and Displacement of Conscious Experience in Speaking and Writing.* Chicago: University of Chicago Press, 1994.

Charlesworth, James H., editor. *Old Testament Pseudepigrapha.* 2 vols. Garden City, NY: Doubleday, 1983, 1985.

Chilton, Bruce. *Pure Kingdom: Jesus' Vision of God.* Grand Rapids: Eerdmans, 1996.

Chilton, Bruce, Darrell Bock, Daniel M. Gartner, Jacob Neusner, Lawrence A. Schiffman and Daniel Oden. *A Comparative Handbook to the Gospel of Mark: Comparisons with Pseudepigrapha, The Qumran Scrolls, and Rabbinic Literature.* Leiden: Brill, 2010.

Clanchy, Michael T. "Looking Back from the Invention of Printing." In *Literacy in Historical Perspective,* edited by Daniel P. Resnick, 7–22. Washington, DC: Library of Congress, 1983.

Clark, Kenneth W. "The Theological Relevance of Textual Variation in Current Criticism of the Greek New Testament." *JBL* 85 (1966) 1–16.

Claussen, Carsten, and Jörg Frey, editors. *Jesus und die Archäologie Galiläas.* Biblisch-theologische Studien 87. Neukirchen-Vluyn: Neukirchener, 2008.

Coates, Jennifer. *Women Talk: Conversations between Women Friends.* Oxford: Blackwell, 1996.

Collins, Adela Yarbro. "Establishing the Text: Mark 1:1." In *Texts and Contexts: Biblical Texts in Their Textual and Situational Contexts—Essays in Honor of Lars Hartman,* edited by Tord Fornberg and David Hellholm, 111–27. Oslo: Scandinavian University Press, 1995.

———. *Mark: A Commentary.* Hermeneia. Minneapolis: Fortress, 2007.

Colwell, Ernest C. *Studies in Methodology in Textual Criticism of the New Testament.* Grand Rapids: Eerdmans, 1969.

Courlander, Harold. *A Treasury of Afro-American Folklore.* New York: Smithmark, 1976, 1996.

Crossan, John Dominic. *The Historical Jesus: The Life of a Mediterranean Jewish Peasant.* San Francisco: Harper, 1991.

D'Angelo, Mary Rose. "Re-Reading Resurrection." *Toronto Journal of Theology* 16 (2000) 109–29.

Davis, Adam. "Agon and Gnomon: Forms and Functions of the Anglo-Saxon Riddle." In *De Gustibus: Essays for Alain Renoir,* edited by John Miles Foley, 110–50. Albert Bates Lord Studies in Oral Tradition 11. New York: Garland, 1992.

Deissmann, Adolf. *Bible Studies.* Translated by A. Grieve. 1901. Reprinted, Eugene, OR: Wipf & Stock, 2004.

———. *Light from the Ancient East.* Translated by Lionel R. M. Strachan. 1910. Reprinted, Eugene, OR: Wipf & Stock, 2004.

———. *Philology of the Greek Bible: Its Present and Future.* Translated by Lionel R. M. Strachan. London: Hodder & Stoughton, 1908.

Derrenbacker, R. A. Jr. *Ancient Compositional Practices and the Synoptic Problem.* BETL 186. Leuven: Leuven University Press, 2005.

Dewey, Joanna. "From Storytelling to Written Text: The Loss of Early Christian Women's Voices." *BTB* 26 (1996) 71–78.

———. "The Gospel of Mark as an Oral-Aural Event." In *The New Literary Criticism and the New Testament,* edited by Elizabeth Struthers Malbon and Edgar V. McKnight, 145–63. JSNTSup 109. Sheffield: Sheffield Academic, 1994.

———. *Markan Public Debate: Literary Technique, Concentric Structure and Theology in Mark 2:1—3:6.* SBL Dissertation Series 48. Chico, CA: Scholars, 1979.

———. "Oral Methods of Structuring Narrative in Mark." *Int* 43 (1989) 32–44.

———. "The Survival of Mark's Gospel: A Good Story?" *JBL* 123 (2004) 495–507.

———. "What Did the Audiences of Mark Hear?" forthcoming.

———. "Women in the Synoptic Gospels: Seen but not Heard." *BTB* 27 (1997) 53–60.

Dibelius, Martin. *The Formation of the Gospel Tradition.* Translated by Bertram Lee Woolf. New York: Scribner, 1935.

Doane, A. N. "Oral Texts, Intertexts, and Intratexts: Editing Old English." In *Influence and Intertextuality in Literary History,* edited by Jay Clayton and Eric Rothstein, 75–113. Madison: University of Wisconsin Press, 1991.

Dodd, C. H. "The Appearances of the Risen Christ: An Essay in Form-Criticism of the Gospels." In *Studies in the Gospels: Essays in Memory of R. H. Lightfoot,* edited by D. E. Nineham, 9–35. Oxford: Blackwell, 1955.

Dorson, Richard M. *Folklore: Selected Essays.* Bloomington: Indiana University Press, 1972.

DuBois, Thomas A. *Finnish Folk Poetry and the Kalevala.* New Perspectives in Folklore 1. New York: Garland, 1995.

Dundes, Alan. "Text Texture and Context." *Southern Folklore Quarterly* 20 (1965) 251–61. Reprinted in *Interpreting Folklore,* 20–32. Bloomington: Indiana University Press, 1980.

Dunn, James D. G. "Altering the Default Setting: Re-envisaging the Early Transmission of the Jesus Tradition." *NTS* 49 (2003) 139–75. Reprinted with gospel texts in English in Dunn, *A New Perspective on Jesus: What the Quest for the Historical Jesus Missed,* 79–125. Grand Rapids: Baker Academic, 2005.

———. *Jesus Remembered.* Christianity in the Making 1. Grand Rapids: Eerdmans, 2003.

———. "Living Tradition." In *What Is It That the Scripture Says? Essays in Biblical Interpretation, Translation and Reception in Honor of Henry Wansborough OSB,* edited by Philip McCosker, 275–89. Library of New Testament Studies 316. London: T. & T. Clark, 2006.

Ehrman, Bart D. *The Orthodox Corruption of Scripture: The Effect of Early Christological Controversies on the Text of the New Testament.* Oxford: Oxford University Press, 1993.

Elliott, J. K. "Can We Recover the Original Text of the New Testament? An Examination of the Role of Thoroughgoing Ecclecticism." In *Essays and Studies in New Testament Textual Criticism*, 17–44. Estudios de filologa neotestamentaria 3. Córdoba: El Almendro, 1992.

———. "Mark 1.1–3—A Later Addition to the Gospel?" *NTS* 46 (2000) 584–88.

———. "T. C. Skeat on the Dating and Origin of Codex Vaticanus." In *The Collected Biblical Writings of T. C. Skeat*, introduced and edited by J. K. Elliott, 281–94. NovTSup 113. Leiden: Brill, 2004.

Elliott, J. K., Christian-Bernard Amphoux and Jean-Claude. Haelewyck. "The Marc Multilingual Project." *Filologia Neotestamentaria* 15 (2002) 3–17.

Epp, Eldon J. "Ancient Texts and Versions of the New Testament." In *The New Interpreters Bible: A Commentary in Twelve Volumes*, edited by Leander E. Keck et al., 8:1–11. Nashville: Abingdon, 1995.

———. "The Significance of the Papyri for Determining the Nature of the New Testament Text in the Second Century: A Dynamic View of Textual Transmission." In *Gospel Traditions in the Second Century: Origins, Recensions, Text, and Transmission*, edited by William L. Petersen, 84–103. Christianity and Judaism in Antiquity 3. Notre Dame: University of Notre Dame Press, 1990.

Eusebius. *Eusebius, Life of Constantine: Introduction, Translation and Commentary.* Edited by Averil Cameron and Stuart G. Hill. Oxford: Clarendon, 1999.

Fine, Elizabeth C. *The Folklore Text: From Performance to Print.* Bloomington: Indiana University Press, 1994.

Fine, Gary. "Rumor, Trust and Civil Society: Collective Memory and Cultures of Judgment." *Diogenes* 54 (2007) 5–18.

Fish, Stanley. *Is There a Text in This Class? The Authority of Interpretative Communities.* Cambridge: Harvard University Press, 1980.

Fisher, Raymond. "The Empty Tomb Story in Mark: its Origin and Significance." *Neot* 33 (1999) 59–79.

Fishman, Joshua A., editor. *The Sociology of Language*, vol. 1 in *Advances in the Sociology of Language*. Contributions to the Sociology of Language 3. The Hague: Mouton, 1971.

Fitzmyer, Joseph A. "The Languages of Palestine in the First Century A.D." In *The Language of the New Testament*, edited by Stanley E. Porter, 126–62. Sheffield: Sheffield Academic, 1991. (Orig. pub. *CBQ* 32 [1970] 501–31.)

Foley, John Miles. *How to Read an Oral Poem.* Urbana: University of Illinois Press, 2002.

———. *Homer's Traditional Art.* University Park: Pennsylvania State University Press, 1999.

———. *Immanent Art: From Structure to Meaning in Traditional Oral Epic.* Bloomington: Indiana University Press, 1991.

———, editor. *Oral Tradition in Literature: Interpretation in Context.* Congress of Missouri Oral Literature Symposium, 1984. Colombia: University of Missouri Press, 1986.

———. *The Singer of Tales in Performance.* Voices in Performance and Text. Bloomington: Indiana University Press, 1995.

# Bibliography

Fredriksen, Paula. *From Jesus to Christ: The Origins of the New Testament Images of Jesus.* New Haven: Yale University Press, 1988.

Freyne, Seán. *Galilee from Alexander the Great to Hadrian: A Study of Second Temple Judaism.* Wilmington, DE: Glazier, 1980.

———. *Galilee, Jesus and the Gospels: Literary Approaches and Historical Investigations.* Philadelphia: Fortress, 1988.

Gaventa, Beverly R., and Patrick D. Miller, editors. *The Ending of Mark and the Ends of God: Essays in Memory of Donald Harrisville Juel.* Louisville: Westminster John Knox, 2005.

Gilfillian Upton, Bridget. *Hearing Mark's Ending: Listening to Ancient Popular Texts through Speech Act Theory.* Biblical Interpretation Series 79. Leiden: Brill, 2006.

Ginsberg, Louis. *Legends of the Jews.* 7 vols. Baltimore: Johns Hopkins University Press, 1928. Reprinted, 1998.

Gray, Rebecca. *Prophetic Figures in Late Second Temple Jewish Palestine: The Evidence from Josephus.* New York: Oxford University Press, 1993.

Greeven, Heinrich. *Textkritik des Markusevangeliums.* Edited by Eberhard Güting. Theologie, Forschung und Wissenschaft 11. Münster: Lit, 2005.

Greimas, A. J. *On Meaning: Selected Writings in Semiotic Theory.* Translation by Paul J. Perron and Frank H. Collins. Theory and History of Literature 38. Minneapolis: University of Minnesota Press, 1987.

———. *Structural Semantics: An Attempt at a Method.* Translation by Daniele McDowell, Ronald Schleifer, and Alan Velie. Lincoln: University of Nebraska Press, 1983.

Haelewyck, J. C., and S. Arbache. "Presentation." *Mélanges de science religieuse* 62/2 (2005) 3–4.

Halliday, Michael A. K. *Explorations in the Functions of Language.* Explorations in Language Study. New York: Elsevier North-Holland, 1977.

Hamers, Josiane, and Michel Blanc. *Bilinguality and Bilingualism.* Rev. ed. Cambridge: Cambridge University Press, 1989.

Harris, William V. *Ancient Literacy.* Cambridge: Harvard University Press, 1989.

Haverly, Thomas P. "Oral Traditional Literature and the Composition of Mark's Gospel." Ph.D. diss., University of Edinburgh, 1983.

Hearon, Holly E. *The Mary Magdalene Tradition: Witness and Counter-Witness in Early Christian Communities.* Collegeville, MN: Liturgical, 2004.

———. "Storytelling in Oral and Written Media Contexts of the Ancient Mediterranean World." In *Jesus, the Voice, and the Text: Beyond 'The Oral and the Written Gospel',* edited by Tom Thatcher, 89–110. Waco, TX: Baylor University Press, 2008.

Hearon, Holly E., and Linda M. Maloney. "Listen to the Voices of the Women." In *Distant Voices Drawing Near: Essays in Honor of Antoinette Clark Wire,* edited by Holly E. Hearon, 33–53. Collegeville, MN: Liturgical, 2004.

Hengel, Martin. "Das Begräbnis Jesu bei Paulus und die leibliche Auferstehung aus dem Grabe." In *Auferstehung Resurrection: The Fourth Durham-Tübingen Research Symposium,* edited by Friedrich Avemarie and Hermann Lichtenberger, 119–83. WUNT 135. Tübingen: Mohr/Siebeck, 1999.

Hezser, Catherine. *Jewish Literacy in Roman Palestine.* Text and Studies in Ancient Judaism 81. Tübingen: Mohr/Siebeck, 2001.

# Bibliography

Honko, Lauri. "Text as Process and Practice: The Textualization of Oral Epics." In *The Textualization of Oral Epics*, edited by Lauri Honko, 3–54. Trends in Linguistics: Studies and Monographs 128. Berlin: de Gruyter, 2000.

———, editor. *Textualization of Oral Epics*. Trends in Linguistics: Studies and Monographs 128. Berlin: de Gruyter, 2000.

Honko, Lauri, and Anneli Honko. "Multiforms in Epic Composition." In *The Epic: Oral and Written*, edited by Lauri Honko, Jawaharlal Handoo, and John Miles Foley, 31–79. Mysore, India: Central Institute of Indian Languages, 1998.

Honko, Lauri, Jawaharlal Handoo, and John Miles Foley, editors. *The Epic: Oral and Written*. Mysore, India: Central Institute of Indian Languages, 1998.

Hooker, Morna D. *Endings: Invitations to Discipleship*. London: SCM, 2003.

Hopkins, Dwight N., and George C. L. Cummings. *Cut Loose Your Stammering Tongue: Black Theology in the Slave Narratives*. 2nd ed. Louisville: Westminster John Knox, 2003.

Horsley, Richard. *Galilee: History, Politics, People*. Valley Forge, PA: Trinity, 1995.

———. *Hearing the Whole Story: The Politics of Plot in Mark's Gospel*. Louisville: Westminster John Knox, 2001.

———. *Jesus and the Spiral of Violence: Popular Jewish Resistance in Roman Palestine*. 1987. Reprinted, Minneapolis: Fortress, 1993.

———. "A Prophet Like Moses and Elijah: Popular Memory and Cultural Patterns in Mark." In *Performing the Gospel: Orality, Memory and Mark: Essays Dedicated to Werner Kelber*, edited by Richard Horsley, Jonathan A. Draper, and John Miles Foley, 166–90. Minneapolis: Fortress, 2006.

Horsley, Richard, with Jonathan A. Draper. *Whoever Hears You Hears Me: Prophets, Performance, and Tradition in Q*. Harrisburg, PA: Trinity, 1999.

Horsley, Richard, Jonathan A. Draper, and John Miles Foley, editors. *Performing the Gospel, Orality, Memory and Mark: Essays Dedicated to Werner Kelber*. Minneapolis: Fortress, 2006.

Hurtado, Larry W. *Text-Critical Methodology and the Pre-Caesarean Text: Codex W in the Gospel of Mark*. Grand Rapids: Eerdmans, 1981.

Hymes, Dell. *"In Vain I Tried to Tell You": Essays in Native American Poetics*. Studies in Native American Literature 1. Philadelphia: University of Pennsylvania Press, 1981.

———. "Sung Epics and Native American Ethnopoetics." In *The Epic: Oral and Written*, edited by Lauri Honko, Jawaharlal Handoo and John Miles Foley, 291–342. Mysore, India: Central Institute of Indian Languages, 1998.

———. "Tonkawa Poetics: John Rush Buffalo's 'Coyote and Eagle's Daughter.'" In *Native American Discourse: Poetics and Rhetoric*, edited by Joel Sherzer and Anthony C. Woodbury, 17–61. Cambridge Studies in Oral and Literate Culture 13. Cambridge: Cambridge University Press, 1987.

Jaffee, Martin S. "Honi the Circler in Manuscript and Memory: An Experiment in 'Reoralizing' the Talmudic Text." In *Jesus in Memory: Traditions in Oral and Scribal Perspectives*, edited by Samuel Byrskog and Werner Kelber, 87–112. Waco, TX: Baylor University Press, 2009.

———. *Torah in the Mouth: Writing and Oral Tradition in Palestinian Judaism, 200 BCE–400 CE*. Oxford: Oxford University Press, 2001.

# Bibliography

Jakobson, Roman, and Petr Begatyrev. "On the Boundary between Studies of Folklore and Literature." In *Readings in Russian Poetics: Formalist and Structuralist Views*, edited by Ladislav Matejko and Krystyna Pomorska, 91–93. Michigan Slavic Contributions 8. Ann Arbor: Michigan Slavic Publications, 1978.

Jason, Heda. "A Model for Narrative Structure in Oral Literature." In *Patterns in Oral Literature*, edited by Heda Jason and Dimitri Segal, 99–139. Chicago: Aldine, 1977.

Jensen, Minna Skafte. "Albert B. Lord's Concept of Transitional Texts in Relation to the Homeric Epics." In *Textualization of Oral Epics*, edited by Lauri Honko, 94–114. Trends in Linguistics: Studies and Monographs 128. Berlin: Gruyter, 2000.

Jolles, Andre. *Einfache Formen: Legende, Sage, Mythe, Rätsel, Spruch, Kasus, Memorabile, Märchen, Witz.* 1929. Reprinted, Tübingen: Niemeyer, 1982.

Kähler, Martin. *The So-called Historical Jesus and the Historic, Biblical Christ.* Translated by Carl Braaten. Philadelphia: Fortress, 1964; German ed. 1896.

Kapferer, Jean Noë. *Rumor: Uses, Interpretations and Images.* Translated by Bruce Fink. New Brunswick, NJ: Transaction, 1990.

Kelber, Werner H. *The Oral and the Written Gospel: The Hermeneutics of Speaking and Writing in the Synoptic Tradition, Mark, Paul and Q.* 1983. Reprinted with a new Introduction, Bloomington: Indiana University Press, 1997.

———. "The Oral-Scribal-Memorial Arts of Communication in Early Christianity." In *Jesus, the Voice and the Text: Beyond 'The Oral and the Written Gospel,'* edited by Tom Thatcher, 234–62. Waco, TX: Baylor University Press, 2008.

Kelber, Werner H., and Tom Thatcher. "'It's Not Easy to Take a Fresh Approach': Reflections on *The Oral and the Written Gospel* (An Interview with Werner Kelber)." In *Jesus, the Voice and the Text: Beyond 'The Oral and the Written Gospel,'* edited by Tom Thatcher, 27–43. Waco, TX: Baylor University Press, 2008.

Kelhoffer, James A. *Miracle and Mission: The Authentication of Missionaries and Their Message in the Longer Ending of Mark.* WUNT 2/112. Tübingen: Mohr/Siebeck, 2000.

Kenyon, Frederic G., editor. *The Gospels and Acts.* Vol. 2 of *The Chester Beatty Biblical Papyri: Descriptions and Texts of Twelve Manuscripts on Papyrus of the Greek Bible;* London: Walker, 1933–34.

King, Nathalia. "'Summoning Together all the People': Variant Tellings of the Mwindo Epic as Social and Political Deliberation." In *Politics of Orality*, edited by Craig Cooper, 39–52. Orality and Literacy in Ancient Greece 6. Leiden: Brill, 2007.

Kirk, Alan. "Manuscript Tradition as a *Tertium Quid*: Orality and Memory in Scribal Practices." In *Jesus, the Voice, and the Text: Beyond 'The Oral and the Written Gospel,'* edited by Tom Thatcher, 215–34. Waco, TX: Baylor University Press, 2008.

Klauck, Hans-Josef. *Allegorie und Allegorese in synoptischen Gleichnistexten.* Neutestamentliche Abhandlungen 13. Münster: Aschendorff, 1978.

Kleist, James. *The Gospel of Saint Mark Presented in Greek Thought-Units and Lines with a Commentary.* Milwaukee: Bruce, 1936.

Kort, Wesley A. *"Take, Read": Scripture, Textuality, and Cultural Practice.* University Park: Pennsylvania State University Press, 1996.

Kuhn, Peter. *Bat Qol, die Offenbarungsstimme in der rabbinischen Literatur: Sammlung, Übersetzung und Kurzkommentierung der Texte.* Eichstätter Materialien 13. Regensburg: Pustet, 1989.

# Bibliography

————. *Offenbarungsstimmen im Antiken Judentum: Untersuchungen zur Bat Qol und verwandten Phänomenen.* Texte und Studien zum antiken Judentum 20. Tübingen: Mohr/Siebeck, 1989.

Langelliur, Kristin M., and Eric E. Peterson. "Spinstorying: An Analysis of Women's Storytelling." In *Performance, Culture and Identity*, edited by Elizabeth C. Fine and Jean Haskell Speer, 157–79. Westport, CT: Praeger, 1992.

Levenson, Jon. *The Death and Resurrection of the Beloved Son: The Transformation of Child Sacrifice in Judaism and Christianity.* New Haven: Yale University Press, 1993.

————. *Resurrection and the Restoration of Israel: The Ultimate Victory of the God of Life.* New Haven: Yale University Press, 2006.

Levi-Strauss, Claude. *The Raw and the Cooked.* Translated by John and Doreen Weightman. Introduction to a Science of Mythology 1. New York: Harper & Row, 1969.

Lightfoot, Robert Henry. *Locality and Doctrine in the Gospels.* London: Hodder & Stoughton,, 1938.

Lindbeck, Kristen H. *Elijah and the Rabbis: Story and Theology.* New York: Colombia University Press, 2010.

Llewelyn, S. R., with R. A. Kearsley. *New Documents Illustrating Early Christianity.* Vol. 7, *A Review of the Greek Inscriptions and Papyri Published in 1982–83.* New South Wales, Australia: Ancient History Documentary Research Centre, Macquarie University, 1994.

Lohmeyer, Ernst. *Das Evangelium des Markus.* 16th ed. Kritisch-exegetischer Kommentar über das Neue Testament 2. Göttingen: Vandenhoeck & Ruprecht, 1963.

————. *Galiläa und Jerusalem.* Forschungen zur Religion und Literatur des Alten und Neuen Testaments 52. Göttingen: Vandenhoeck & Ruprecht, 1936.

Lord, Albert B. "The Gospels as Oral Traditional Literature." In *The Relationships among the Gospels: An Interdisciplinary Dialogue*, edited by William O. Walker, 33–91. Trinity University Monograph Series in Religion 5. San Antonio, TX: Trinity University Press, 1978.

————. "The Merging of Two Worlds: Oral and Written Poetry as Carriers of Ancient Values." In *Oral Tradition in Literature: Interpretation in Context*, edited by John Miles Foley, 19–64. Columbia: University of Missouri Press, 1986.

————. *The Singer of Tales.* 1960. Reprinted, New York: Atheneum, 1978. 2nd ed. with audio and video by Stephen Mitchell and Gregory Nagy; Cambridge: Harvard University Press, 2000.

————. *The Singer Resumes the Tale.* Edited by Mary Louise Lord. Ithaca, NY: Cornell University Press, 1995.

Mack, Burton L. *A Myth of Innocence: Mark and Christian Origins.* Philadelphia: Fortress, 1988.

MacKinnon, Kenneth. "Power at the Periphery: The Language Dimension—and the Case of Gaelic Scotland." *Journal of Multilingual and Multicultural Development* 5.6 (1984) 491–510.

Madigan, Daniel A. *The Qur'ān's Self-Image: Writing and Authority in Islam's Scripture.* Princeton: Princeton University Press, 2001.

Malbon, Elizabeth Struthers. *Mark's Jesus: Characterization as Narrative Christology.* Waco, TX: Baylor University Press, 2009.

# Bibliography

Martini, C. M. *Il problema della recensionalità del codice B alla luce del papiro Bodmer XIV.* Analecta Biblica 26. Rome: Pontifical Biblical Institute Press, 1966.

Marx, Jennifer Rebecca. "Bat Kol—A Divine Voice." In *Theological Terms in the Talmud: A First Book,* edited by Eugene B. Borowitz, 65–76. New York: Ilona Samek Institute at HUC—JIR, 1998.

Marxsen, Willi. *Mark the Evangelist: Studies in the Redaction History of the Gospel.* Translated by James Boyce et al. Nashville: Abingdon, 1969.

Metzger, Bruce M. *A Textual Commentary on the Greek New Testament.* London: United Bible Societies, 1971.

Minchin, Elizabeth. "The Language of Heroes and the Language of Heroines: Storytelling in Oral Traditional Epics." In *Politics of Orality,* edited by Craig Cooper, 3–38. Orality and Literacy in Ancient Greece 6. Leiden: Brill, 2007.

Mitchell, Joan. *Beyond Fear and Silence: A Feminist-Literary Approach to the Gospel of Mark.* New York: Continuum, 2001.

Morrison, Ken. "Stabilizing the Text: The Institutionalization of Knowledge in Historical and Philosophical Forms of Argument." *Canadian Journal of Sociology* 12 (1987) 242–74.

Mournet, Terence C. *Oral Tradition and Literary Dependency: Variability and Stability in the Synoptic Tradition and Q.* WUNT 2/195. Tübingen: Mohr/Siebeck, 2005.

Mussies, Gerard. "Greek as the Vehicle of Early Christianity." *NTS* 29 (1983) 356–69.

Myers, Ched. *Binding the Strong Man: A Political Reading of Mark's Story of Jesus.* Maryknoll, NY: Orbis, 1988. 2ND ED., 2008.

Nadich, Judah. *Jewish Legends of the Second Commonwealth.* Philadelphia: Jewish Publication Society of America, 1983.

Nagy, Gregory. *The Best of the Achaeans: Concepts of the Hero in Archaic Greek Poetry.* Baltimore: Johns Hopkins University Press, 1979.

———. *Poetry as Performance: Homer and Beyond.* Cambridge: Cambridge University Press, 1996.

Najman, Hindy. *Seconding Sinai: The Development of Mosaic Discourse in Second Temple Judaism.* Supplements to the Journal for the Study of Judaism 77. Leiden: Brill, 2003.

Neirynck, Frans. *Duality in Mark: Contributions to the Study of the Markan Redaction.* Rev. ed. BETL 31. Leuven: Leuven University Press, 1988.

Nestle, Eberhard, and Erwin Nestle, Barbara and Kurt Aland, Johannes Karavidopoulos, Carlo M. Martini, and Bruce M. Metzger, editors [Nestle-Aland]. *Novum Testamentum Graece.* 27th edition. Stuttgart: Deutsche Bibelgesellschaft, 1898 and 1993.

Neusner, Jacob. *Building Blocks of the Rabbinic Tradition: The Documentary Approach to the Study of Formative Judaism.* Studies in Judaism. Lanham, MD: University Press of America, 2008.

———. *Development of a Legend: Studies on the Traditions concerning Yohanan ben Zakkai.* Studia Post-Biblica 16. Leiden: Brill, 1970.

———. *A Life of Yohanan ben Zakkai: ca. 1–80 CE.* 2nd ed. Studia Post-Biblica 6. Leiden: Brill, 1970.

———. *What Exactly Did the Sages Mean by "The Oral Torah?": An Inductive Answer to the Question of Rabbinic Judaism.* South Florida in the History of Judaism 196. Atlanta: Scholars, 1999.

# Bibliography

Neuwirth, Angelika. "Psalmen—in Koran neu gelesen (Ps 104 und 136)." In *Im vollen Licht der Geschichte: Die Wissenschaft der Judentums und die Anfänge der kritischen Koranforschung*, edited by Dirk Hartwig, Walter Homolka, Michael Marx, and Angelika Neuwirth, 157–90. Ex Oriente Lux 8. Würzburg: Ergon, 2008.

———. *Studien zur Komposition der mekkanischen Suren: Die literarische Form der Koran—ein Zeugnis seiner Historizität?* 1991. Reprinted with a new introduction, Berlin: de Gruyter, 2007.

———. Two Faces of the Qur'an: *qur'an* and *mushaf*." A paper presented on April 13, 2008, at Rice University, in a conference on Orality & Literacy VII: Judaism, Christianity, Islam.

———. "Von Rezitationstext über die Liturgie zum Kanon: Zu Entstehung und Wiederauflösung der Surenkomposition im Verlauf der Entwicklung eines islamischen Kultes." In *The Qur'an as Text*, edited by Stefan Wild, 69–106. Islamic Philosophy, Theology, and Science 27. Leiden: Brill, 1996.

———. "Zur Struktur der Yūsuf-Sure." In *Studien aus Arabistik und Semitistik: Anton Spitaler zum siebzigsten Geburtstag von seinen Schülern überreicht*, edited by Werner Diem and Stefan Wild, 123–52. Wiesbaden: Harrassowitz, 1980.

Newman, Carey C. "Glory, Glorify." In *New Interpreter's Dictionary of the Bible*, edited by Katherine Doob Sakenfeld, 2:576–80. Nashville: Abingdon, 2007.

Nickelsburg, George W. E. "The Genre and Function of the Markan Passion Narrative." *HTR* 73 (1980) 153–84.

Niditch, Susan. *Folklore and the Hebrew Bible*. Guides to Biblical Scholarship. Minneapolis: Fortress, 1993.

———. *Oral World and Written Word: Ancient Israelite Literature*. Library of Ancient Israel. Louisville: Westminster John Knox, 1996.

Oakman, Douglas E. *Jesus and the Economic Questions of His Day*. Studies in the Bible and Early Christianity 8. Lewiston, NY: Mellen, 1986.

Ong, Walter. *Fighting for Life: Contest, Sexuality and Consciousness*. Ithaca, NY: Cornell University Press, 1981.

Park, Eung Chun [Eugene]. "The Problem of the APOUSIA of Jesus in the Synoptic Resurrection Traditions." In *Antiquity and Humanity: Essays on Ancient Religion and Philosophy Presented to Hans Dieter Betz on His 70th Birthday*, edited by Adela Yarbro Collins and Margaret M. Mitchell, 121–35. Tübingen: Mohr/Siebeck, 2001.

Parker, David C. *Codex Bezae: An Early Christian Manuscript and Its Text*. Cambridge: Cambridge University Press, 1992.

———. *An Introduction to the New Testament Manuscripts and Their Texts*. Cambridge: Cambridge University Press, 2008.

———. *The Living Text of the Gospels*. Cambridge: Cambridge University Press, l997.

———. "Professor Amphoux's History of the New Testament Text: A Response." *New Testament Textual Research Update* 4 (1996) 41–45.

Parker, David C., and S. R. Pickering. "New Testament 4968. Acta Apostolorum 10–12, 15–17." In *The Oxyrhynchus Papyri*, vol. 74, edited by D. Leith, D. C. Parker, S. R. Pickering, N. Gones and M. Malonta, 7–8. London: Egypt Exploration Society, 2009.

Parry, Milman. *The Making of Homeric Verse: The Collected Papers of Milman Parry*. Edited by Adam Parry. Oxford: Clarendon, 1971.

# Bibliography

Paulston, Christina Bratt. "Language Repetoire and Diglossia in First-Century Palestine: Some Comments." In *Diglossia and Other Topics in New Testament Linguistics*, edited by Stanley E. Porter, 79–89. JSNTSup 193. Sheffield: Sheffield Academic, 2000.

Perrin, Norman. "The Christology of Mark." In *Journal of Religion* 51 (1971) 173–87. Reprinted in Perrin, *Parable and Gospel*, edited by K. C. Hanson, 73–84. Fortress Classics in Biblical Studies. Minneapolis: Fortress, 2003.

Porter, Stanley E. "Jesus and the Uses of Greek in Palestine." In *Studying the Historical Jesus: Evaluation of the State of Current Research*, edited by Bruce Chilton and Craig A. Evans, 123–54. New Testament Tools and Studies 19. Leiden: Brill, 1994.

———, editor. *The Language of the New Testament: Classic Essays*. JSNTSup 60. Sheffield: Sheffield Academic, 1991.

Propp, Vladimir. *Morphology of the Folktale*. Translated by Laurence Scott with introductions by Svatava Pirkova-Jakobson and Alan Dundes. 2nd ed. Austin: University of Texas Press, 1968.

Reed, Jonathan L. *Archaeology and the Galilean Jesus: A Reexamination of the Evidence*. Harrisburg, PA: Trinity, 2000.

———. "Instability in Jesus' Galilee: A Demographic Perspective." *JBL* 129 (2010) 343–65.

Reinhardt, Michael. *Endgericht durch den Menschensohn? Zur eschatologischen Funktion des Menschensohnes im Markusevangelium*. Stuttgarter Biblische Beiträge 62. Stuttgart: Katholisches Bibelwerk, 2009.

Reiser, Marius. *Sprache und literarische Formen des Neuen Testaments: Eine Einführung*. UTB für Wissenschaft 2197. Paderborn: Schöningh, 2001.

———. *Syntax und Stil des Markusevangeliums im Licht der hellenistischen Volksliteratur*. WUNT 2/11. Tübingen: Mohr/Siebeck, 1984.

Renoir, Alain. "Oral Formulaic Rhetoric and the Interpretation of Written Texts." In *Oral Tradition in Literature: Interpretation in Context*, edited by John Miles Foley, 103–35. Columbia: University of Missouri Press, 1986.

Riedo-Emmenegger, Christoph. *Prophetisch-messianische Provokateure der Pax Romana: Jesus von Nazaret und andere Störenfriede im Konflikt mit dem Römischen Reich*. Novum Testamentum et Orbis Antiquus 56. Göttingen: Vandenhoeck & Ruprecht, 2005.

Royse, James R. *Scribal Habits in Early Greek New Testament Papyri*. New Testament Tools, Studies and Documents 36. Leiden: Brill, 2008.

Rüegger, Hans Ulrich. *Verstehen, was Markus erzählt: Philologisch-hermeneutische Reflexionen zum Übersetzen von Markus 3,1–6*. WUNT 2/155. Tübingen: Mohr/Siebeck, 2002.

Saenger, Paul. "Separation of Words and the Physiology of Reading." In *Literacy and Orality*, edited by David R. Olson and Nancy Torrance, 198–214. Cambridge: Cambridge University Press, 1991.

Sawicki, Marianne. *Crossing Galilee: Architectures of Contact in the Occupied Land of Jesus*. Harrisburg, PA: Trinity, 2000.

———. *Seeing the Lord: Resurrection and Early Christian Practices*. Minneapolis: Fortress, 1994.

Schjerve, Rosita Rindler, and Eva Vetter. "Historical Sociolinguistics and Multilingualism: Theoretical and Methodological Issues in the Development of a Multifunctional Framework." In *Diglossia and Power: Language Policies and Practice*

# Bibliography

*in the 19th Century Habsburg Empire*, edited by Rosita Rindler Schjerve, 35–68. Language, Power, and Social Process 9. Berlin: de Gruyter, 2003.

Schmidt, Karl Ludwig. *The Place of the Gospels in the General History of Literature.* Translated by Bryan R. McCane. Colombia: South Carolina University Press, 2002.

Schottroff, Luise. "Maria Magdalena und die Frauen am Grabe Jesu." *EvT* 42 (1982) 3–25.

Schüssler Fiorenza, Elisabeth. "The Followers of the Lamb: Visionary Rhetoric and Social-Political Situation." In *Discipleship in the New Testament,* edited by Fernando F. Segovia, 386–403. Philadelphia: Fortress, 1985. Reprinted in Schüssler Fiorenza, *The Book of Revelation: Justice and Judgment,* 159–80. Philadelphia: Fortress, 1985.

———. *In Memory of Her: A Feminist Theological Reconstruction of Christian Origins.* New York: Crossroad, 1983.

Sellew, Philip. "Oral and Written Sources in Mark 4:1–34." *NTS* 36 (1990) 235–67.

Sevenster, J. N. *Do You Know Greek? How Much Greek Could the First Jewish Christians Have Known?* NovTSup 19. Leiden: Brill, 1968.

Shibutani, Tamotsu. *Improvised News: A Sociological Study of Rumor.* Indianapolis: Bobbs-Merrill, 1966.

Silva, Moisés. "Bilingualism and the Character of Palestinian Greek." In *The Language of the New Testament: Classic Essays,* edited by Stanley E. Porter, 213–16. JSNTSup 60. Sheffield: Sheffield Academic, 1991. (Orig. pub. *Biblica* 61 [1980] 206–9.)

Sinai, Nicolas. "Quranic Self-Referentiality as a Strategy of Self-Authorization." In *Self-Referenitiality in the Qur'an,* edited by Stefan Wild, 103–34. Diskurs der Arabistik 11. Wiesbaden: Harrassowitz, 2006.

Skeat, T. C. "The Codex Sinaiticus, the Codex Vaticanus and Constantine." In *The Collected Biblical Writings of T. C. Skeat,* introduced and edited by J. K. Elliott, 193–235. NovTSup 113. Leiden: Brill, 2004.

———. "A Codicological Analysis of the Chester Beatty Papyrus Codex of the Gospels and Acts ($P^{45}$)." In *The Collected Biblical Writings of T. C. Skeat,* Introduced and edited by J. K. Elliott, 141–59. NovTSup 113. Leiden: Brill, 2004.

Steck, Odil Hannes. *Israel und das gewaltsame Geschick der Propheten: Untersuchungen zur Überlieferung des deuteronomistischen Geschichtsbildes im Alten Testament, Spätjudentum und Urchristentum.* Wissenschaftliche Monographien zum Alten und Neuen Testament 23. Neukirchen-Vluyn: Neukirchener, 1967.

Stern, David. *Parables in Midrash: Narrative and Exegesis in Rabbinic Literature.* Cambridge: Harvard University Press, 1991.

Taylor, David G. K. "Bilingualism and Diglossia in Late Antique Syria and Mesopotamia." In *Bilingualism in Ancient Society: Language Contact and the Written Text,* edited by J. N. Adams, Mark Janse, and Simon Swain, 298–331. Oxford: Oxford University Press, 2002.

Tedlock, Dennis. "From Voice and Ear to Hand and Eye." *JAF* 103 (1990) 133–56.

———. *Popol Vuh: The Mayan Book of the Dawn of Life.* Rev. ed. New York: Simon & Schuster, 1996.

Thatcher, Tom, editor. *Jesus, the Voice, and the Text: Beyond 'The Oral and the Written Gospel.'* Waco, TX: Baylor University Press, 2008.

Theissen, Gerd. *The Miracle Stories of the Early Christian Tradition.* Translated by Frances McDonagh. Edited by John Riches. Edinburgh: T. & T. Clark, 1983.

# Bibliography

Thomas, Rosalind. *Oral Tradition and Written Record in Classical Athens*. Cambridge Studies in Oral and Literate Culture 18. Cambridge: Cambridge University Press, 1989.

Thompson, Stith. *Motif-Index of Folk-Literature: A Classification of Narrative Elements in Folk-tales, Ballads, Myths, Fables, Mediaeval Romances, Exempla, Fabliaux, Jestbooks and Local Legends*. 6 vols. Bloomington: Indiana University Press, 1932–36. Reprinted, 1955–58.

Tolbert, Mary Ann. *Sowing the Gospel: Mark's World in Literary–Historical Perspective*. Minneapolis: Fortress, 1989.

Vouga, François. "'Habt Glauben an Gott': Der Theozentrismus der Verkündigung des christlichen Glaubens im Markusevangelium." In *Texts and Contexts: Biblical Texts in Their Textual and Situational Contexts: Essays in Honor of Lars Hartman*, edited by Tord Fornberg and David Hellholm, 93–109. Oslo: Scandinavian University Press, 1995.

Watson, David F. "The 'Messianic Secret': Demythologizing a Non-Existent Markan Theme." *Journal of Theology* [Deleware, Ohio—Trottwood, Ohio] (summer 2006) 33–44.

Watt, Jonathan M. "The Current Landscape of Diglossia Studies: The Diglossic Continuum in First-Century Palestine." In *Diglossia and Other Topics in New Testament Linguistics*, edited by Stanley E. Porter, 18–36. JSNTSup 193. Sheffield: Sheffield Academic, 2000.

Weeden, Theodore J. *Mark: Traditions in Conflict*. Philadelphia: Fortress, 1971.

Wills, Lawrence M. *The Quest of the Historical Gospel: Mark, John, and the Origins of the Gospel Genre*. London: Routledge, 1997.

Wire, Antoinette Clark. "The God of Jesus in the Gospel of Mark." In *To Break Every Yoke: Essays in Honor of Marvin L. Chaney*, edited by Robert B. Coote and Norman K. Gottwald, 292–310. Social World of Biblical Antiquity, 2/3. Sheffield: Sheffield Phoenix 2007.

———. "The God of Jesus in the Gospel Sayings Source." In *Reading from this Place: Social Location and Biblical Interpretation in the United States*, edited by Fernando F. Segovia and Mary Ann Tolbert, 277–304. Minneapolis: Fortress, 1995.

———. *Holy Lives, Holy Deaths: A Close Hearing of Early Jewish Storytellers*. Studies in Biblical Literature 1. Atlanta: Society of Biblical Literature, 2002.

———. "Mark: News as Tradition." In *The Interface of Orality to Written Text: Speaking, Seeing, Writing in the Shaping of New Genres*, edited by Annette Weissenrieder and Robert B. Coote, 52–70. WUNT 1/260. Tübingen: Mohr/Siebeck, 2010.

———. "The Miracle Story as the Whole Story." *South East Asia Journal of Theology* 22 (1981) 29–37.

———. *The Parable Is a Mirror*. Atlanta: General Assembly Mission Board, Presbyterian Church, U.S., 1983.

———. "The Structure of the Gospel Miracle Stories and Their Tellers." *Semeia* 11 (1978) 83–111.

Yassif, Eli. *The Hebrew Folktale: History, Genre, Meaning*. Translated by Jacqueline S. Teitelbaum. Folklore Studies in Translation. Bloomington: Indiana University Press, 1999.

Zangenberg, Jürgen, editor. *Religion, Ethnicity and Identity in Ancient Galilee: A Region in Transition*. WUNT 210. Tübingen: Mohr/Siebeck, 2007.

# Index of Ancient Documents

# Index of Modern Authors

# Index of Subjects

# Biblical Performance Criticism Series

## David Rhoads, Series Editor

*The Bible in Ancient and Modern Media: Story and Performance*, edited by Holly E. Hearon and Philip Ruge-Jones. 2009. 176pp. $23.00.

Contributors include A. K. M. Adam, Adam Gilbert Bartholomew, Arthur J. Dewey, Dennis Dewey, Joanna Dewey, Robert M. Fowler, Holly E. Hearon, David Rhoads, Phillip Ruge-Jones, Whitney Shiner, Marti J. Steussy, and Richard W. Swanson.

This cutting-edge volume has been brought together in honor of Thomas Boomershine on the occasion of the twenty-fifth anniversary of the SBL section on *The Bible in Ancient and Modern Media*. This volume deals with many issues lifted up in this program unit for over two and a half decades: media history, storytelling and performance in the first century, the contrast between oral and written, the "space" of performance, interpretation in light of media shifts, and more. Recommended for students in college and seminary as well as scholars and teachers seeking an introduction to biblical performance criticism.

> "These essays, written specifically for the generation of students who will shape thinking about both Bible and media in the years to come, provide an accessible introduction to the complex issues involved in this area of scholarship." —*Interpretation*

> "*The Bible in Ancient and Modern Media* is a treasure chest, with every chapter showcasing some of the best gems stemming from each author's work of trying to get around the anachronism of understanding and interpreting the Bible through silent, solitary means and reclaiming an audible, embodied, communal experience of these stories. It's breadth, depth, and accessibility have made it required reading for several of my courses, where it has been widely appreciated by current and future proclaimers of the Word, as well as those responsible for pastoral care, formation,

and evangelism. In fact, one doctoral student claimed it was, by far, the most helpful book he had read while in the program."
—Tracy Radosevic, professional storyteller, Dean of the Academy for Biblical Storytelling, and adjunct professor at Wesley Theological Seminary in Washington, DC, and the Ecumenical Institute of Theology in Baltimore.

∽

*From Orality to Orality: A New Paradigm for Contextual Translation of the Bible*, by James A. Maxey. 2009. 234pp. $26.00.

James A. Maxey is Translations and Biblical Scholar at the Nida Institute for Biblical Scholarship of the American Bible Society.

This exploratory volume intertwines two innovative subjects: a proposal for an alternative paradigm for Bible Translation as contextualization and a discussion of the implications of orality and biblical performance criticism for translation. It is based on original field research of oral performances among the Vuté community in Cameroon. Recommended for biblical scholars and translators and a generation of students seeking new ways to relate to the Bible.

> "In this groundbreaking work, Bible translation is presented as an expression of contextualization that explores the neglected riches of the verbal arts in the New Testament. Going beyond a historical study of media in antiquity, this book explores a renewed interest in oral performance that informs methods and goals of Bible translation today. Such exploration is concretized in the New Testament translation work in central Africa among the Vuté people of Cameroon.
> "This study of contextualization appreciates the agency of local communities—particularly in Africa—who seek to express their Christian faith in response to anthropological pauperization. An extended analysis of African theologians demonstrates the ultimate goals of contextualization: liberation and identity.
> "Oral performance exploits all the senses in experiencing communication while performer, text, and audience negotiate meaning. Performance not only expresses but also shapes identity as communities express their faith in varied contexts. This book contends that the New Testament compositions were initially performed and not restricted to individualized, silent reading.

This understanding encourages a reexamination of how Bible translation can be done. Performance is not a product but a process that infuses biblical studies with new insights, methods, and expressions.

"What does 'orality' and public performance have to do with translating the written Scriptures of God? Many misconceptions about the nature of the biblical texts and their communication in modern world languages are corrected in this thoroughly engaging, wide-ranging book that offers an innovative, multidisciplinary approach to the subject. I can heartily recommend James Maxey's pioneering work on contextualizing the New Testament for effective contemporary, multi-sensory re-presentation. This is a vital resource for all students, exegetes, commentators, teachers, translators, and other communicators of the Word."
—Ernst R. Wendland, Translation Consultant, United Bible Societies and Instructor at Lusaka Lutheran Seminary.

"In this volume, which brings together studies on Bible translation, orality, and performance criticism, James Maxey leads us into new and exciting ways of thinking about and doing Bible translation that takes into serious consideration the local context of the translation. The specific reference to the Vuté New Testament translation in Cameroon takes the reader from theory to actual practice and shows the exciting future of Bible translation for performance."
—Roger L. Omanson, United Bible Societies and Consultant for Scholarly Editions and Helps

"Discarding simplistic communication models and insisting on the role of receptor community in the construction of meaning, James Maxey's From Orality to Orality deploys a strategic array of tools (orality studies, postcolonial critique, performance criticism, contextual case studies) that allows development towards a (contextual) 'missiology of Bible translation' and aids in the much needed redefinition of Bible translation as a power activity. In this way, Dr. Maxey also contributes significantly to the relocation of Bible translation within the broader context of translation studies."
—Philip H. Towner, Dean, The Nida Institute for Biblical Scholarship of the American Bible Society

"Samuel Coleridge once said: 'I have knowledge of your ignorance, but I am ignorant of your knowledge.' Many missionaries

continue to approach the people of cultures other than their own with an implicit prejudice: they judge others on the basis of what those others seem to lack or to be perceived to need, and they attempt to provide as much as they can. But few people in highly literate cultures understand that literacy itself is limited, that its opposite is not *illiteracy* but *orality*, and that in a predominantly oral world, many aspects of literacy are redundant. Jesus lived among people who were predominantly and functionally oral, and his message did not require them to read but to listen *and to be engaged*. James Maxey wonderfully explicates the intricacies of an oral world, and shows how contemporary oral cultures can be more effectively evangelized. This book will open the eyes of many missionaries and pastors to a world of orality that is not only exotic but remains part of the ethos of almost everyone. He shows how we can enrich our preaching and engage with our communities, by using techniques we may have forgotten or never known, in our own literate and televisual cultures. This book is a true ground breaker, and will reward the attentive reader in myriad ways."
—Anthony Gittins, C.S.Sp., Professor of Mission and Culture, Catholic Theological Union, Chicago

"This book brings the latest research on orality to bear on issues of translation and performance of New Testament texts. In doing so, it gives new insights into those texts themselves and opens new avenues for developing contextual theologies. It is a must-read for those working in the field of World Christianity today."
—Robert Schreiter, Professor at the Catholic Theological Union, Chicago and author of *Constructing Local Theologies*

~

*The Case for Mark Composed in Translation.* Antoinette Clark Wire. 2011. 226pp. $26.00.

Antoinette Clark Wire is Professor Emerita at San Francisco Theological Seminary and the Graduate Theological Union in Berkeley. Her writings include *The Corinthian Women Prophets: A Reconstruction Through Paul's Rhetoric* (1990) and *Holy Lives, Holy Deaths: A Close Hearing of Early Jewish Storytellers* (2002).

S